POSTCARD HISTORY SERIES

Lawrence County

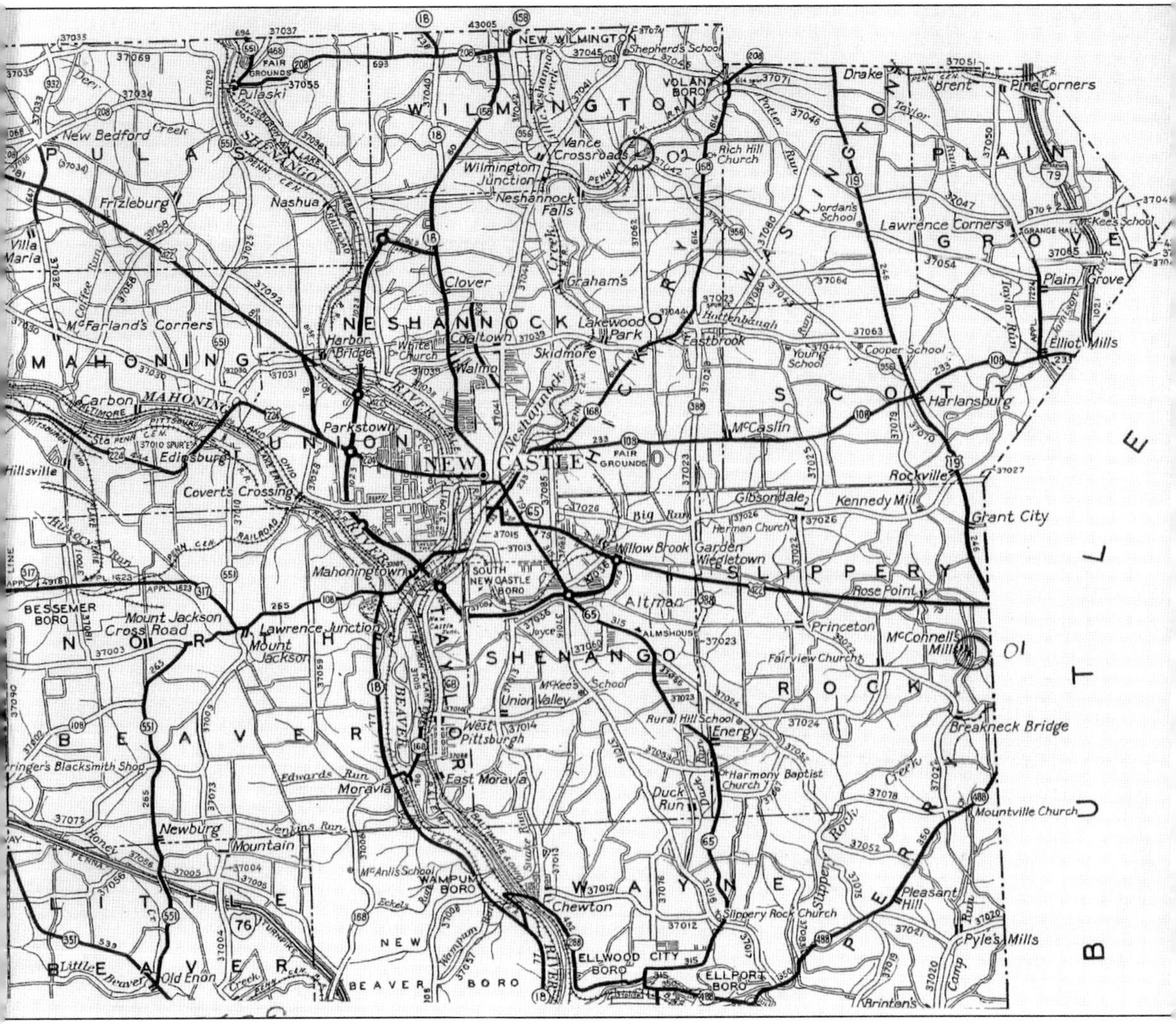

Map of Lawrence County. This map of Lawrence County is from the 1970s. It shows Lawrence County's 17 townships and their various communities, rivers, roads, and some landmarks. It does not show the Beaver Valley Expressway, which was completed after the map was published. (Courtesy of the New Castle Public Library.)

On the front cover: **Railroad Street, Wampum, Early 1900s.** At the end of the street is the Wampum railroad station conveniently located for business travelers. Major employers in Wampum were the cement, limestone, and coal industries. In this view, the banner announces a grand reunion of the Independent Order of Odd Fellows at Cascade Park in New Castle, nine miles away. (Courtesy of Anthony Walczak.)

On the back cover: **Shelby Tube Mill, Ellwood City.** The first seamless steel tubes in the country were manufactured in Ellwood City in 1895 by the Ellwood Weldless Tube Company, which made tubing for bicycles. That firm was acquired by the Shelby Tube Mill. Shelby eventually became part of U.S. Steel. Today seamless steel tubes, many now manufactured in China, are used in the oil, weapons, construction, and other industries. (Courtesy of Anthony Walczak.)

POSTCARD HISTORY SERIES

Lawrence County

Anita DeVivo and Anthony P. Walczak

ARCADIA
PUBLISHING

ISBN 978-0-7385-4996-5

Published by Arcadia Publishing
Charleston, South Carolina

Printed in the United States of America

Library of Congress Catalog Card Number: 2006940091

For all general information contact Arcadia Publishing at:
Telephone 843-853-2070
Fax 843-853-0044
E-mail sales@arcadiapublishing.com
For customer service and orders:
Toll-Free 1-888-313-2665

Visit us on the Internet at www.arcadiapublishing.com

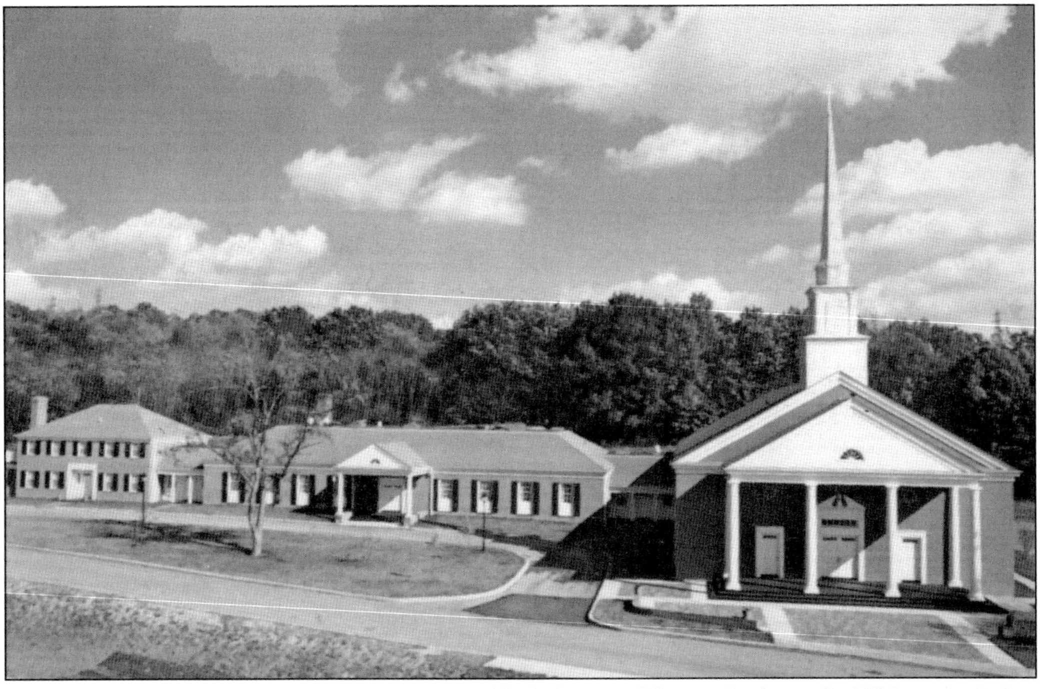

ST. LUCY'S CHURCH, MAHONINGTOWN, *c.* 1979. St. Lucy's began in the early 1900s as a mission church for St. Vitus Church, an Italian ethnic parish in New Castle. In 1912, the first St. Lucy's Church, also an Italian ethnic parish, was built on South Cedar Street in Mahoningtown. A second church, on North Cedar Street, was dedicated in 1931. The third church, on Lucymont Drive, pictured here, was dedicated in 1978. Presently St. Lucy's and three other parishes have merged to form St. Vincent de Paul parish, with St. Lucy's as the parish church.

Contents

ACKNOWLEDGMENTS

The postcards and photographs that make up the major part of this book are from the collection of coauthor Anthony Walczak.

We thank the following people for their special contributions: Brian Hollins for scanning the images, Loretta Walczak for her general assistance, Adam Pivovar for field trips and expertise on Lawrence County, and Bob Presnar, Lynn Slovonsky, Tom Walczak, and Beverly Zona for reviewing the manuscript.

We thank the many generous people and organizations who let us use their cards and photographs. They are mentioned in the courtesy lines that accompany their contributions. The Lawrence County Historical Society, John Hitch Collection, has been abbreviated to LCHS, Hitch Collection, in courtesy lines.

Finally, we thank the people who gave us information, reminiscences, and reference material: Mary Ann Cardella, Faye Costarell, Bebe Coyne, John Daley, Ed and Sally Daytner, Obie Derr, Jim DiBlasio, Tom Duncan, Chris Fabian, Joanne Gardner, Lesley Gent, Carl Hall, Lugene Hudson, Jake and Betty Ippolito, Phyllis Lach, Jack Reed, Joan Whitman, Caroline Winter, and Jean Workman.

INTRODUCTION

It took a long time to form Lawrence County. In 1820, two counties had jurisdiction over the land that became Lawrence County: Mercer County to the north and Beaver County to the south. The inconvenience of crossing the county line to do business, and the politics of the two counties, led to serious demands that a new county be formed. A quarter of a century passed, but in 1849, the Pennsylvania legislature took one part of Beaver County and another part of Mercer County and called it Lawrence County. The name was for James Lawrence, a naval captain during the War of 1812.

Today the county has one city, New Castle, which is the county seat, 10 boroughs, and 16 townships. The census for the year 2000 showed that New Castle had 26,309 people. The 10 boroughs had these populations: Bessemer, 1,172; Ellport, 1,198; Ellwood City, 8,688; Enon Valley, 387; New Beaver, 1,677; New Wilmington, 2,452; SNPJ (*Slovenska Norodna Podporna Jednota*), 14; South New Castle Borough, 808; Volant, 113; and Wampum, 678.

Lawrence County's 16 townships are, with their populations in the year 2000, as follows: Hickory, 2,356; Little Beaver, 1,310; Mahoning, 3,447; Neshannock, 9,216; North Beaver, 4,022; Perry, 1,930; Plain Grove, 854; Pulaski, 3,658; Scott, 2,235; Shenango, 7,633; Slippery Rock, 3,179; Taylor, 1,198; Union, 5,103; Washington, 714; Wayne, 2,328; and Wilmington, 2,760.

Lawrence County is a collection of opposites. One can find tranquil rural areas and noisy industrial areas; scenic views and rundown neighborhoods; steep hills and flat plains; wild gorges and meandering streams; lush green parks and dun-colored limestone mines; the simplicity of the Old Order Amish and the dazzle of fireworks. Many of these contrasts can be found in a day because distances are short. The area of Lawrence County is 363 square miles, .63 percent of it water.

A total of 94,643 people make their homes in the county. Centuries back, in the 1700s, most of the early settlers were Scotch-Irish. Then in the 1800s came the Germans, the Irish, and, to work the tin mill in New Castle, the Welsh. In the 1900s, the ethnic doors opened wide. Workers were needed to make something of Lawrence County's natural resources: iron ore, coal, clay, limestone, sandstone, gravel, and other minerals. More workers were needed for the quarries, railroads, mills, factories, and utilities. They came from Italy, Poland, Slovakia, Slovenia, Greece, Croatia, and Finland. New Castle's population of 6,000 in 1869 doubled at the end of that century, and the county's future was bright.

As the number of people increased, time worked its changes. Wars, depressions, recessions, mergers, layoffs, buyouts, and changes in agriculture drove some people out of the county. Some communities on early maps do not appear on later maps, Oreville, for instance, or Burnstown, Otis, Skidmore, Hoytdale, Coverdale, and Irish Ripple.

Celebrations go on in spite of change. A century later, the county is filled with gatherings that are truly American, or truly ethnic: square dancing at the granges, vintage car rallies at Cascade Park, Light-Up Night with Santa Claus, the county fair, Polish Day, the Greek festival, the Welsh Gymanfa Ganu, the Slovenefest, polka dancing at Bessemer's Croatian Club, and sauerkraut dinners at the Eintracht Singing Society. The German, Italian, and Polish communities each have weekly musical programs on the local radio station.

Lawrence Countians like tradition. Old Timers' Day has been held at Cascade Park for 100 years. The fireworks industry has been putting on shows for the county for almost as many years. Vintage cars shine at the four-day Back-to-the-Fifties rally each year, and more and more families look forward to the annual arts and crafts shows in Ellwood City and New Wilmington. Find a Victorian house in Neshannock Falls, on New Castle's North Hill, or in New Wilmington and you may find a young family restoring it with great care.

History lives in Lawrence County. The Lawrence County Federated Library System's three libraries, in New Castle, Ellwood City, and Bessemer, offer resources for genealogists. The Lawrence County Historical Society brings history alive with events for families. Other community societies are multiplying as history grows longer: Ellwood Area Historical Society, Wampum Historical Society, Pulaski Historical Society, Volant Historical Society, and possibly in the future, a New Bedford historical society.

We regret that we could not include every community in Lawrence County in this book, but the content was determined by the postcards available to us. The postcard photographers who documented Lawrence County on the pages that follow preserved our heritage in a unique way. They were there. We hope this book helps readers step into the past and be there too.

One

McConnell's Mill and Slippery Rock Creek Area

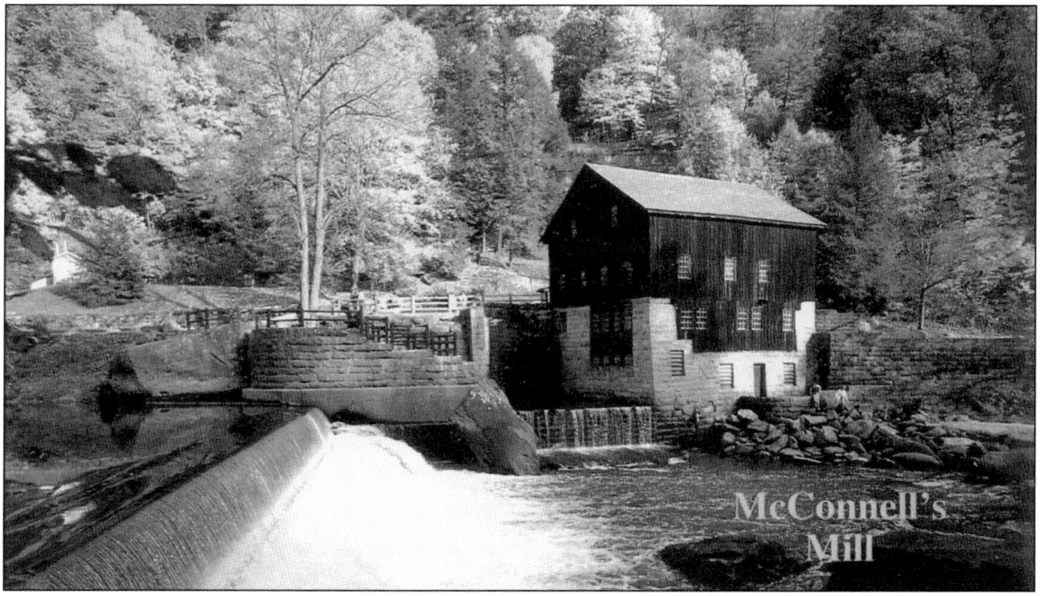

View of McConnell's Mill. McConnell's Mill is a 2,500-acre state park on Slippery Rock Creek. The park's dramatic gorge, nature and hiking trails, white-water kayaking, fishing, and picnic areas draw thousands of tourists each year. The park was dedicated in 1957, and the mill, built in 1868, was restored in the 1960s. The park is located 40 miles north of Pittsburgh near Interstate 79, at the intersection of U.S. Route 422 and State Route 19.

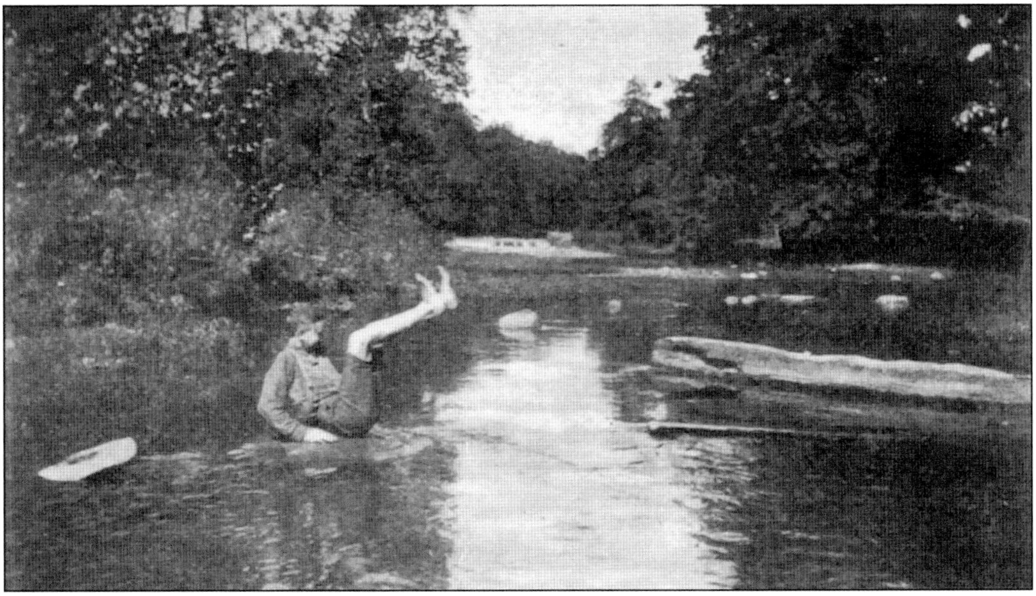

How Slippery Rock Got Its Name. Slippery Rock Creek is named for a shelf of Homewood sandstone where a natural oil seep once flowed. The slick sandstone was on a trail used by Native Americans to cross the creek. The oil seep disappeared in the late 1800s when oil wells were drilled in the area, but the name survived. This historic spot is south of the gorge, below the Armstrong Bridge.

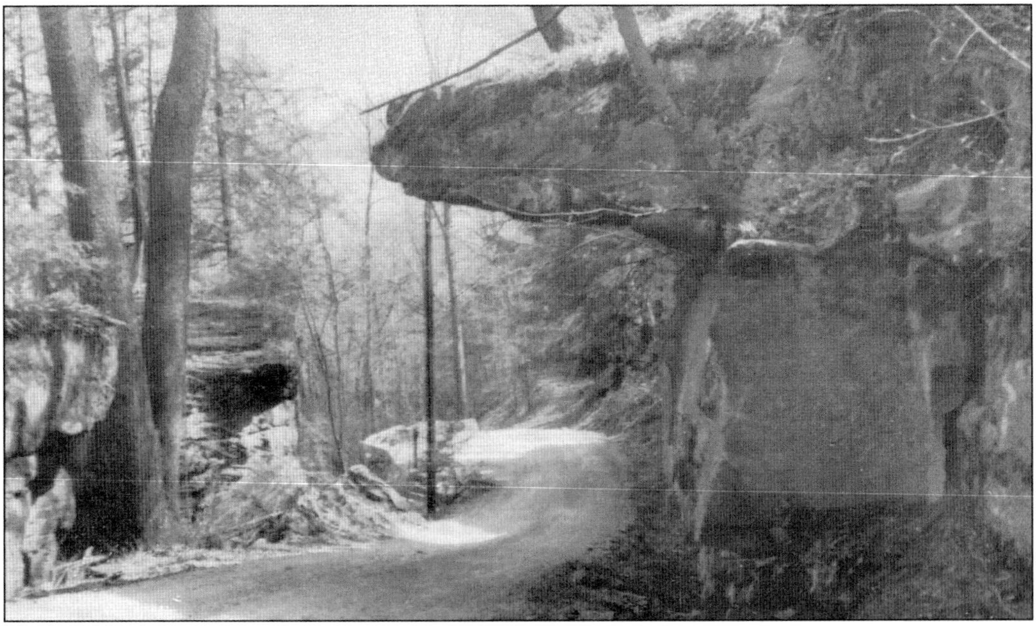

Approach to McConnell's Mill. Massive sandstone formations greet visitors to McConnell's Mill State Park. When the State of Pennsylvania created the park in 1957, it assured the preservation of the historic mill, its dam, covered bridge, and 11 miles of trails. Preservation of the gorge, waterfalls, wildflowers, boulders, caves, and fishing spots is up to the forces of nature.

ENTRANCE TO CAVES AT MCCONNELL'S MILL, EARLY 1900S. This postcard view shows the rugged terrain and bumpy road before McConnell's Mill became a state park. Dramatic views like this one were created by a continental glacier thousands of years ago. The gigantic boulders are enticing to rock climbers who seek out the challenge of formations like "Mr. Smoothy" or "Snake Bite."

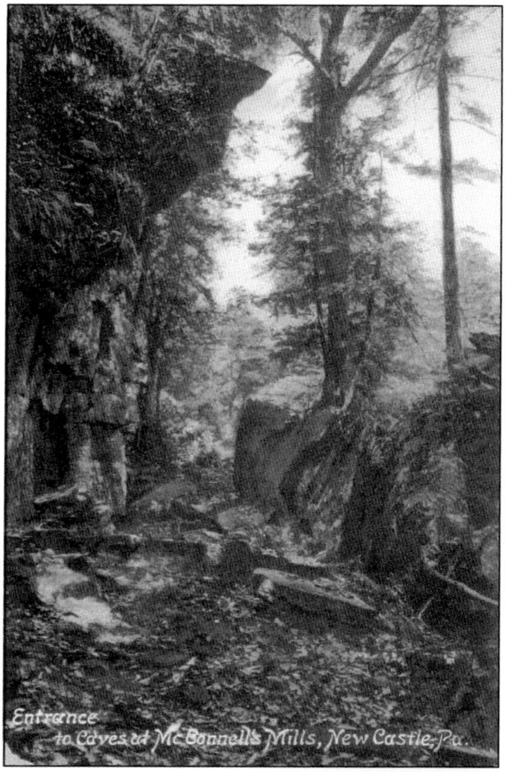

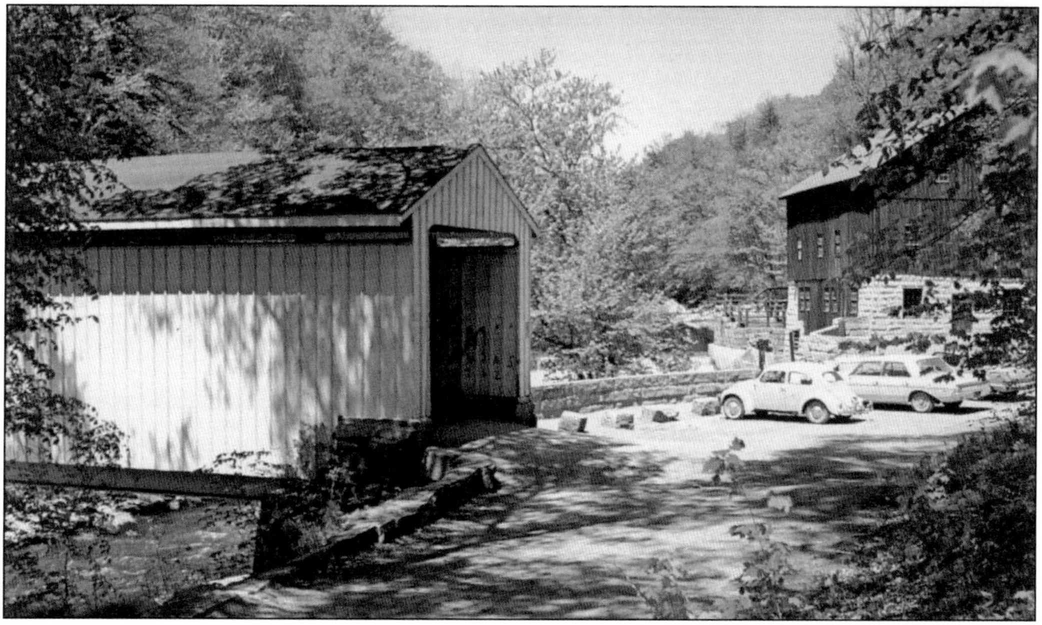

MCCONNELL'S MILL COVERED BRIDGE. This covered bridge, built in 1874 using a Howe Truss, is one of two covered bridges in Lawrence County (the other is Banks Bridge in Neshannock Falls). The North Country National Scenic Trail, a hiking trail to be 4,600 miles long when completed, passes through the bridge. The bridge is owned by Lawrence County, and it is a national historic landmark.

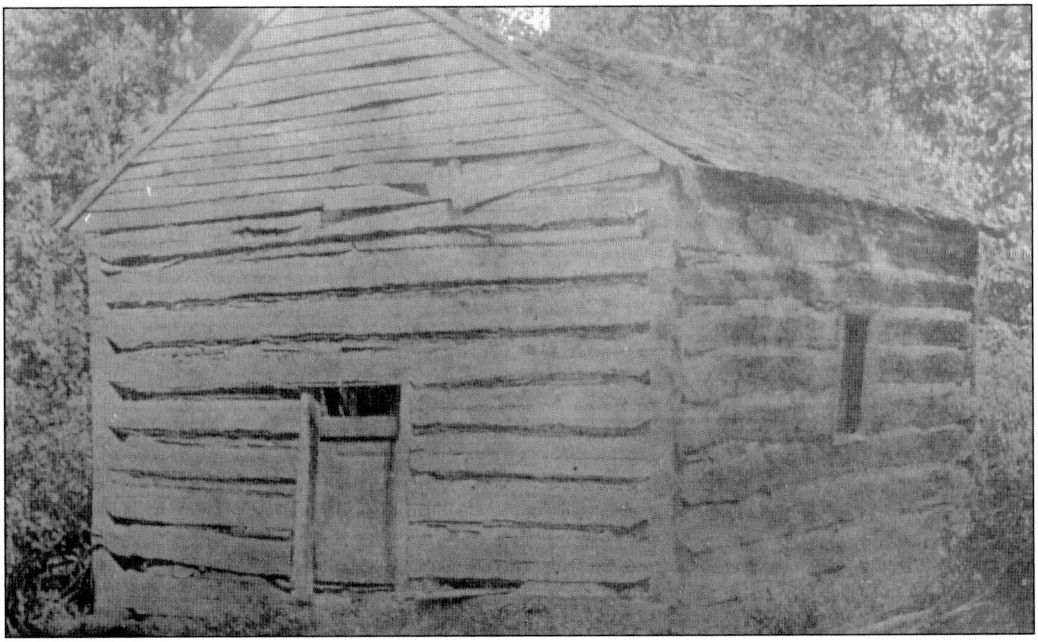

JERUSALEM (OLD LOG) CHURCH. This primitive log church was built on Fisher Road, near McConnell's Mill, in 1825 for a German Evangelical Lutheran congregation. It was eventually replaced by a brick church, located a mile and a half west of the log church, called the Jerusalem Evangelical Lutheran Church. (Courtesy of LCHS, Hitch Collection.)

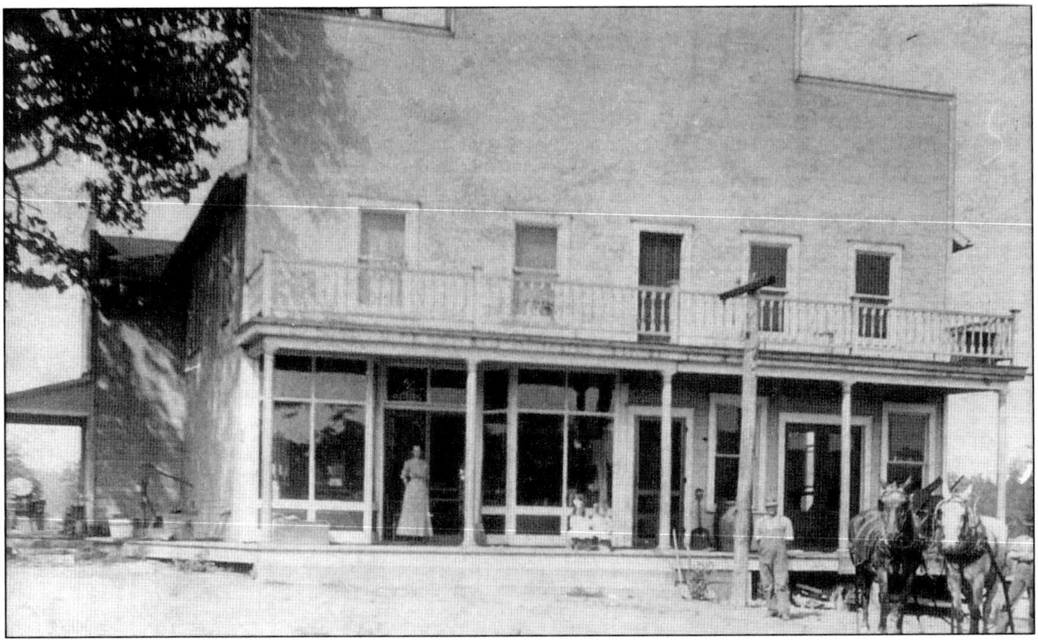

GENERAL STORE AND STATION, PRINCETON AREA, EARLY 1900S. When early settler John Frew's daughter Rosa and John Randolph from Princeton, New Jersey, married, around 1840, Frew gave them 50 acres as a wedding present. Randolph laid out a town in 1841 and named it for his former home. Princeton grew into the largest station on the Western Allegheny Railroad Line. (Courtesy of LCHS, Hitch Collection.)

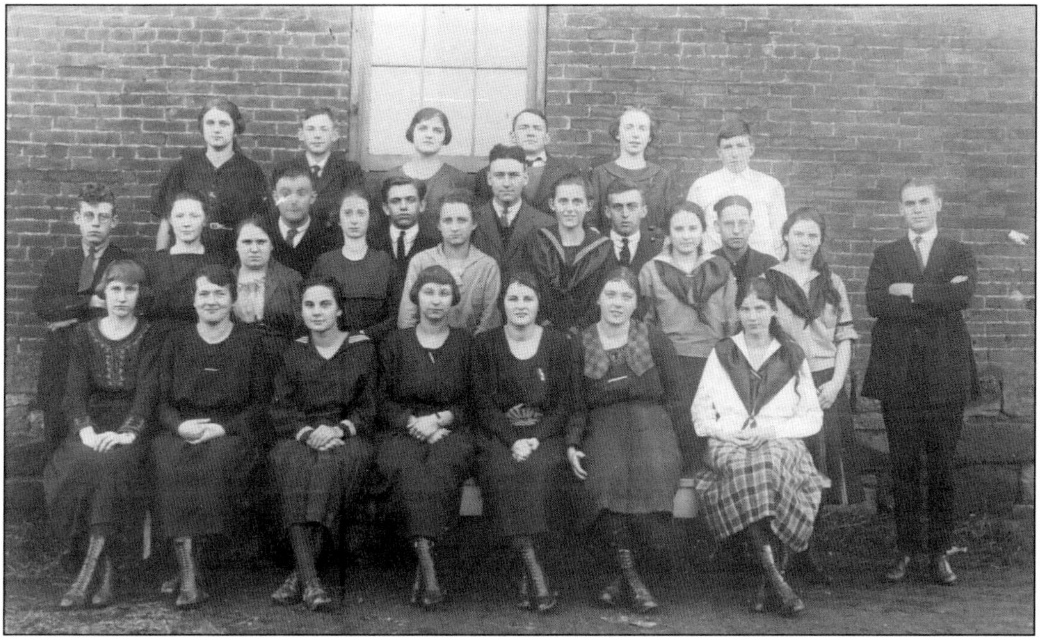

PRINCETON SCHOOL, 1914. Princeton's two-story brick schoolhouse was built in 1876. This 1914 real-photo postcard of a Princeton School class was probably taken in the spring because the pupils are not wearing coats. Records show that in 1908, Slippery Rock Township had 11 schools and 11 teachers.

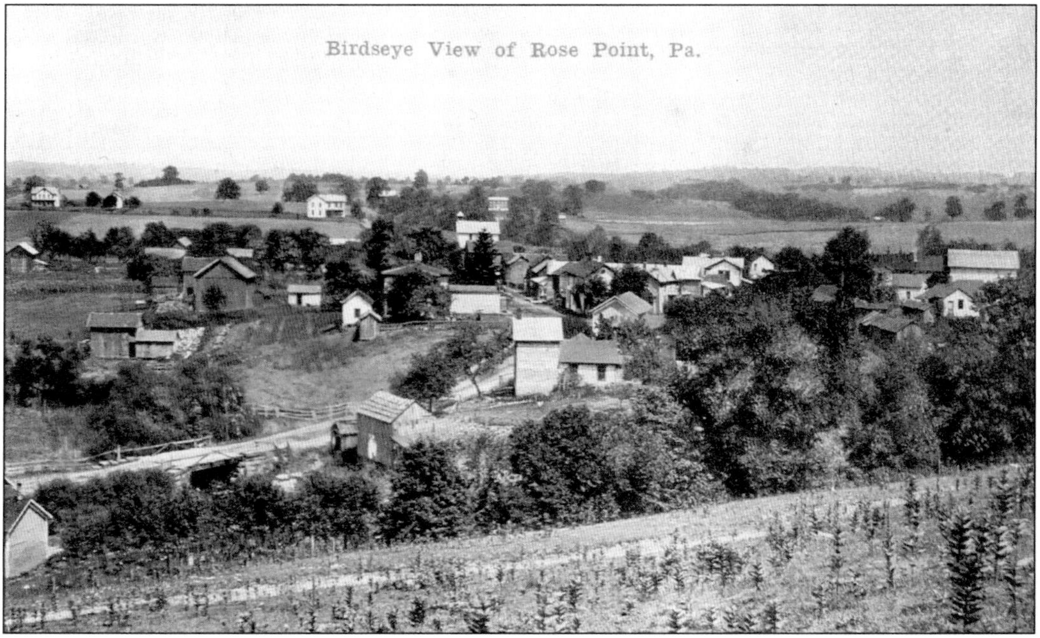

BIRD'S-EYE VIEW OF ROSE POINT, EARLY 1900S. Rose Point was originally called Stonertown for John Stoner, a settler in 1850. Pennsylvania had another Stonertown so the town was renamed Rose Point for the rose bush at the intersection of two main roads. Here the bridge at lower left crosses Slippery Rock Creek. From 1852 to 1865, Rose Point was a station on the Underground Railroad. Rose Point Academy was incorporated there in 1891.

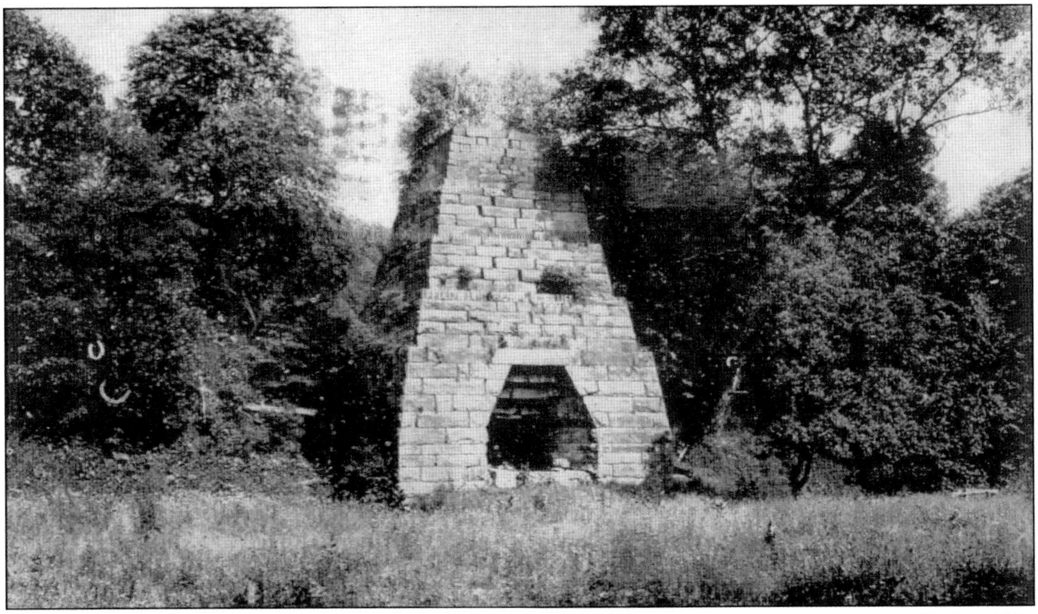

FIRST IRON FURNACE, ROSE POINT, 1846. The Wilroy iron furnace, sometimes called Willie Roy, was named for Will and Roy Foltz, sons of owner Samuel Foltz. On the east shore of Slippery Rock Creek, the furnace used nearby iron ore, limestone, and timber charcoal. During the Civil War, iron from Wilroy was in demand for cannons and cannonballs. The furnace, still standing, is on the National Register of Historical Places.

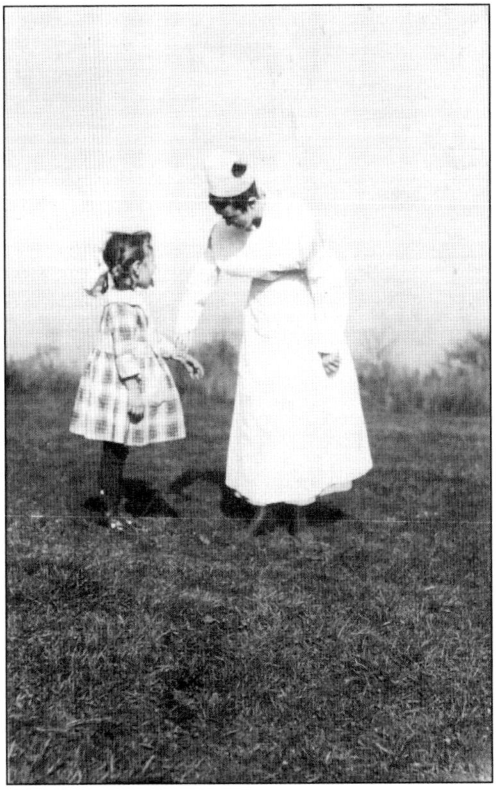

NURSE AND LITTLE GIRL, ROSE POINT, 1920S. This real-photo postcard shows a nurse taking the pulse of a little girl. The nurse is Mary Henry of Rose Point. Mary worked at the Shenango Valley Hospital in New Castle. The little girl is her sister Ruth Henry. (Courtesy of Beverly Zona.)

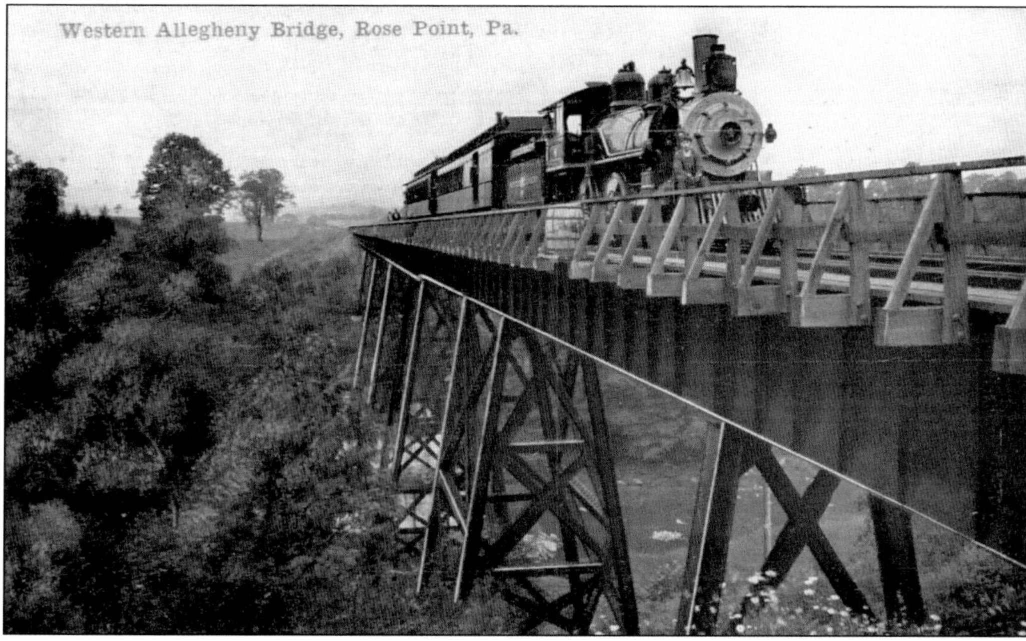

WESTERN ALLEGHENY RAILROAD BRIDGE, ROSE POINT, EARLY 1900S. This railroad, built in the early 1900s, ran from West Pittsburg to Queens Junction in Butler County. The trestle shown here crossed the Slippery Rock Creek near Muddy Creek Falls. It was 540 feet long and stood 107 feet above the water. The Western Allegheny later merged with the Buffalo, Rochester, and Pittsburgh Railroad, which then was taken over by the Baltimore and Ohio Railroad (B&O).

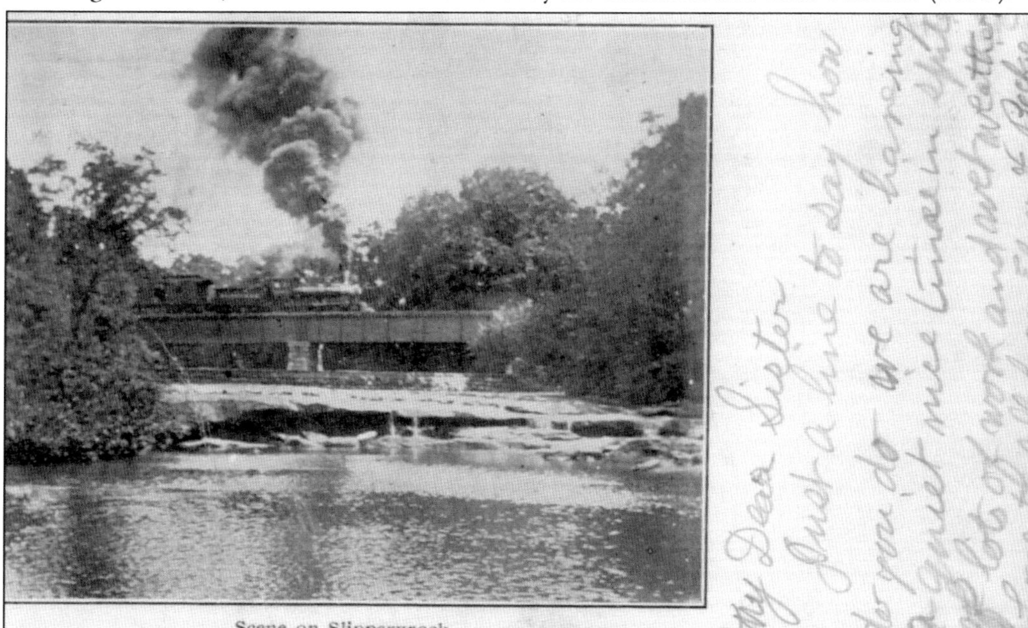

SCENE ON SLIPPERY ROCK CREEK, EARLY 1900S. The Western Allegheny Railroad was the last steam short-line railroad to be built in Lawrence County. One passenger train ran each day, stopping in East New Castle (Punkintown), Princeton, Rose Point, Grant City, and Grantboro. People who wanted to picnic at Muddy Creek Falls got off the train at Grantboro.

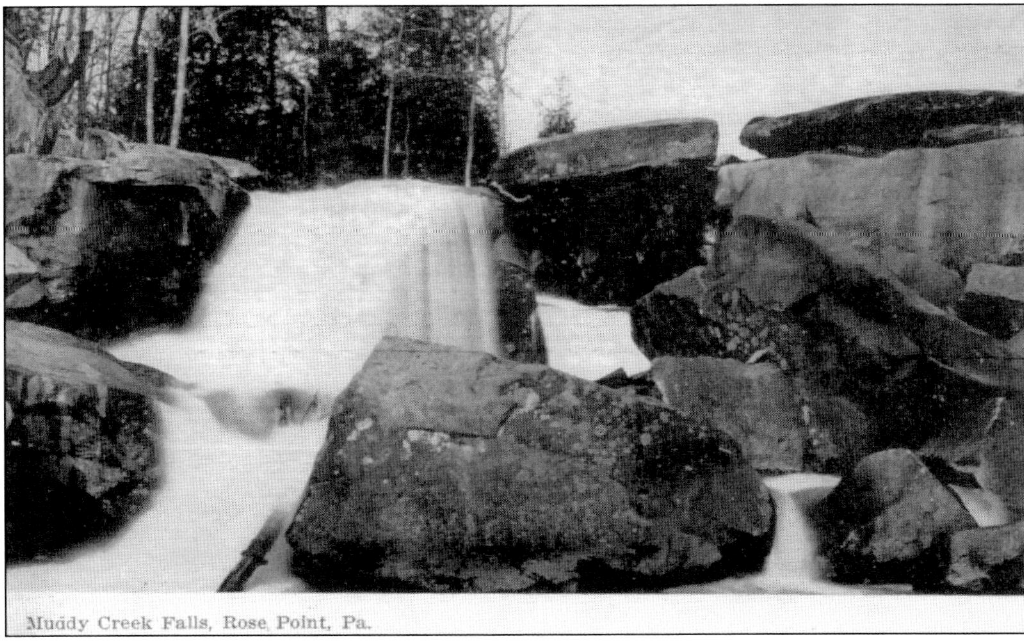

MUDDY CREEK FALLS, ROSE POINT. Muddy Creek joins Slippery Rock Creek just above Rose Point. About a half mile up from there, Muddy Creek has eroded a 60-foot-deep gorge. Its history of glaciers can be seen in the huge boulders scattered along the creek bed, creating cascades of water.

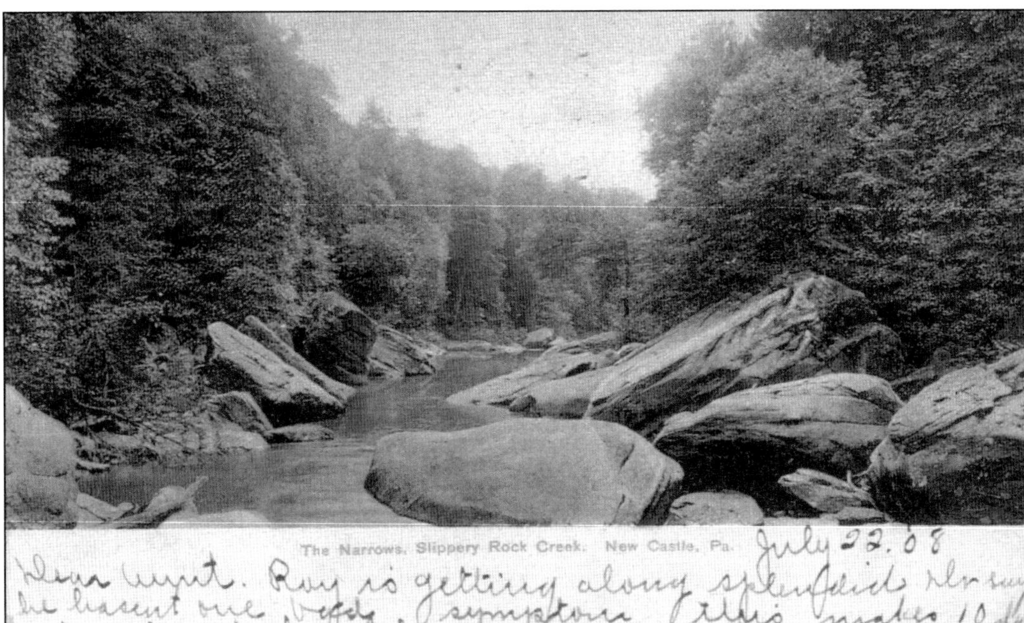

THE NARROWS, SLIPPERY ROCK CREEK, *C.* 1908. Slippery Rock Creek, running 49 miles through a variety of rugged settings, is a favorite of trout fishermen and white-water enthusiasts. It enters eastern Lawrence County from Butler County near Elliot Mill and Harlansburg, then runs south past Rose Point, McConnell's Mill, and Wurtemburg. It joins the Connoquenessing Creek and the Beaver River near Ellwood City.

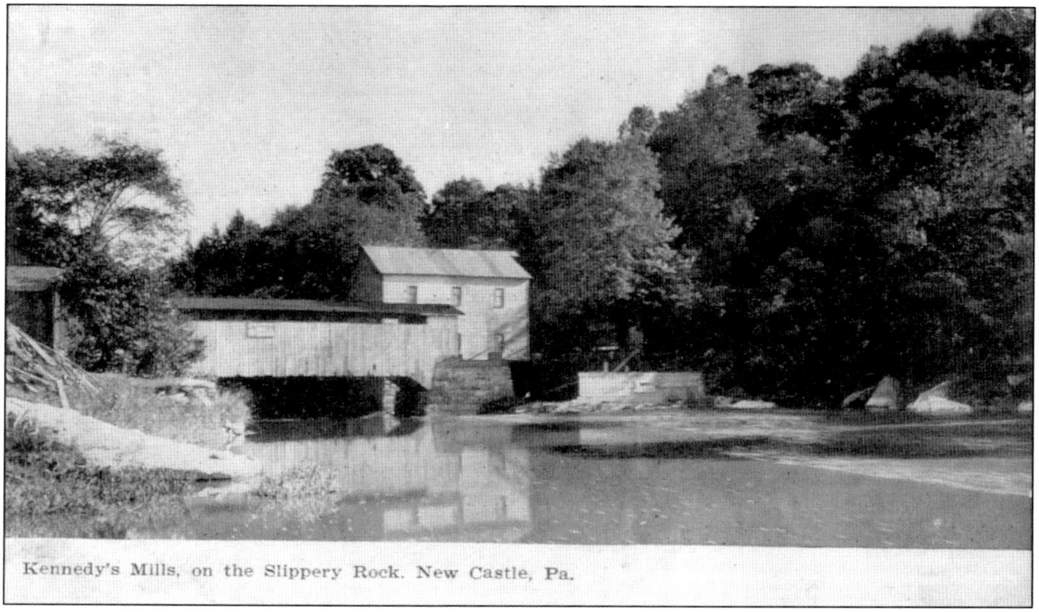

KENNEDY'S MILLS, DAM SIDE, *C.* 1908. Many people consider Slippery Rock Township the most scenic in Lawrence County. County historians S. W. and P. A. Durant wrote in 1877, "there are many localities of nearly primitive wildness" with "rocky gorges and gloomy dells." This tranquil view often changes into rapids as Slippery Rock Creek flows under the bridge toward Muddy Creek, Rose Point, and McConnell's Mill.

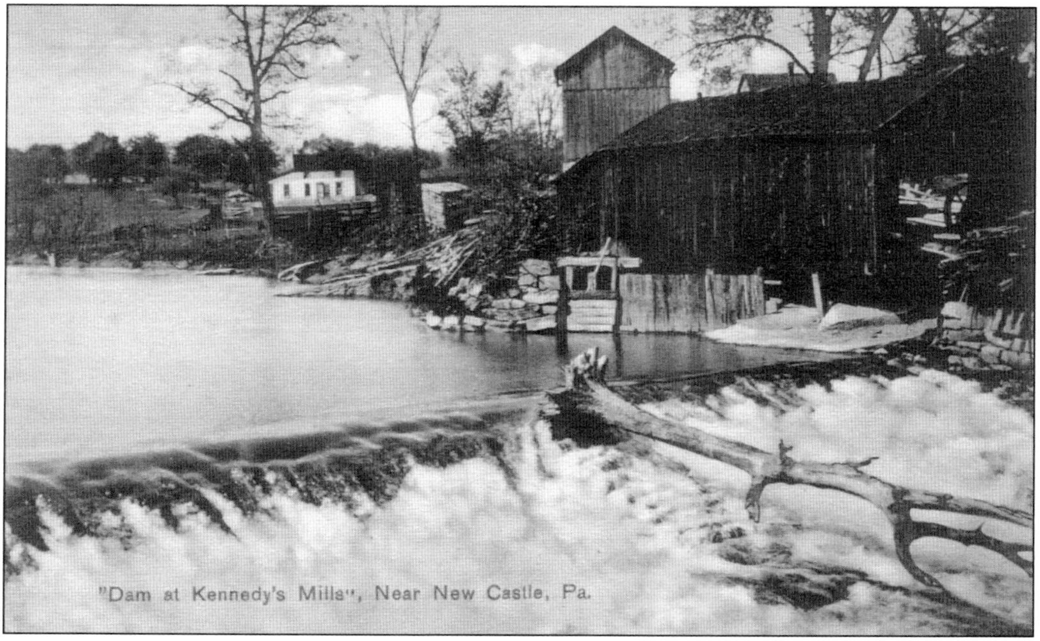

DAM AT KENNEDY'S MILLS, 1918. Kennedy's Mills were a sawmill and a gristmill on Slippery Rock Creek about three miles upstream from McConnell's Mill. The sawmill used an up-and-down vertical saw operated by water power. Because log cutting was slow, the miller could start a log through the saw, leave to work in the gristmill, then return to the sawmill when he thought the cutting was finished. The mills were torn down in the late 1930s.

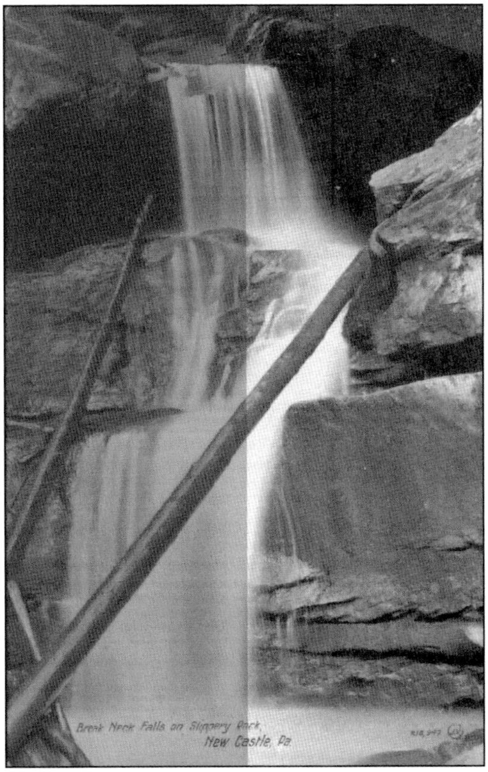

BREAKNECK FALLS, C. 1910. Breakneck Falls is south of McConnell's Mill. This postcard shows the 11-foot stream of water falling down terraced rocks into Slippery Rock Creek. In the area of the falls, glacial meltwater gradually erodes the sandstone, creating irregularities in the landscape that cause boulders to shift over time.

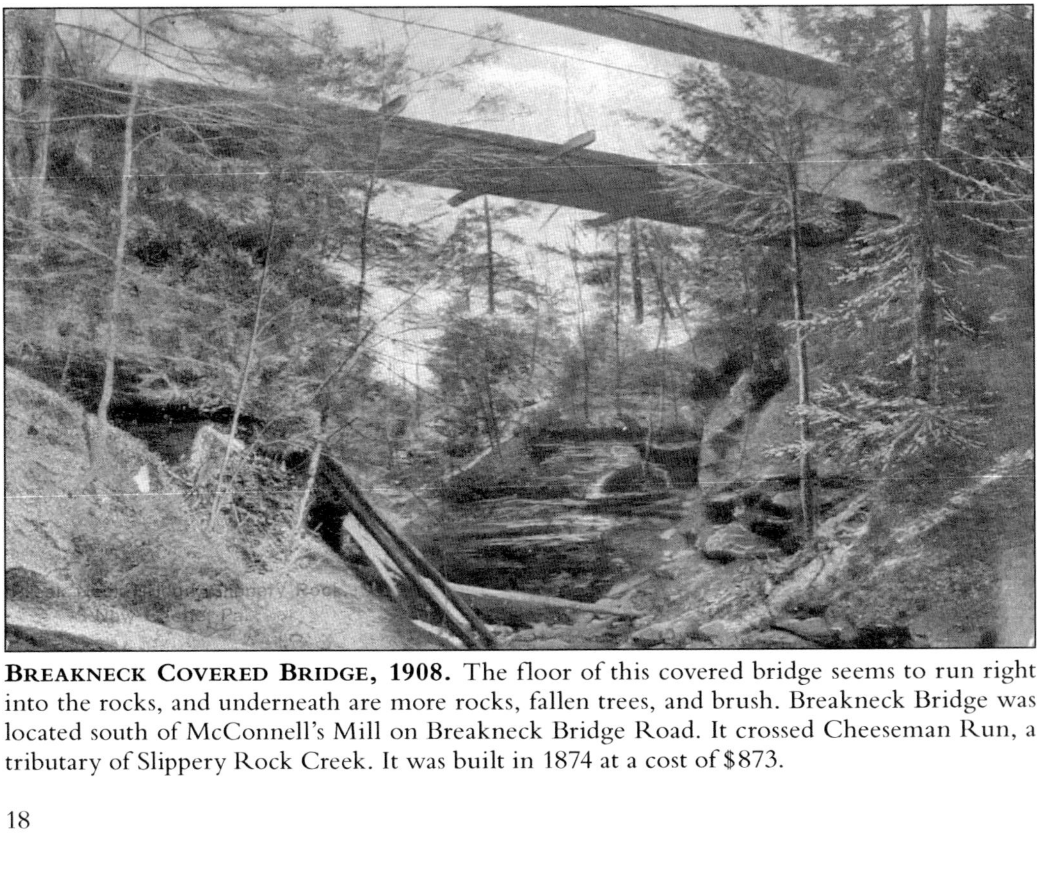

BREAKNECK COVERED BRIDGE, 1908. The floor of this covered bridge seems to run right into the rocks, and underneath are more rocks, fallen trees, and brush. Breakneck Bridge was located south of McConnell's Mill on Breakneck Bridge Road. It crossed Cheeseman Run, a tributary of Slippery Rock Creek. It was built in 1874 at a cost of $873.

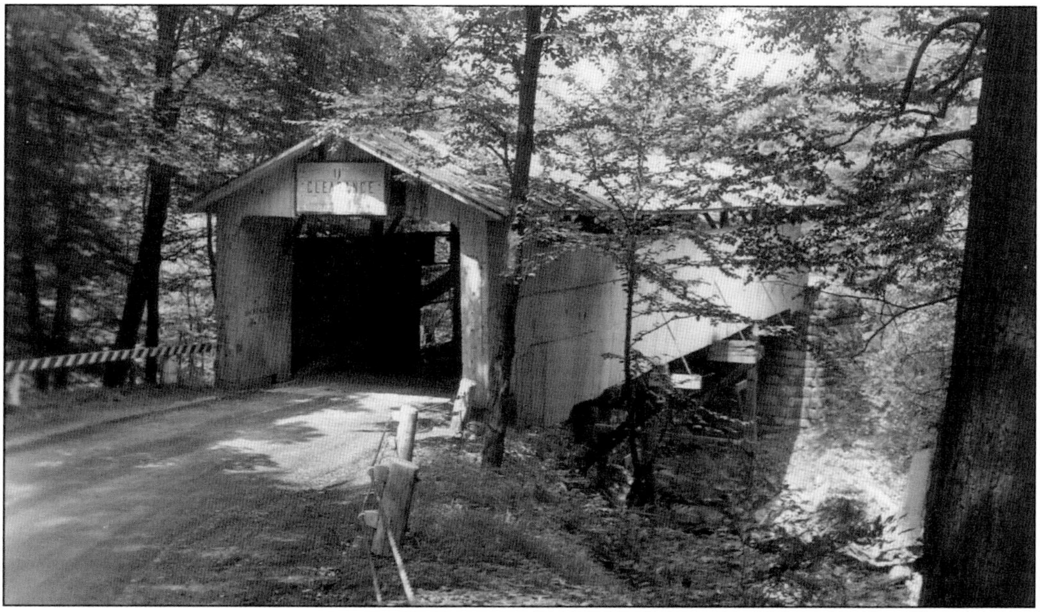

BREAKNECK BRIDGE. On August 16, 1952, Breakneck Bridge lived up to its name. An overweight coal truck crashed through its floor and went up in flames. The driver escaped but died of injuries soon thereafter. The covered bridge was replaced by a concrete bridge, but the concrete bridge is now closed because of low traffic and the expense of maintaining the area. (Courtesy of Tom Walczak.)

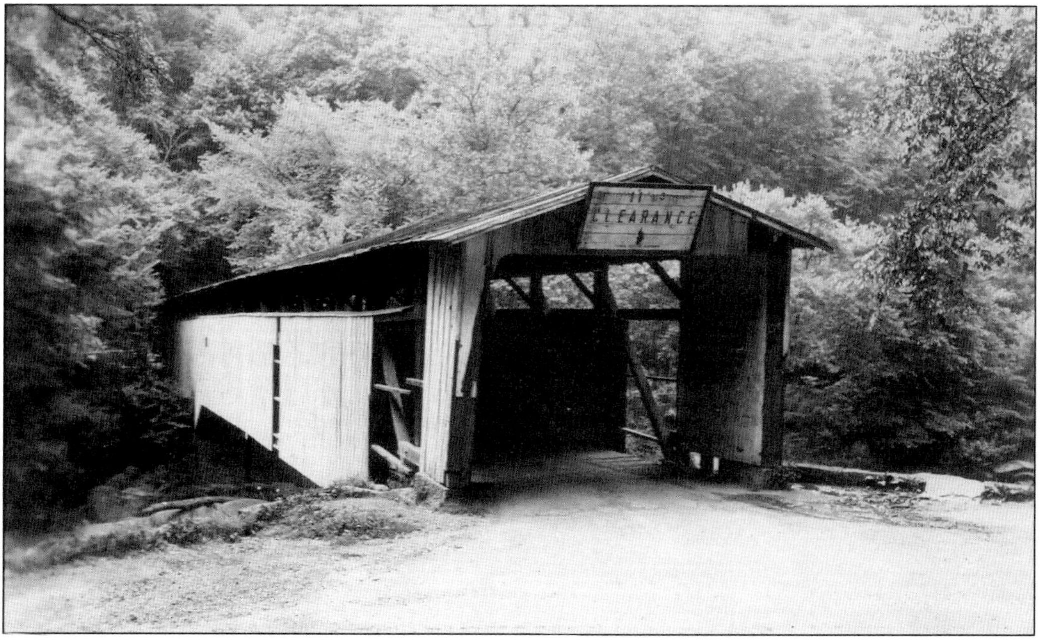

ECKERT'S BRIDGE. Eckert's Bridge was built in 1852, crossing Slippery Rock Creek south of McConnell's Mill on Eckert Bridge Road. It was a two-span, 175-foot covered bridge with spans of unequal length. A natural rock formation in the creek served as a pier for the bridge. It was replaced in the 1950s. Like Breakneck Bridge, Eckert's is closed because of low traffic and maintenance costs. (Courtesy of Tom Walczak.)

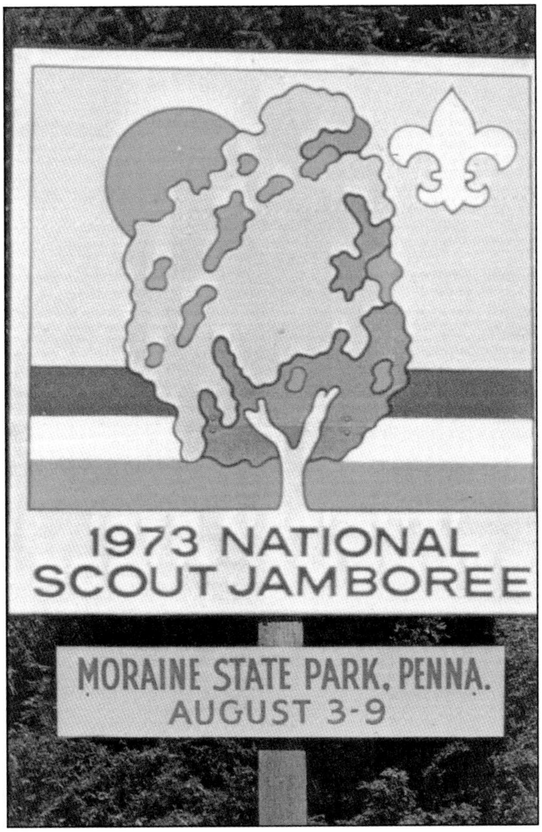

National Scout Jamboree, Moraine State Park, 1973. McConnell's Mill and Lawrence County were visited by many of the 40,000 Boy Scouts at this jamboree at Moraine State Park, just over the Lawrence County line in Butler County. A tent city at Moraine accommodated local Scouts who attended as well as 500 busloads of Scouts from all over the United States and some foreign countries.

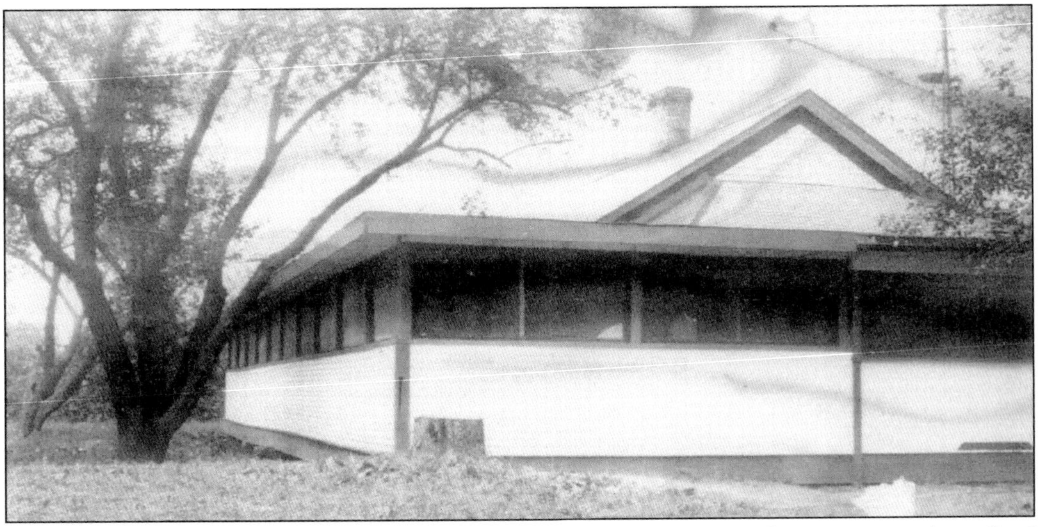

Camp Agawam, Rose Point, *c.* 1940. Many former Boy Scouts and Scoutmasters have fond memories of Camp Agawam on Frew Mill Road. This dining hall was originally a farmhouse. The Scouts used it as a kitchen, and added porches to make a dining area. The camp is still active with programs largely directed to Cub Scouts. (Courtesy of King Beaver District, Moraine Trails Council.)

Two

Wampum Area

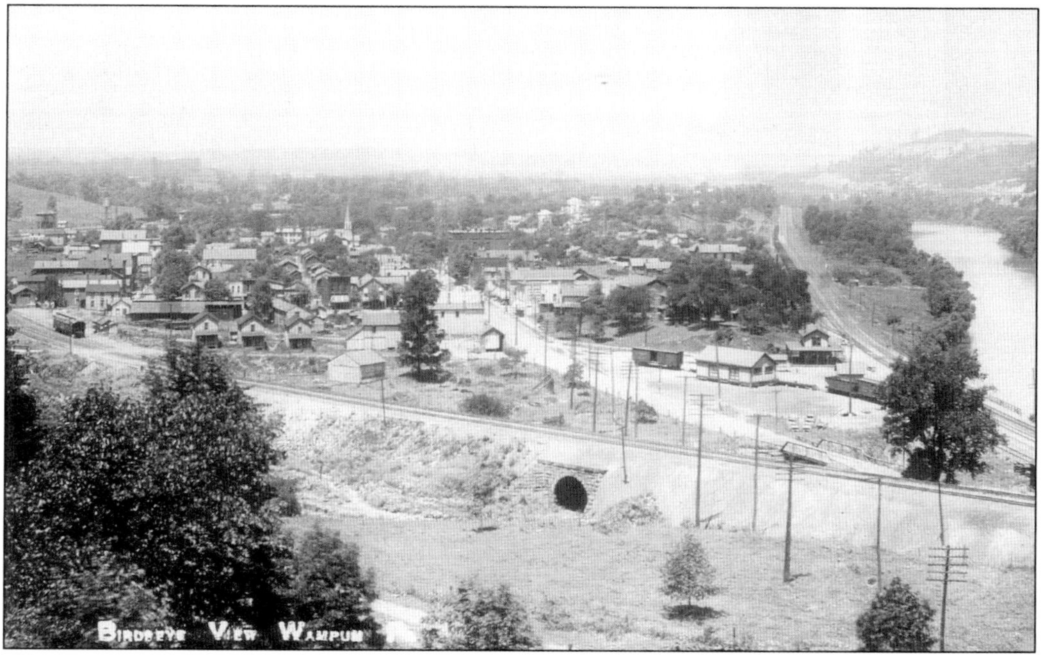

Bird's-Eye View of Wampum, Looking North, Early 1900s. In this view, the Beaver River is to the right, flowing south. The Pittsburgh and Lake Erie Railroad (P&LE) and the B&O run along the river with the train station at center right. The rail line in the foreground is the Pennsylvania. Main Street runs through the center of the view. The Presbyterian church steeple can be seen in the distance.

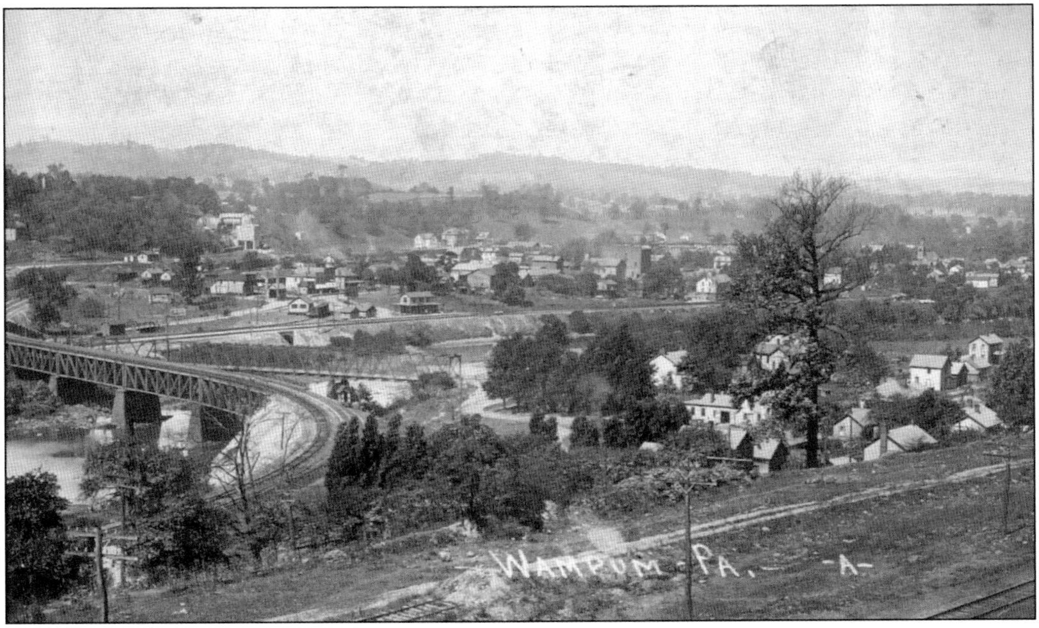

Bird's-Eye View of Wampum, Looking Northwest, Early 1900s. This postcard shows the P&LE and B&O station at center, above the tracks. Lower Chewton is at the right. At right center is St. Monica's steeple, and at left center a tipple for a limestone crusher. The first furnace in Wampum was built in 1856. It was eventually established as the Wampum Furnace Company, which produced 20 tons of metal daily, manufacturing pig iron.

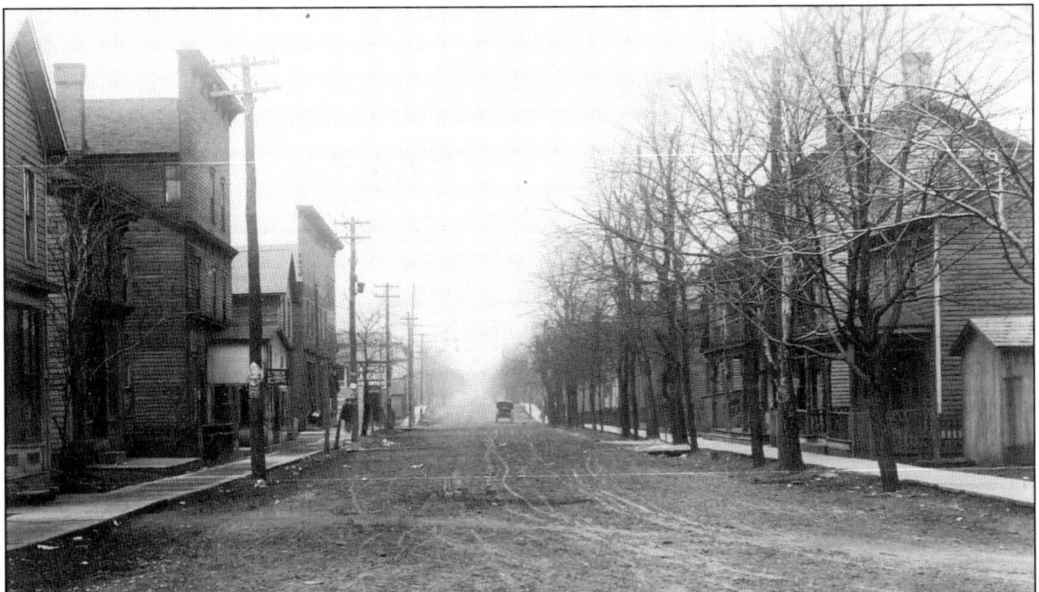

Beaver Street, Wampum, c. 1909. Wampum's early business district can be seen in this card. A lunchroom is behind the telephone pole on the left, and a blacksmith shop is farther down. In 1910, two fires in one month destroyed buildings on both sides of the street and some on Church Street. Main Street soon became the town's commercial district.

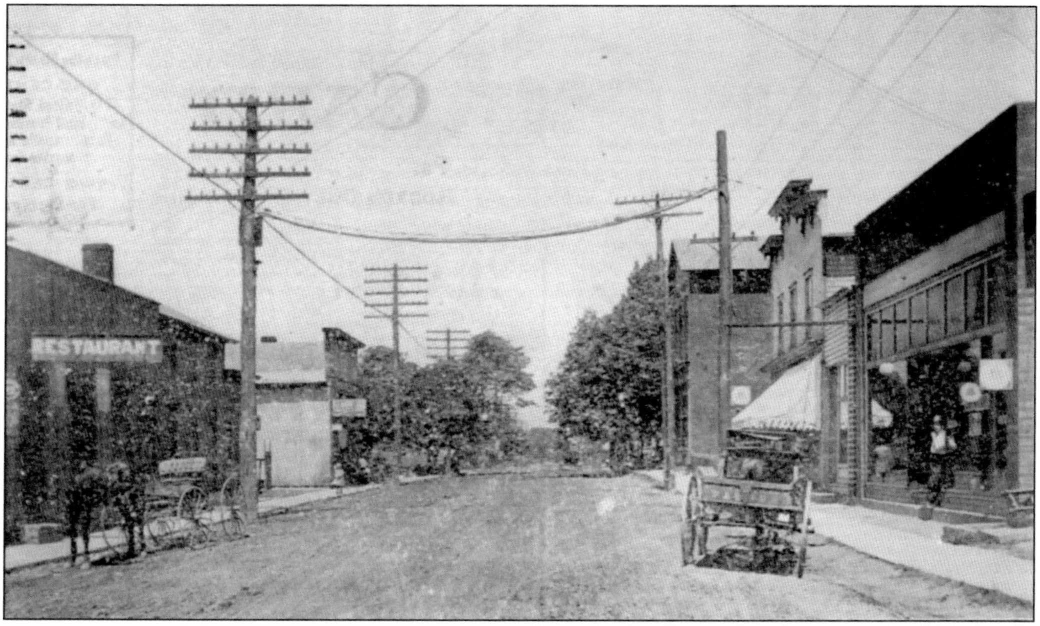

MAIN STREET, WAMPUM, C. 1913. Wampum was first settled in 1796. The post office was established north of the town in 1832. It was called Irish Ripple for the rapids in the Beaver River, and for the first settlers who were Irish. Wampum was incorporated as a borough in 1876. Some of the stores in this view have facades rising above the buildings in the style of the times.

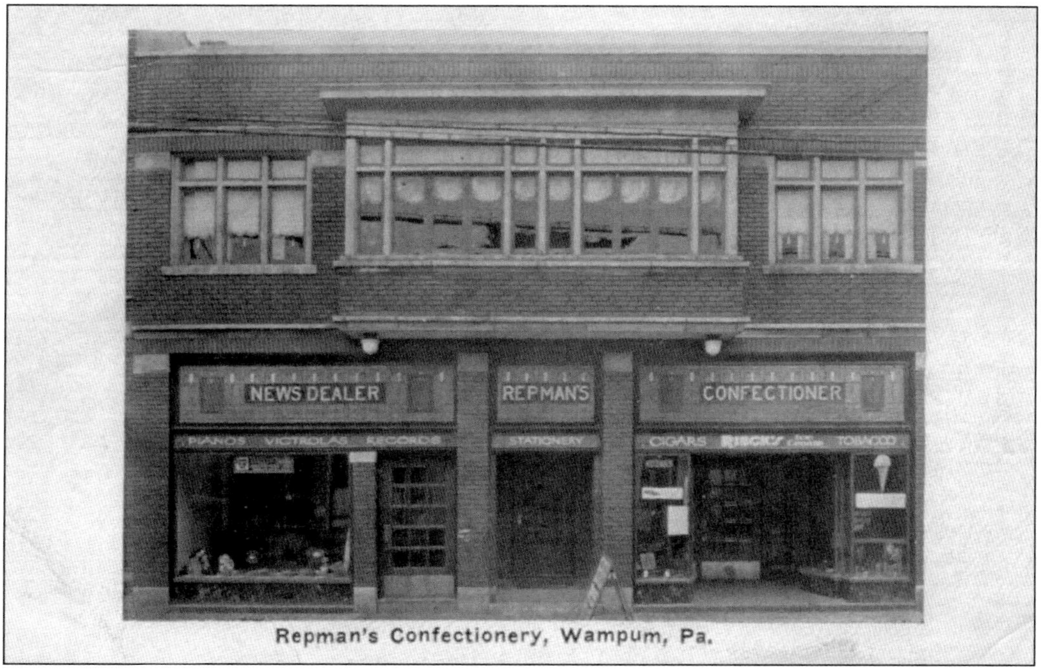

REPMAN'S CONFECTIONERY, WAMPUM, 1920S. Repman's was more than a confectionery store. According to this postcard, pianos, Victrolas, tobacco, ice cream, and newspapers could also be bought there. The architectural details and stylish window dressings on the second floor of the building indicate Wampum's growing prosperity. The building is still standing.

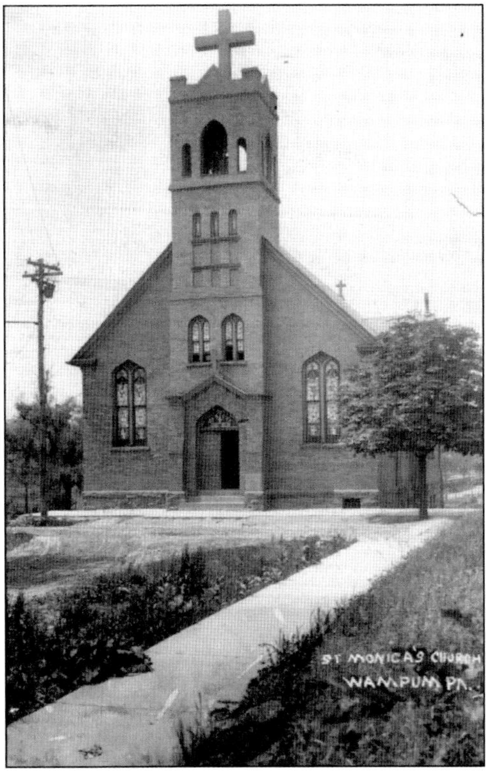

ST. MONICA'S CATHOLIC CHURCH, WAMPUM, *C.* 1911. St. Monica's was established in 1902 and dedicated in 1905. In 1992, St. Monica's and St. Teresa's church in Koppel merged to form a new Queen of Heaven parish with St. Monica's still in use. In 2005, after many major improvements to the building, lightning struck, making the church unsafe. Now behind safety warning signs, the church building has an uncertain future.

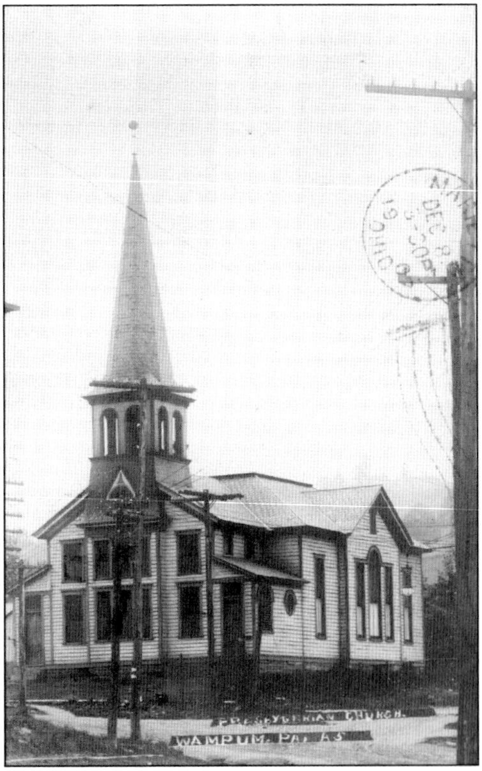

PRESBYTERIAN CHURCH, WAMPUM, *C.* 1907. The stately Wampum Presbyterian Church was built in 1889 when the Presbyterian Church in nearby Newport was moved to Wampum. Two churches preceded this one in the town, the Methodist Episcopal Church, organized in 1871, and the United Presbyterian Church, organized in 1875. This church is still standing.

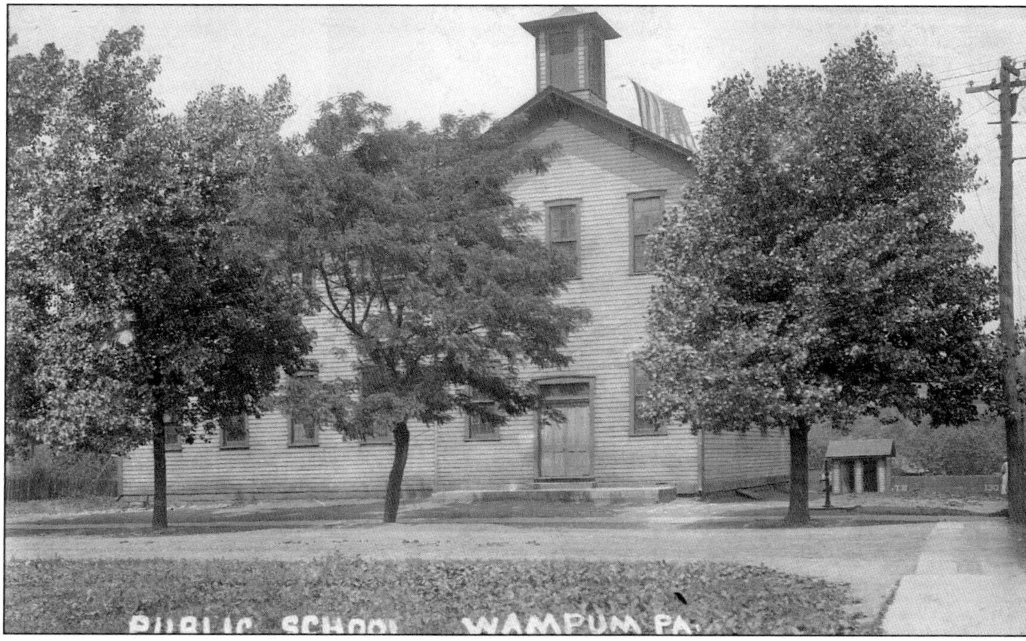

PUBLIC SCHOOL, WAMPUM, EARLY 1900S. This frame building was built in 1877 following a fire in the fall of 1875. Other school buildings followed. Before area schools were consolidated, the Wampum schools produced some distinguished athletes such as basketball coach Butler Hennon, his son All-American Don Hennon, and major-league baseball players Harold, Richard, and Ron Allen.

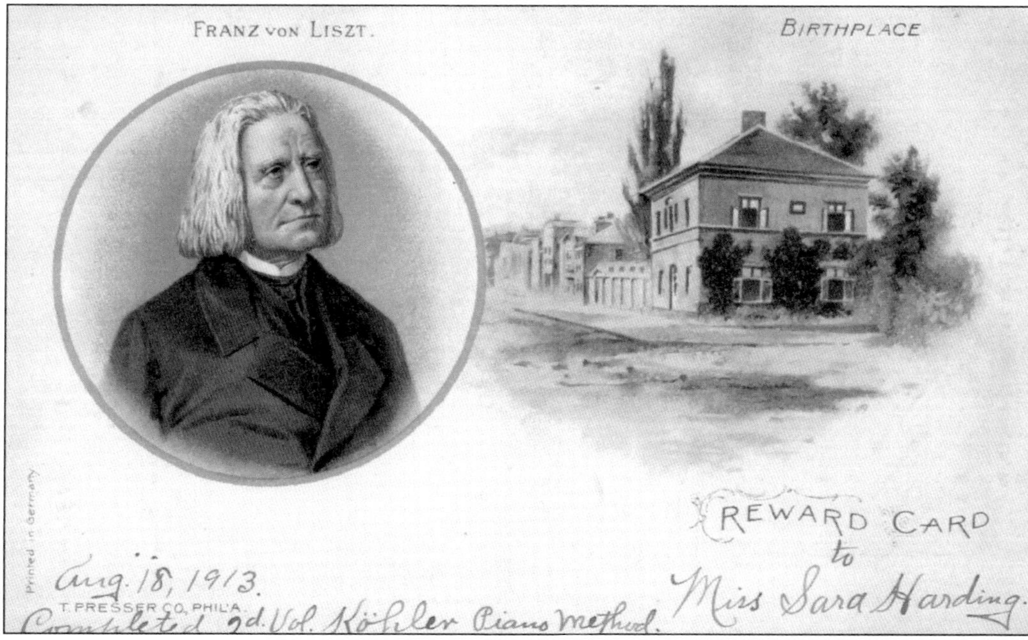

FRANZ VON LISZT REWARD CARD, 1913. Piano teacher J. W. Guy of Wampum gave this reward card to his student Sara Harding for completing her study of the Kohler piano method. The card shows Franz Liszt, who was considered one of the greatest pianists of his time (mid-1800s). As a composer, he is identified with Hungarian Rhapsodies and other musical works.

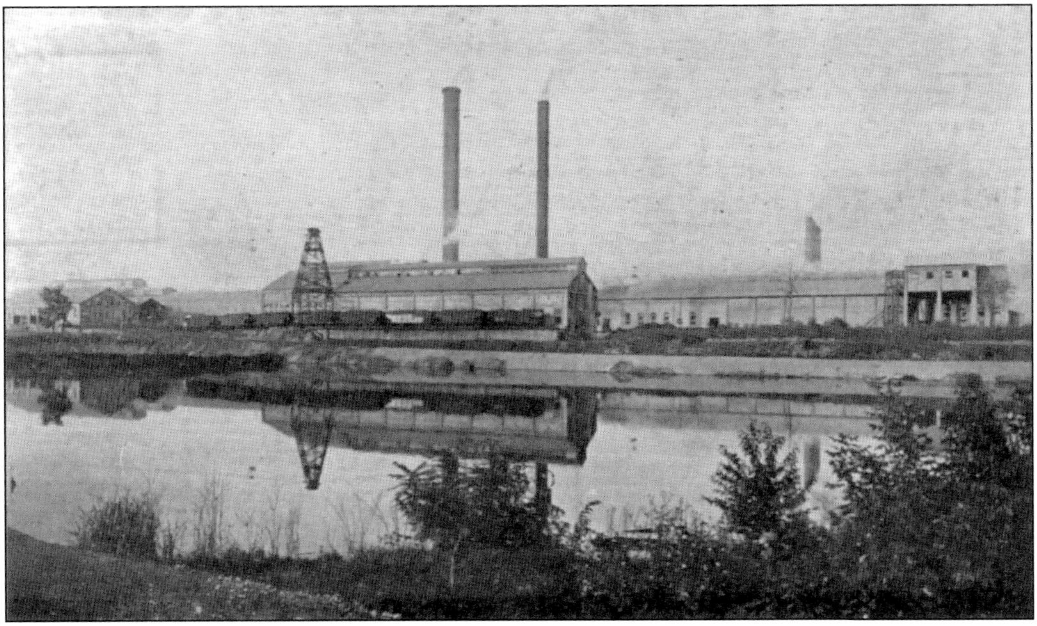

Crescentdale Cement Works, Wampum, *c.* 1913. Portland cement was formulated on the Isle of Portland in England in 1824. This cement plant, first known as the Wampum Mining and Manufacturing Company, was built in 1870. In 1874, it became the Wampum Cement and Lime Company. Around 1900, it became the Crescent Portland Cement Company. Over time, its name has changed to Medusa, then Southdown, and today Cemex (pronounced Semex).

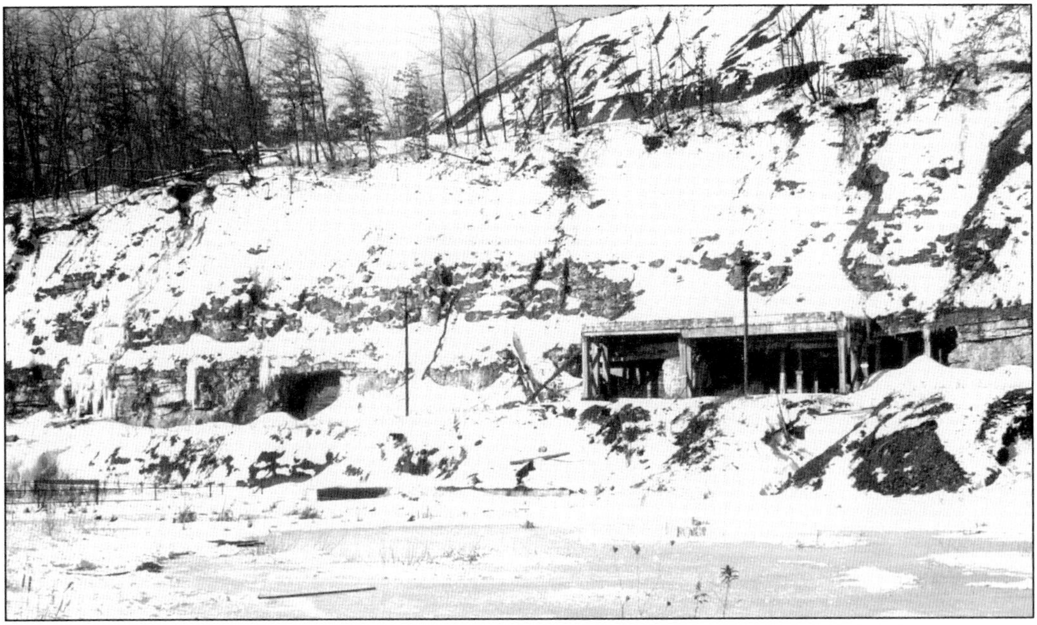

Wampum Mines in Winter. Snow-covered hills cover the Gateway Commerce Center entrance on Pennsylvania's Route 18. The center is a two-and-a-half-million-square-foot limestone mine active from the 1870s to the 1940s. Doorways are large enough to admit trucks, vans, buses, boats, the world's largest telescope lens, and the equipment to polish it. (Courtesy of LCHS, Hitch Collection.)

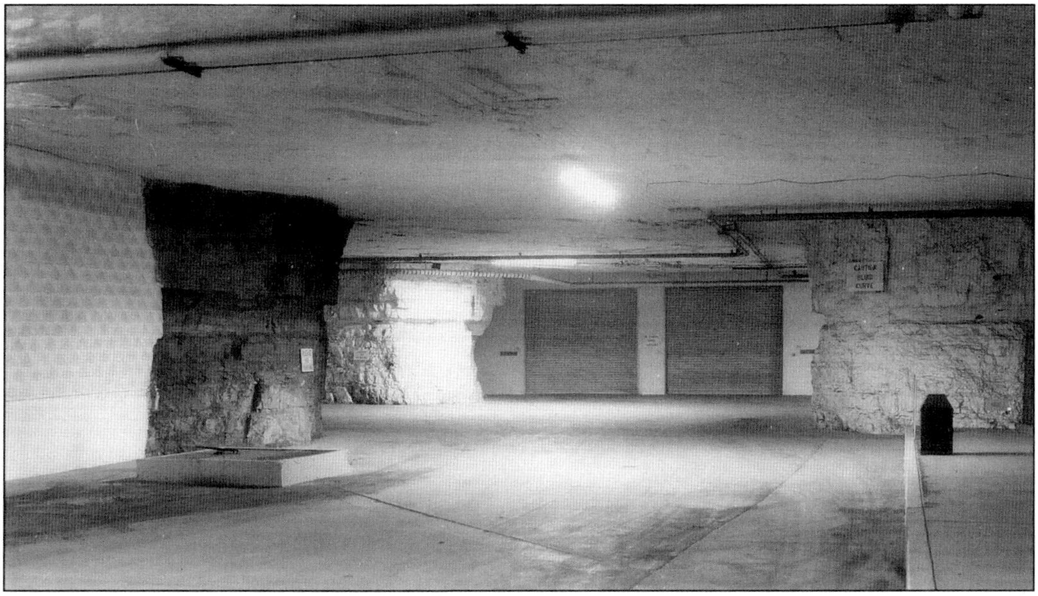

PILLARS IN THE WAMPUM MINES. When the mines were active and limestone was removed, the miners left supporting pillars 30 feet in diameter, 16 feet high, and 50 feet apart. The resulting space was first developed by Medusa Cement Company, which adapted it for future use with electricity, water, sewers, ventilation, temperature controls, flooring, and partitions. Although considered an ideal bomb shelter, the facility was never actually used that way. (Courtesy of LCHS, Hitch Collection.)

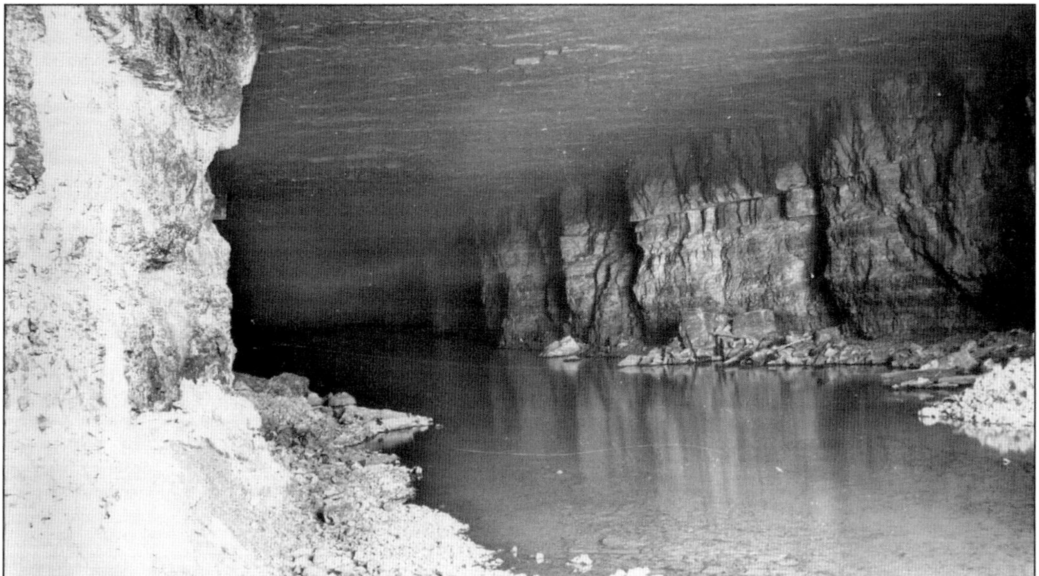

LAKE IN THE WAMPUM MINES. In addition to vehicles, these spaces have housed in the past U.S. government medical supplies, Hollywood film negatives, bank records, experimental hydroponic gardens, pet food, civil defense equipment, and a Medusa Cement technical center. They have also been used as a location for a Hollywood film. Contrary to popular belief, this space has not been used to grow mushrooms, although mushroom caves are in the vicinity. (Courtesy of LCHS, Hitch Collection.)

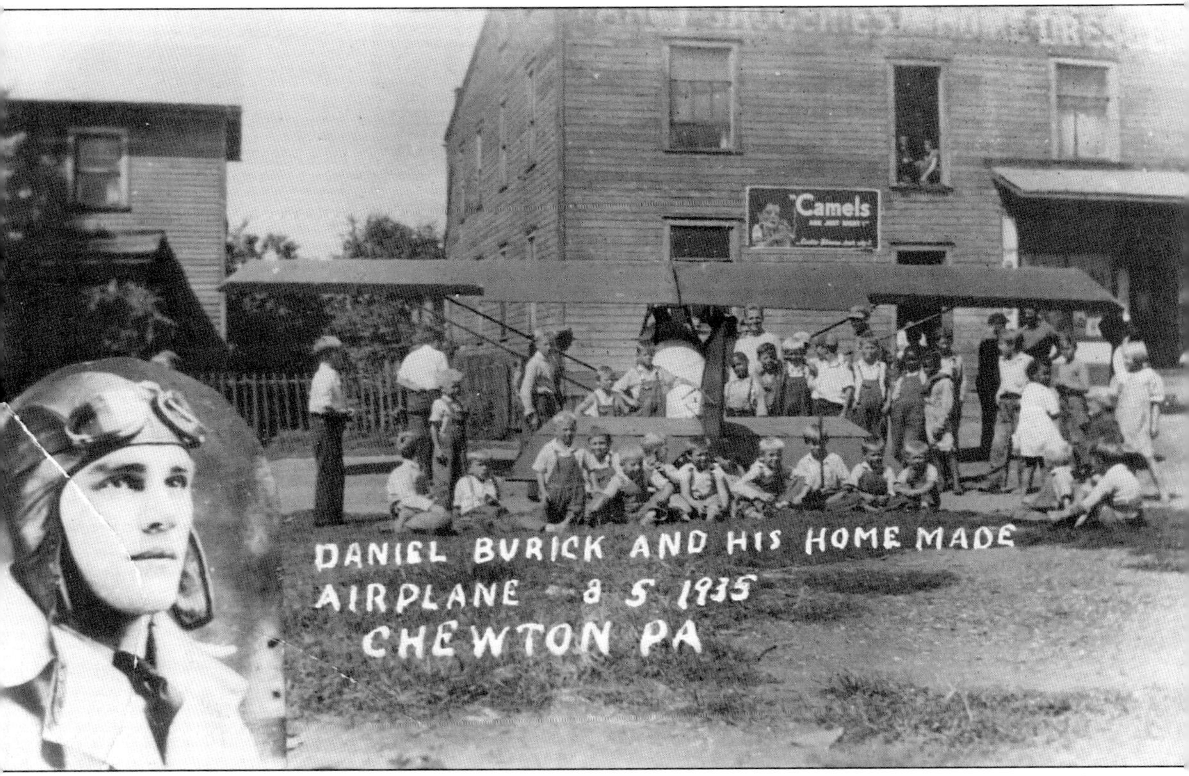

DANIEL BURICK AND HIS HOMEMADE AIRPLANE, CHEWTON, 1935. There were no airplanes in Chewton when Benjamin Chew Jr. started laying out the town in 1830. The area was rich in limestone, and quarries owned by the Lawrence Limestone Company were worked until 1919. One hundred and five years after Chew laid out the town, Daniel Burick built an airplane inside a Chewton farmhouse. A wall of the brick farmhouse had to be removed in order to get the plane out. This composite photograph of Burick and his plane, taken in August 1935, shows Chewton's general store and the children of Chewton proudly posing with the plane. Two years later, on November 7, 1937, Burick, then 26 years old, and his friend Alex Sroczynski, 21 years old, died in an airplane crash when the plane engine failed during a loop over Castlewood. The plane was not the one Burick had built; it had been rented in Youngstown, Ohio.

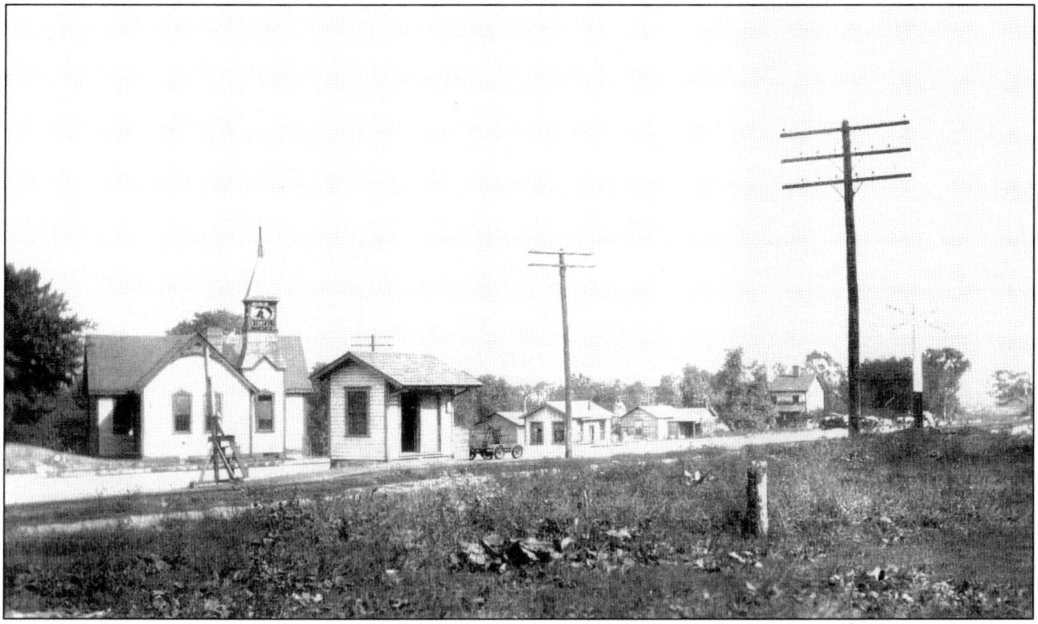

Church and Station at Moravia. Around 1770, Moravian missionaries, the first white settlers in what was to become Lawrence County, established a mission for Native American converts on the Beaver River. They called it Friedensstadt, City of Peace. Although the Moravians moved to Ohio in 1773, the village they founded survived. In 1888, residents of Moravia bought land behind this railroad station for a Presbyterian church. (Courtesy of LCHS, Hitch Collection.)

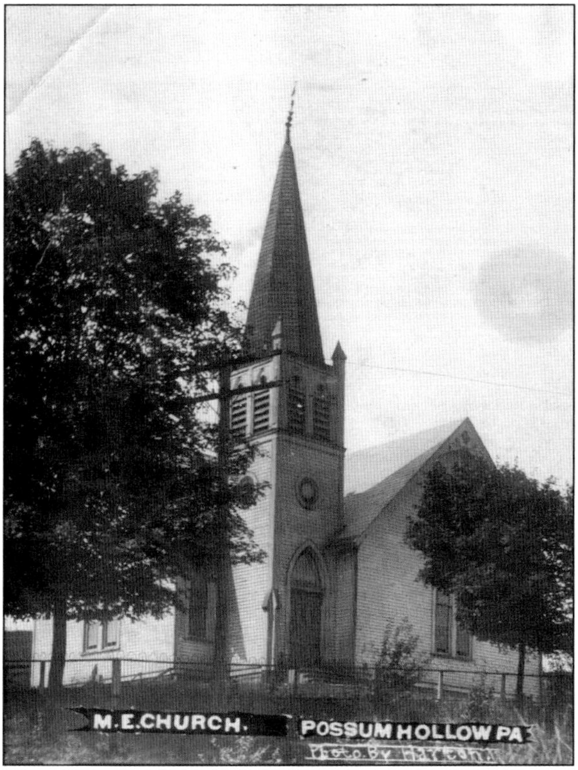

Methodist Episcopal Church, Possum Hollow, Early 1900s. Possum Hollow is located southwest of Wampum near the Beaver County line. Coal was mined on a large scale there in the mid-1800s. The terrain required horses to carry the sacks of coal downhill for loading onto canal boats. Although shipping got easier with the railroads, and in the next century with the opening of Route 18, eventually the mining stopped.

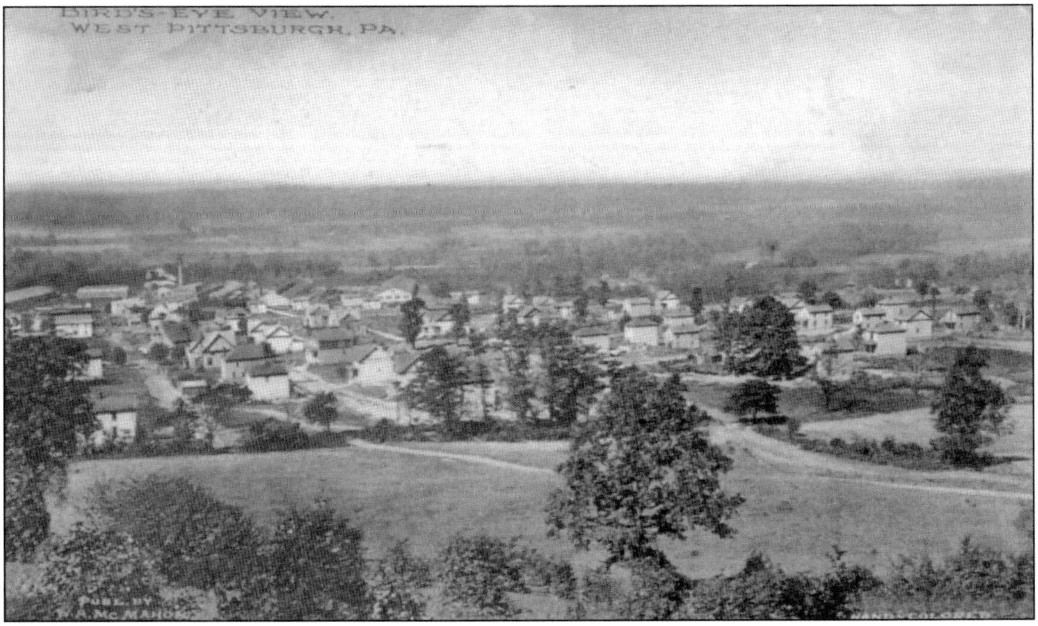

Bird's-Eye View of West Pittsburg, c. 1909. In the early 1900s, West Pittsburg was a thriving community with a limestone quarry, a four-story hotel, small businesses, and trains running through. The West Pittsburg Water Company, owned by the Garland Corporation, was incorporated in 1902, and a waterworks was built in 1905. In this view, several West Pittsburg industries can be seen in the last row of buildings.

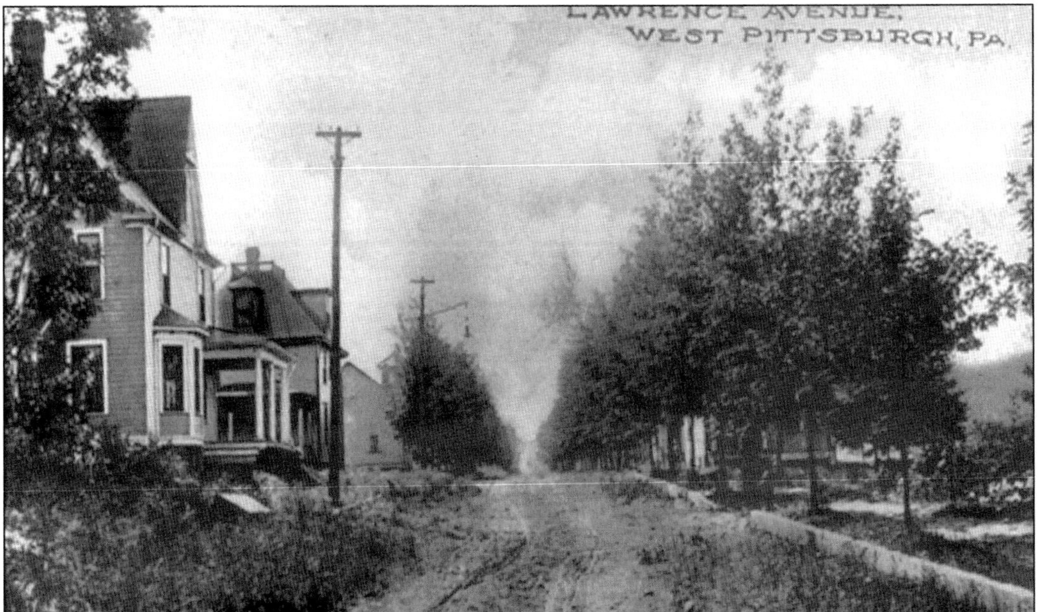

Lawrence Avenue, West Pittsburg, c. 1905. Even though this was West Pittsburg's main street, it was not yet paved in the early 1900s. Called Lawrence Avenue then, eventually this street's name was changed to Center Avenue. The tracks in the muddy street are probably from horse-and-buggy traffic. (Courtesy of Taylor Township Board of Supervisors.)

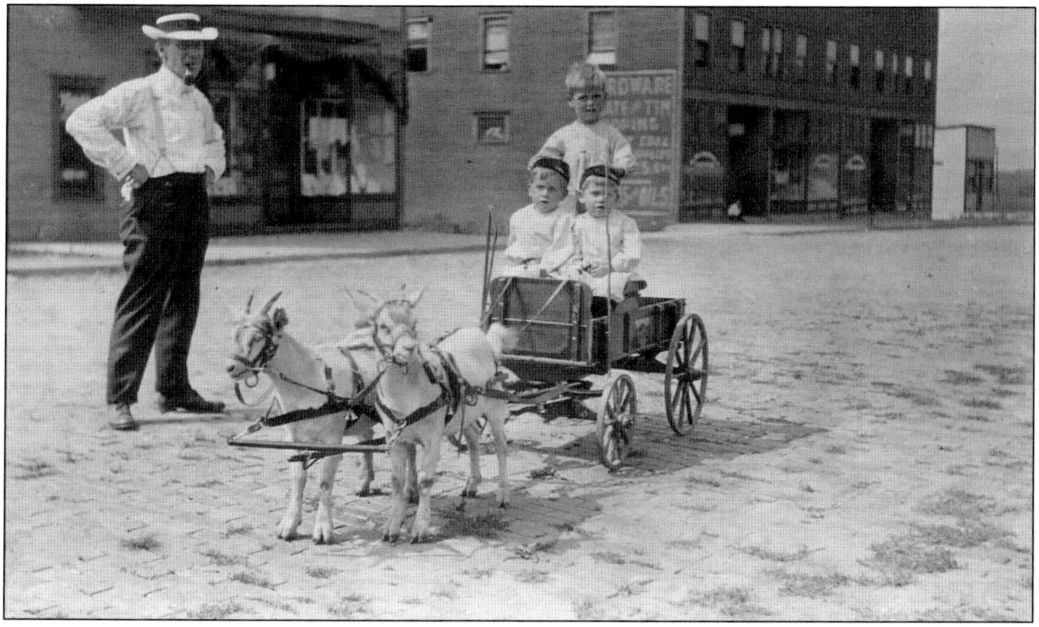

CENTER AVENUE GOAT WAGON, WEST PITTSBURG, 1920S. Here is Center Avenue with brick paving and storefronts. At center, a sign on the building advertises hardware, tin roofing, coal, and other necessities. In this photograph, John Elsesser is watching his children Richard and John drive the goat wagon while an unidentified child looks on. The goats seem to be posing too. (Courtesy of Mary Ann Elsesser.)

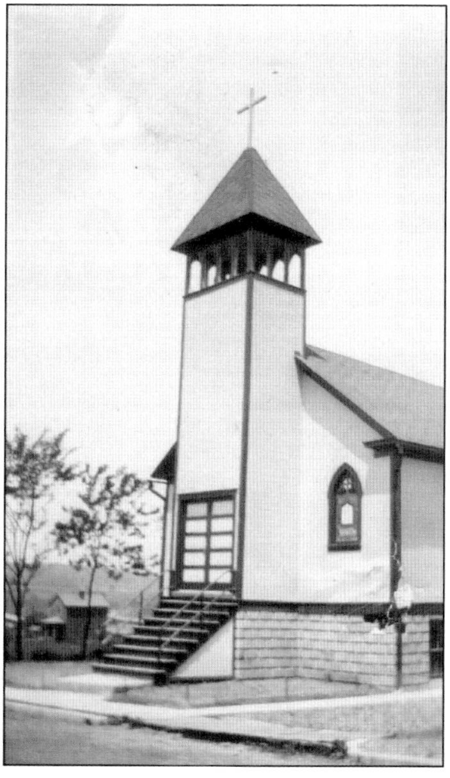

HOLY CROSS CATHOLIC CHURCH, WEST PITTSBURG, LATE 1920S. Before this church was built in 1925, West Pittsburg Catholics traveled to New Castle, Mahoningtown, or Wampum for services. Eventually services were in the city building once a month. The church was remodeled through the 1960s and 1970s. In 1993, Holy Cross merged with three other parishes in New Castle to form St. Vincent de Paul parish. (Courtesy of Mary Ann Elsesser.)

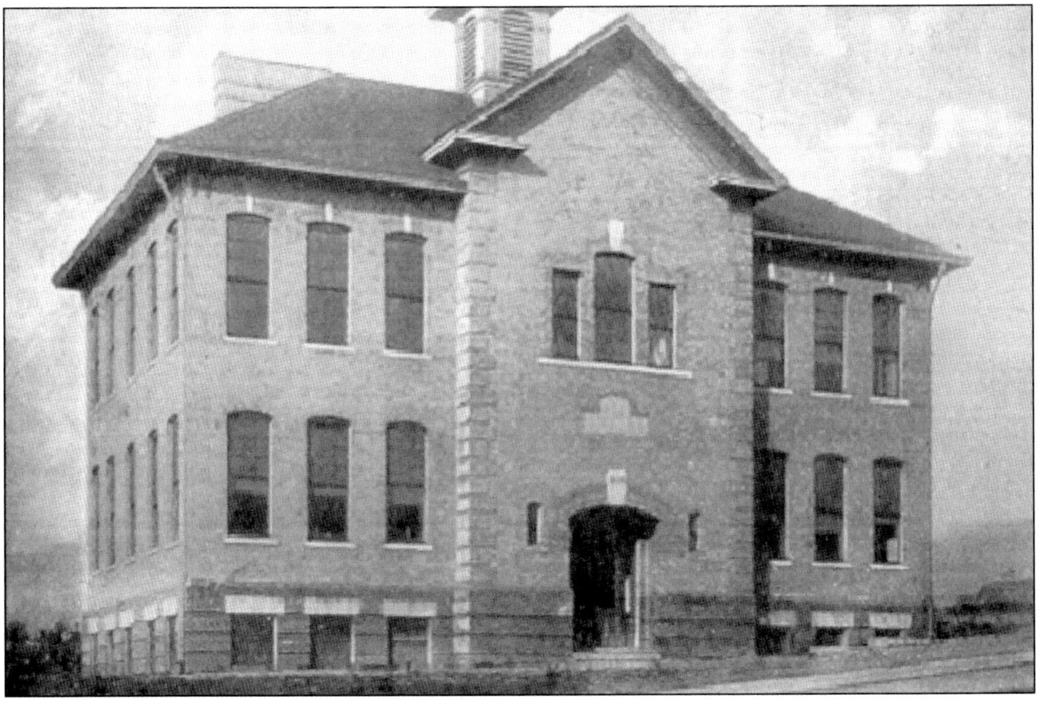

PUBLIC SCHOOL, WEST PITTSBURG, C. 1900. West Pittsburg children attended this sturdy brick schoolhouse, a far cry from the one-room schoolhouses attended by so many students in Lawrence County. In the early 1900s, teachers did not need more than a high school education, but by the 1920s, a two-year diploma from a normal school or teachers college was required. (Courtesy of Taylor Township Board of Supervisors.)

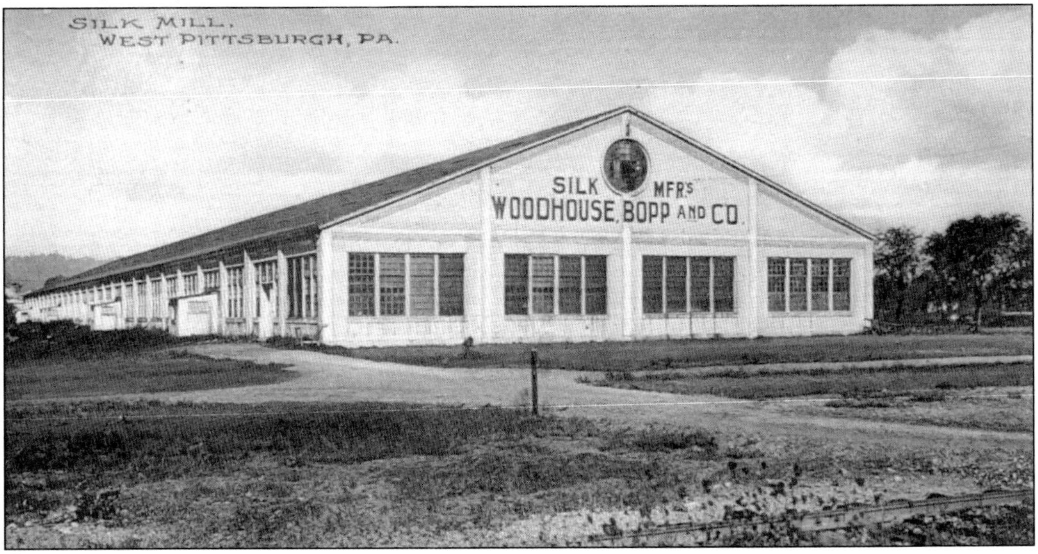

SILK MILL, WEST PITTSBURG, C. 1910. Woodhouse, Bopp and Company were silk manufacturers in the early 1900s. Women and children were the primary labor force in silk mills then, making Pennsylvania a leader in silk production in the United States. Many strong protests against child labor led to compulsory school attendance for children, and the U.S. silk industry diminished as the Japanese silk industry flourished. This building is still standing.

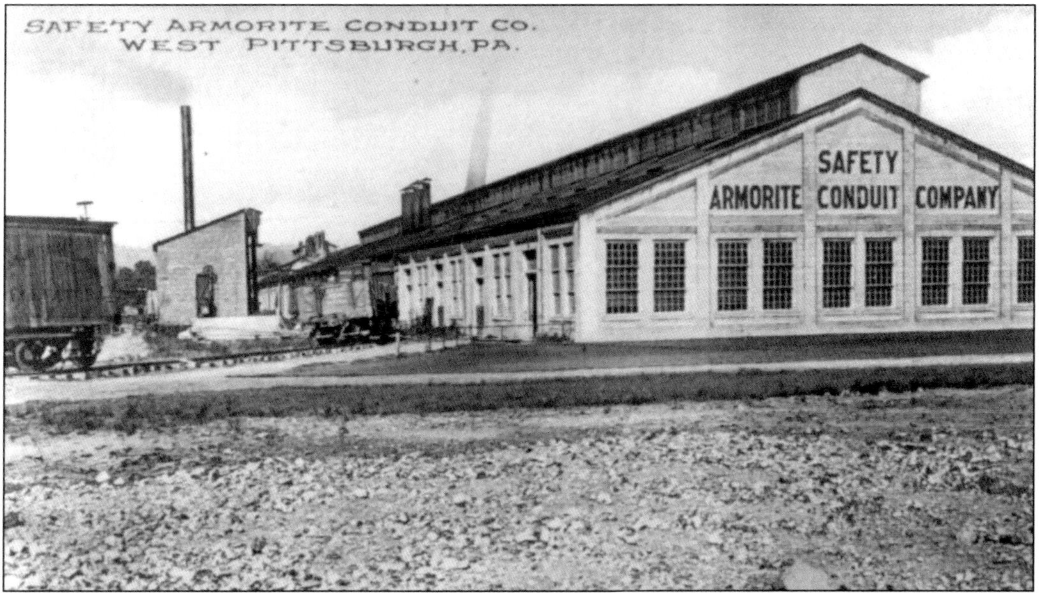

SAFETY ARMORITE CONDUIT COMPANY, WEST PITTSBURG, *C.* 1904. In the early 1900s, West Pittsburg's railroads, limestone, and willing workers began to attract industries. A major one was the Garland Manufacturing Company, which owned this building. It did well because electricity for households was still a young industry and conduit wiring was becoming essential. Safety Armorite eventually became a part of the General Electric Corporation. (Courtesy of Taylor Township Board of Supervisors.)

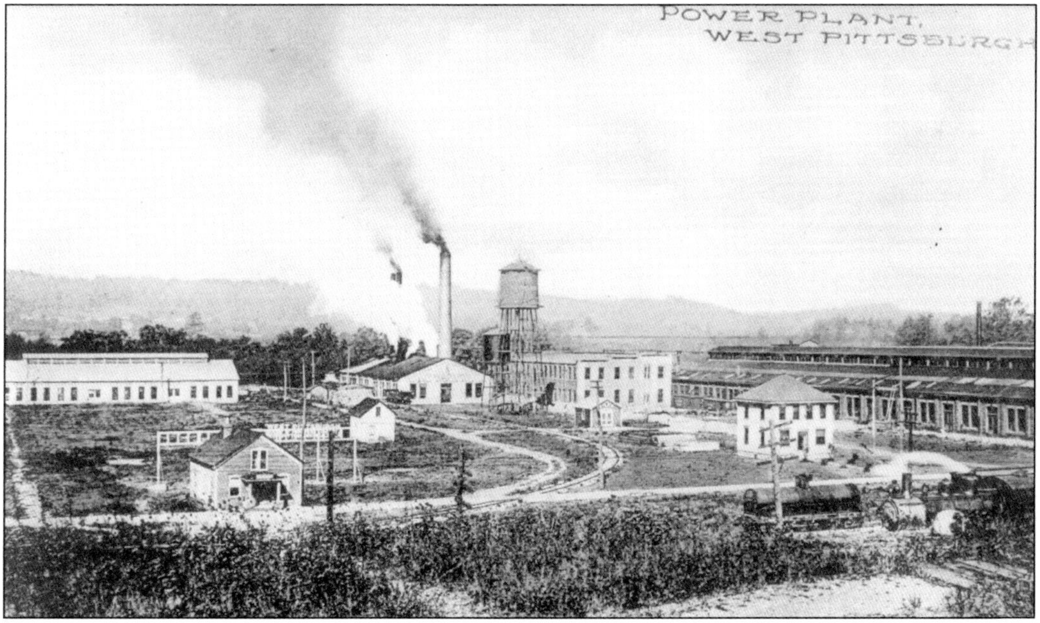

WEST PITTSBURG POWER PLANT, *C.* 1905. This early power plant was in the midst of the new industries in West Pittsburg. It preceded the Pennsylvania Power Company's power plant built in 1939. That power plant, enlarged many times since it was built, was dedicated by Wendell Willkie, who was a candidate for U.S. president in 1940. (Courtesy of Taylor Township Board of Supervisors.)

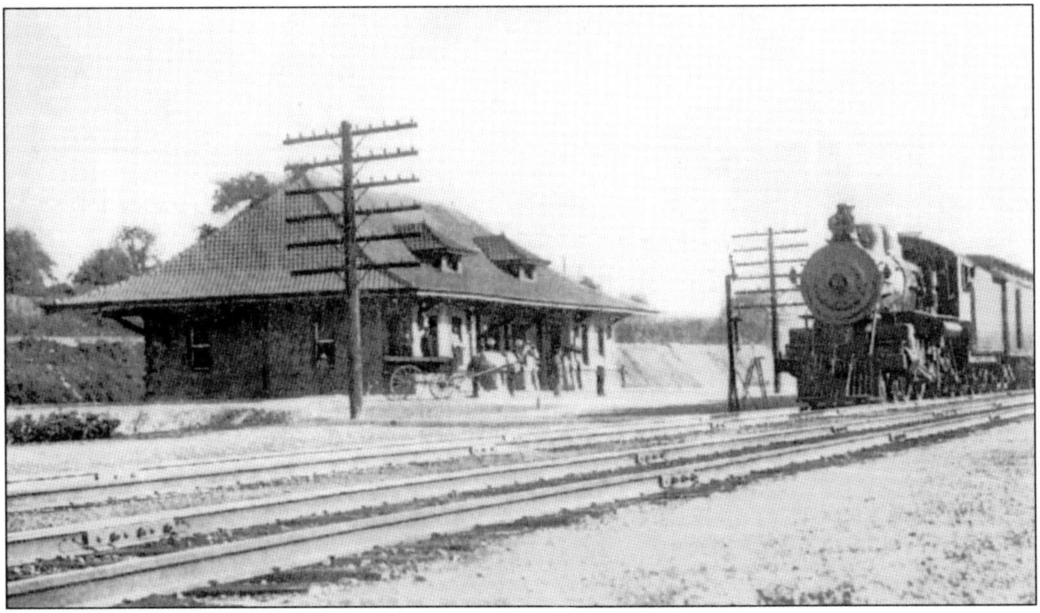

P&LE Railroad Station, West Pittsburg, c. 1909. This station, 100 years old in 2007, is being restored by the Beaver Valley Junction chapter of the National Railroad Historical Society. Pres. Harry Truman drove a train past the station in 1948 when he was campaigning for reelection. A new diesel engine was hooked up to the campaign train at New Castle Junction, and Truman sat in the engineer's seat until the train reached Cumberland, Maryland. (Courtesy of Don Gee.)

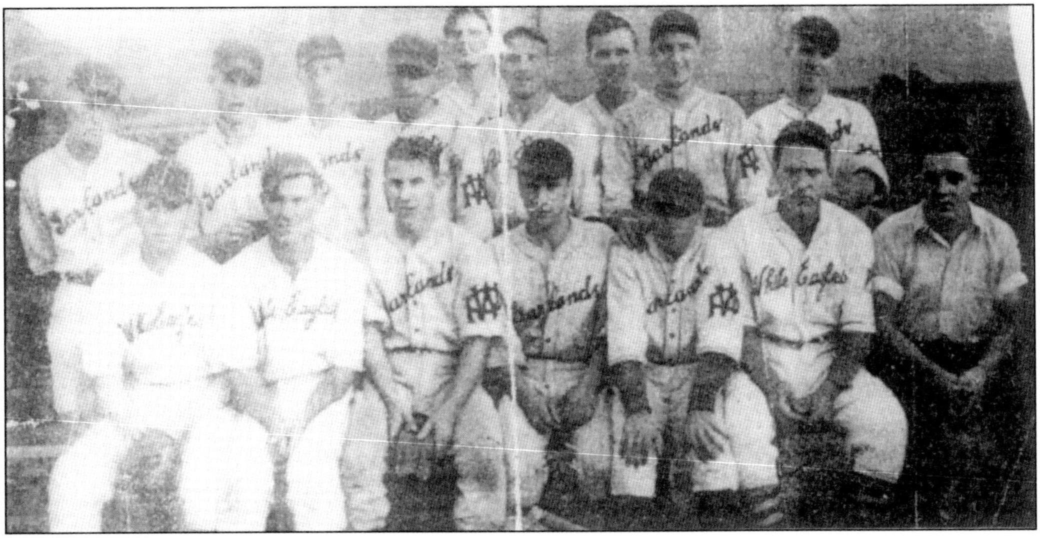

Gas House Gang, West Pittsburg, 1937. The Garland Manufacturing Company sponsored this local baseball team known as the Gas House Gang. From left to right are (first row) Frank Powell, John Winters, John Marcantino, Ralph Fundoots, George Tonsetic, Steve Winters, and manager Daniel DeGenova; (second row) Richard Elsesser, John Elsesser, Albert DeMonaco, James Marcantino, "Dutch Hill" Kolick, John Kolick, Tony Kosier, John DeMonaco, and ? Dombeck. (Courtesy of Mary Ann Elsesser.)

Three

Ellwood City Area

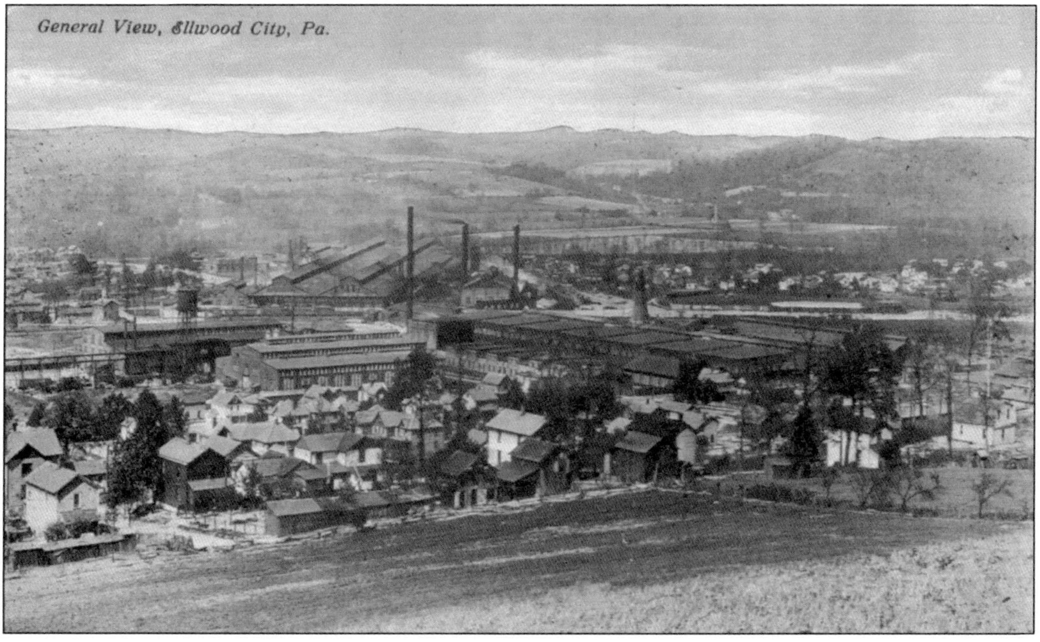

Bird's-Eye View of Ellwood City, Early 1900s. Ellwood City was founded in 1889 by Henry Waters Hartman, a steel industrialist from Beaver Falls. Hartman broke ground for the town in 1890 and named it for his friend Isaac L. Ellwood, who invented barbed wire fencing. In 1892, Ellwood City became a borough. This view, looking north toward the borough of Hazel Dell, shows how much industry had already come into the town in its earliest years.

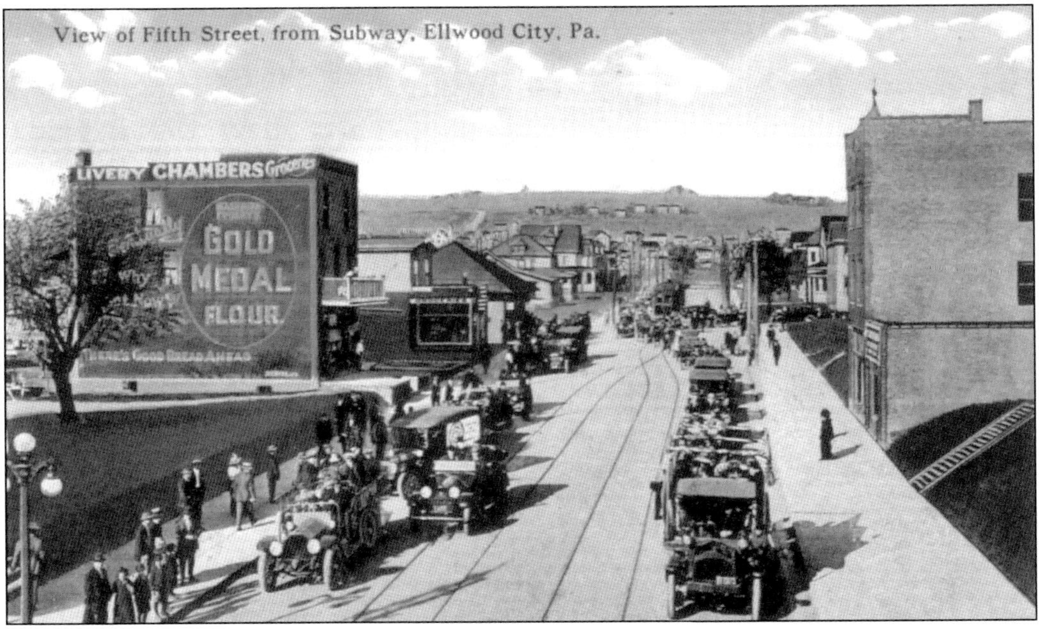

VIEW OF FIFTH STREET FROM ELLWOOD CITY SUBWAY, *c*. 1914. This motorcade was probably organized to mark the formal opening of the Fifth Street Subway adjacent to union station. In the distance is the borough of Hazel Dell on Ellwood City's north side, which became the fourth ward of Ellwood City in 1914. The Fifth Street Bridge does not appear in this view; it was completed in 1915.

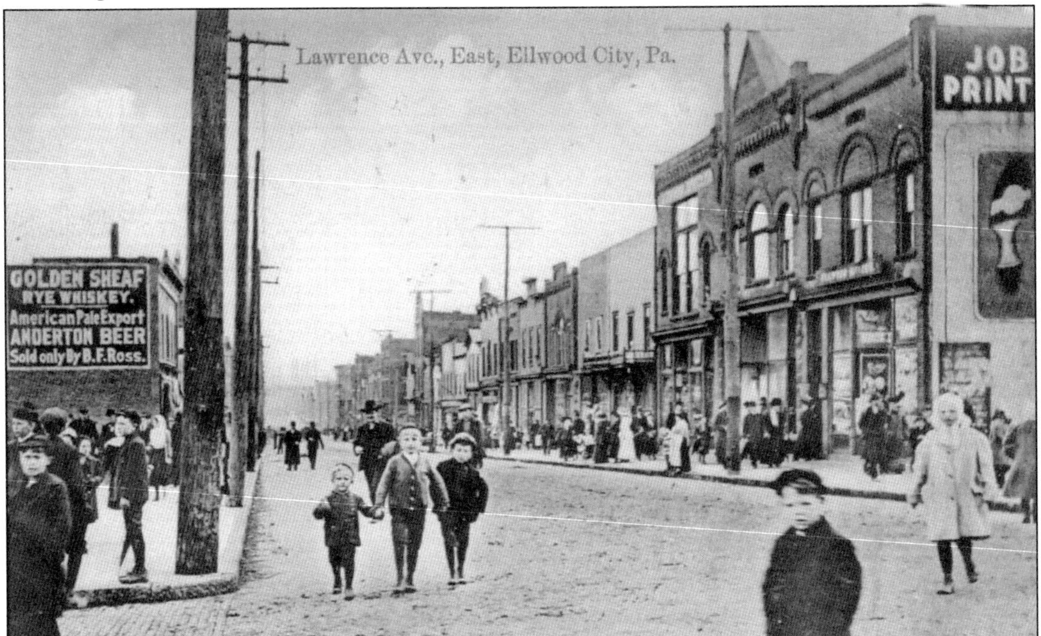

LAWRENCE AVENUE LOOKING EAST, ELLWOOD CITY, *c*. 1911. Before Ellwood City became a borough in 1892, the area was largely rural. With the development of rail lines, industries, and small businesses, Lawrence Avenue became a commercial center, the place for city residents to transact business, do shopping, and run errands. The street was paved in 1906.

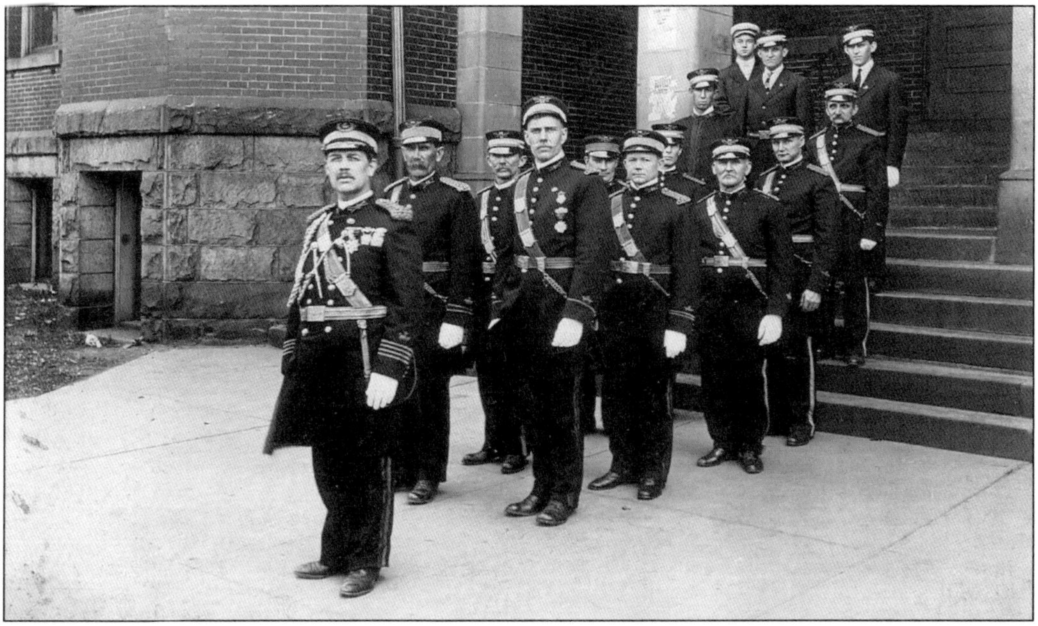

Odd Fellows in Uniform, Early 1900s. The Independent Order of Odd Fellows (IOOF) was founded in 1819 in Baltimore. It was based on a fraternal organization in England. By 1899, Ellwood City had two lodges of the IOOF. Here members of one of the lodges appear in full regalia. Carl Daellenbach leads the group. Also in the photograph are Bert Roupe, second row, right, and a Mr. Shanor, fifth row, left.

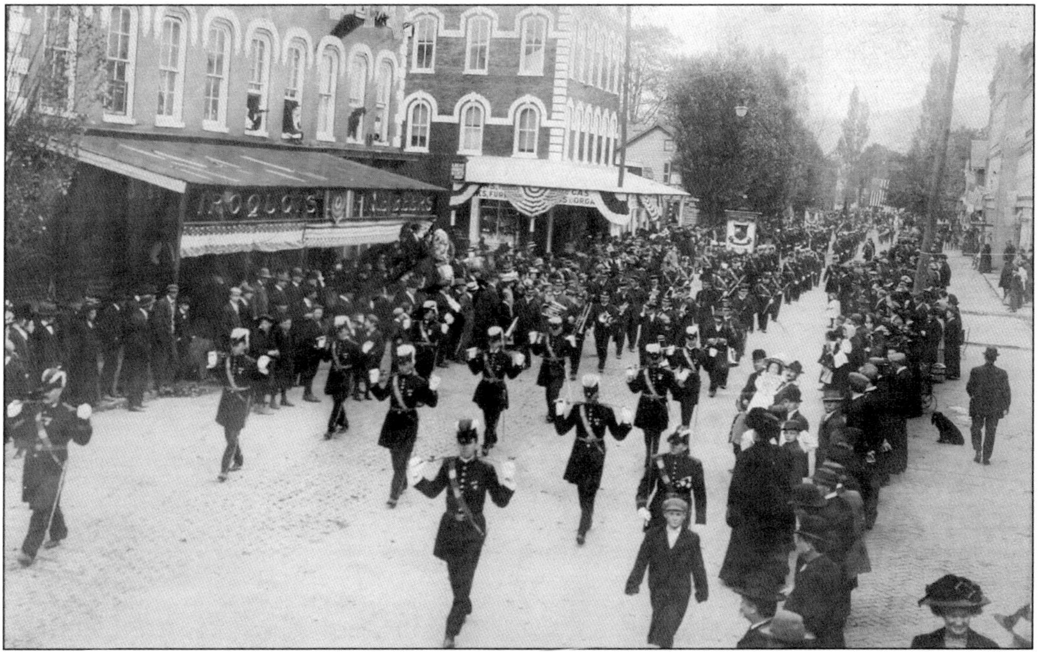

Odd Fellows on Parade, Early 1900s. In this view, the Odd Fellows hold their swords in a drill as they march ahead of the band. The sign on the left reads "Iroquois Beer." On the sidewalk at right center sits a little black dog enjoying the outing.

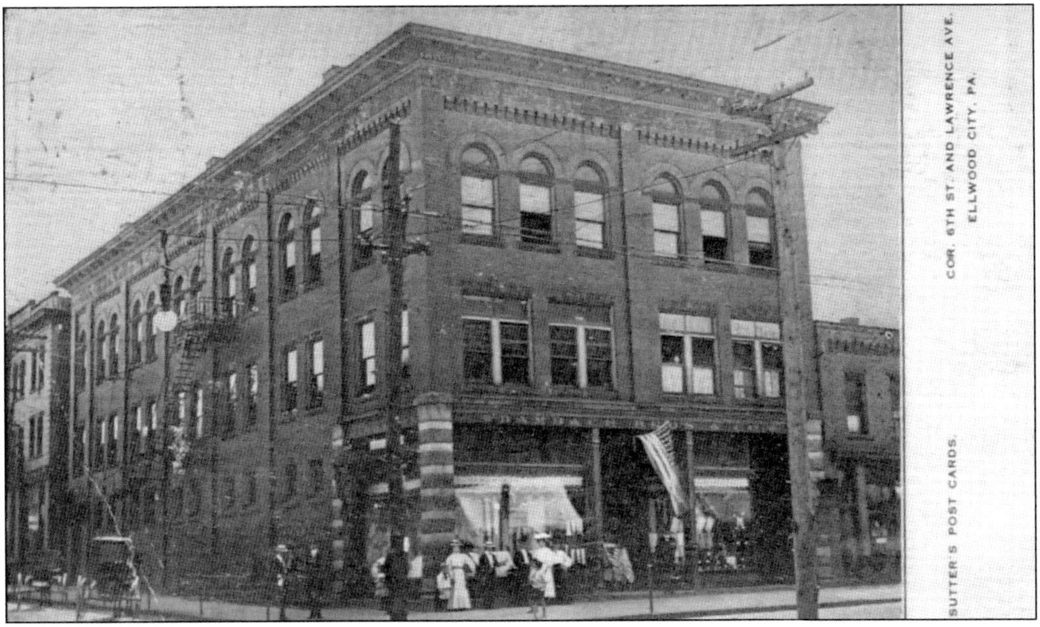

DAMBACH BUILDING, EARLY 1900S. Dambach Brothers and Company was a clothing retail store on the southwest corner of Lawrence Avenue and Sixth Street. The pedestrians near the building are well dressed, good advertising for the store. The two little boys on the sidewalk appear to be walking without shoes.

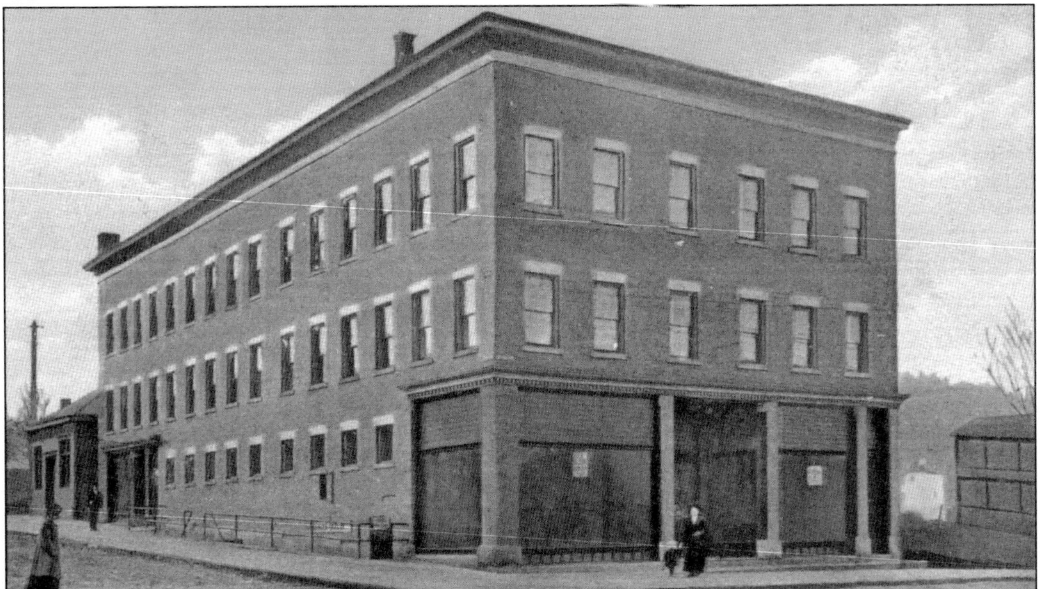

STIEFEL BUILDING, EARLY 1900S. Much of the industrial life of Ellwood City can be credited to Ralph C. Stiefel, a mechanical engineer who started at the Ellwood Seamless Tube Company, then moved on to the Shelby Steel Tube Company. After Shelby was absorbed by the U.S. Steel Corporation, Stiefel became general superintendent of all U.S. Steel plants in the United States. The Stiefel Building (spelling inncorrectly on this postcard) stands on the southwest corner of Lawrence Avenue and Fifth Street.

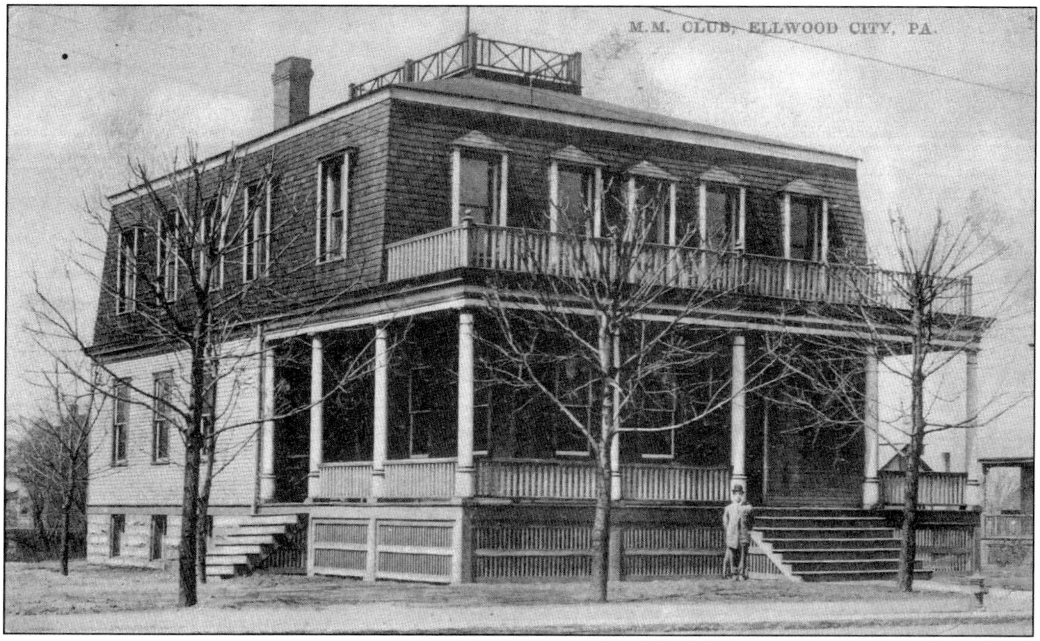

M and M Club, Early 1900s. At a banquet in 1900, the leading merchants and manufacturers of Ellwood City decided to form the M and M Club. In 1902, they built this clubhouse on the west side of Fourth Street. The building was later occupied by the Veterans of Foreign Wars.

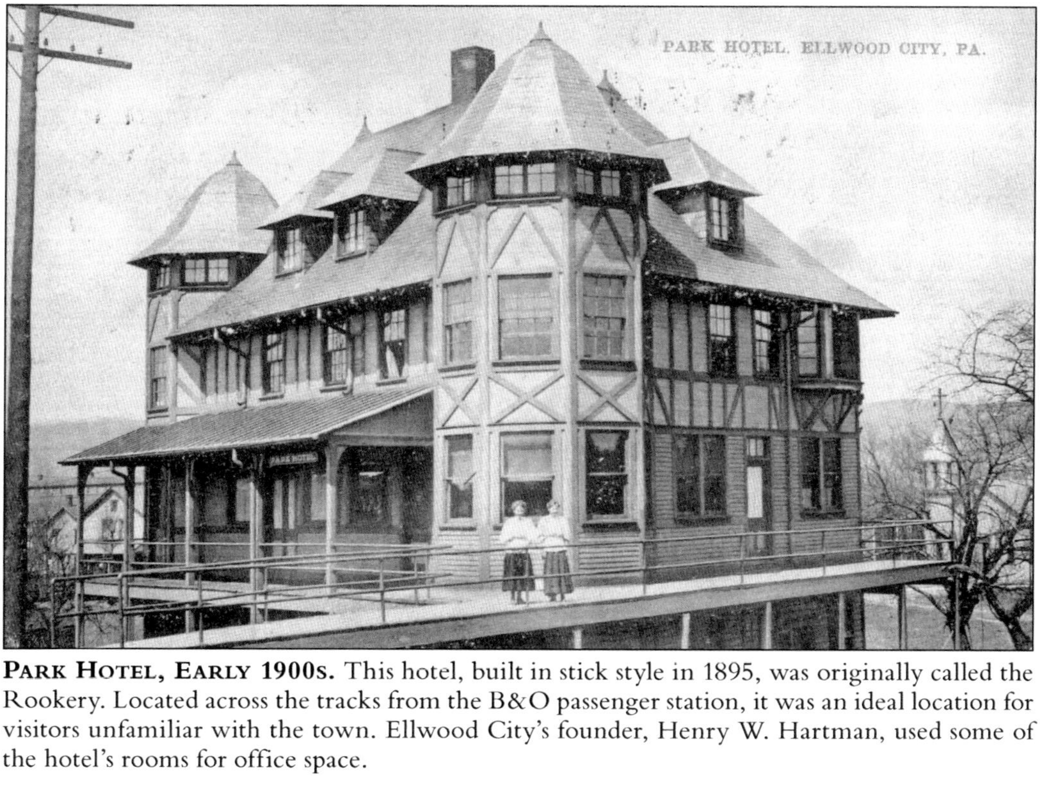

Park Hotel, Early 1900s. This hotel, built in stick style in 1895, was originally called the Rookery. Located across the tracks from the B&O passenger station, it was an ideal location for visitors unfamiliar with the town. Ellwood City's founder, Henry W. Hartman, used some of the hotel's rooms for office space.

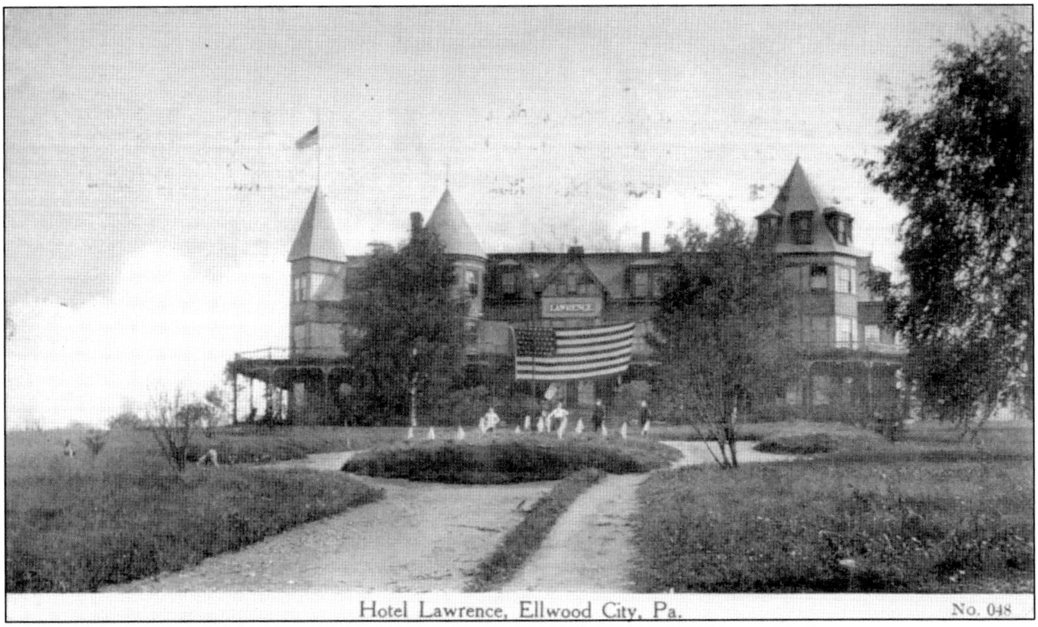

HOTEL LAWRENCE, EARLY 1900S. The first hotel in Ellwood City was the gracious Hotel Oliver, built in 1890 at the southern end of Fifth Street. In 1896, after several changes of management, it was renamed Hotel Lawrence. In 1914, the hotel became the Lawrence Building when it was sold to Ellwood City's board of education for classroom use. The building was torn down in 1925, and it was replaced by the Lincoln School building.

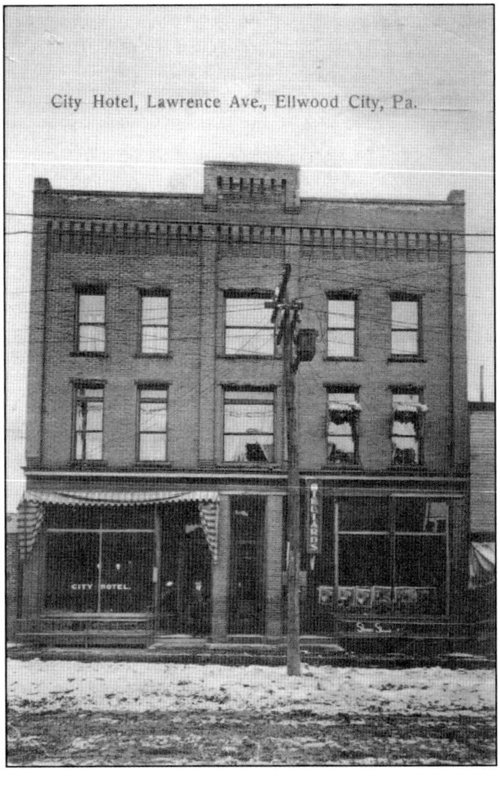

CITY HOTEL, EARLY 1900S. The building that housed the City Hotel on Lawrence Avenue also housed a billiard parlor where hotel guests could get their shoes shined. The 28-room hotel was renovated in 1905 with the latest in conveniences for guests.

CENTRAL HOUSE, EARLY 1900S. The hotel shown in this postcard was also known as the Grand Central Hotel on Lawrence Avenue between Seventh and Eighth Streets. Built in 1903, it had 30 rooms and a large commercial trade. It was later known as the McDowell Hotel.

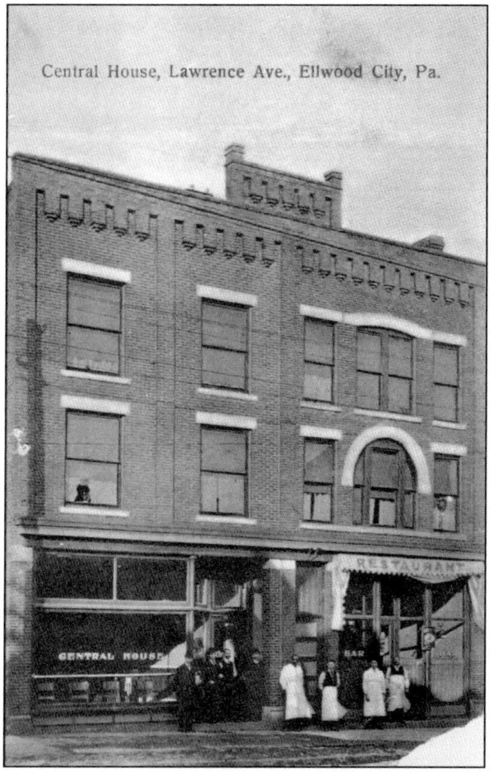

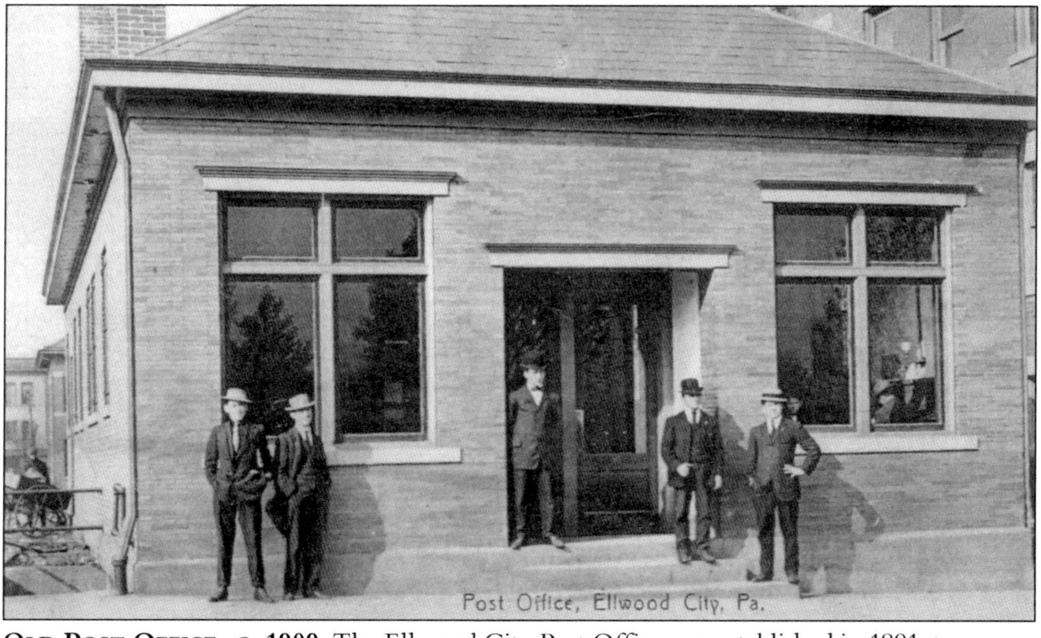

OLD POST OFFICE, *C.* 1909. The Ellwood City Post Office was established in 1891, two years after the city was founded. It had several addresses on Lawrence Avenue and Seventh Street, then moved into this building on Fifth Street behind the Stiefel Building. The post office is now located at Seventh Street and Crescent Avenue, and this building, beautifully restored, now houses the Ellwood City Area Historical Society.

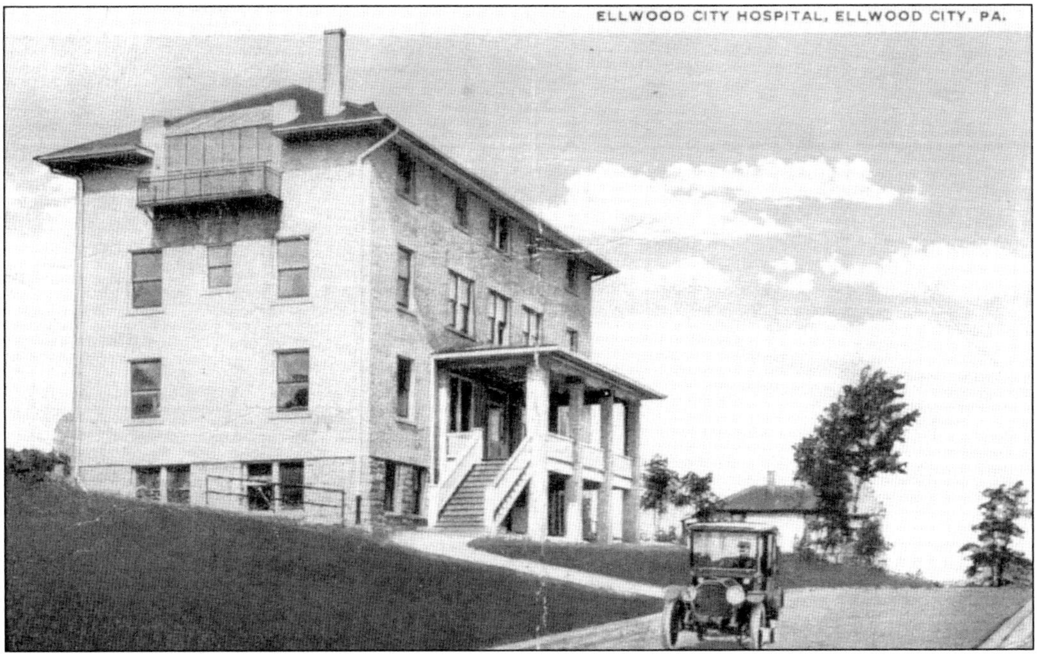

ELLWOOD HOSPITAL, *C.* 1920. Ellwood City's first hospital was founded by N. Belle Drake, M.D. Drake bought the H. S. Blatt residence on Seventh Street and Crescent Avenue and remodeled it to include a surgery and laboratory, nurses' stations, and accommodations for 10 patients. She admitted the hospital's first patient in December 1910.

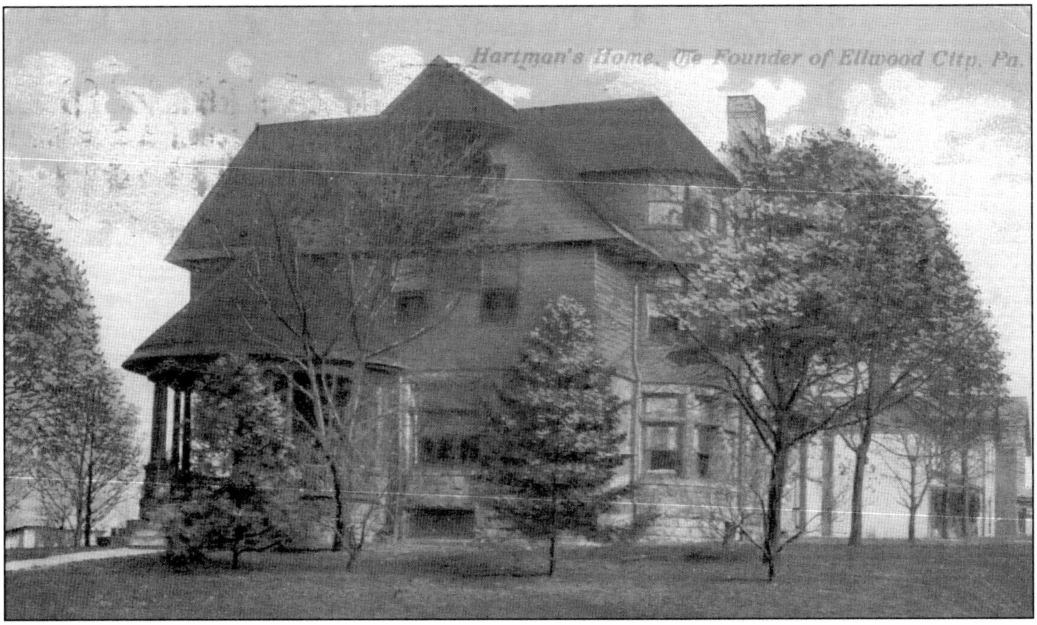

HARTMAN RESIDENCE, EARLY 1900S. Henry W. Hartman, founder of Ellwood City, built this home on Fourth Street and Crescent Avenue in 1893. Hartman was president of the Pittsburgh Company, which developed the new city. As successful as he was as a businessman, and as the first burgess of the city, he failed to establish a street railway system. Disappointed, he moved to Denver, Colorado, where he died in 1914.

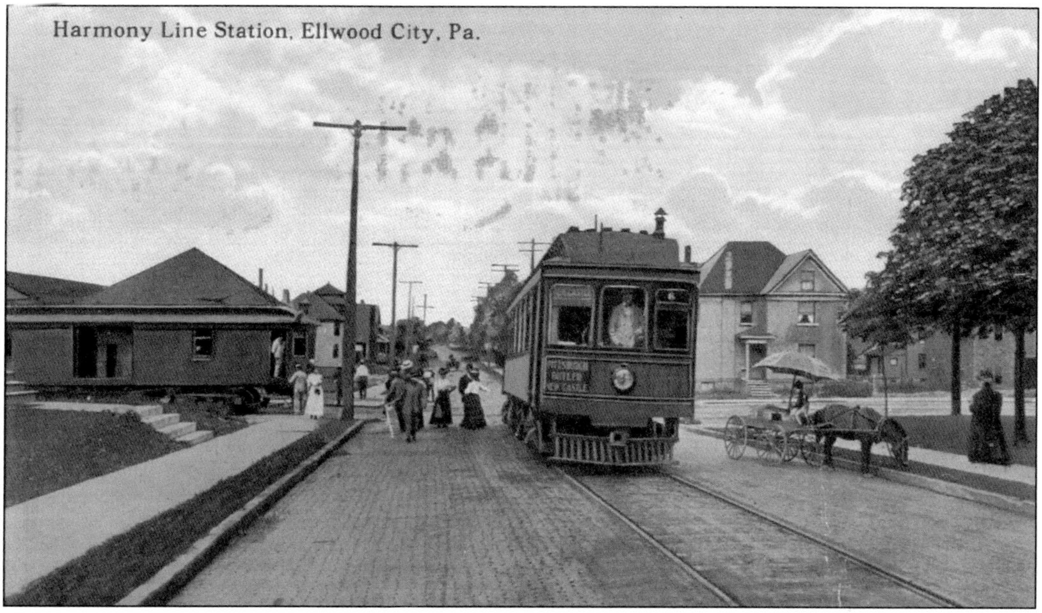

HARMONY LINE STATION, EARLY 1900S. This station of the Pittsburgh, Harmony, Butler, and New Castle Railway Company was on the southwest corner of Fifth Street and Spring Avenue, near union station. The Harmony Line played an important role in the communities it served from 1908 to 1931; citizens could afford to travel faster and more often to nearby Pittsburgh, and to neighboring towns. The last car, called "the Bummer," ran in August 1931.

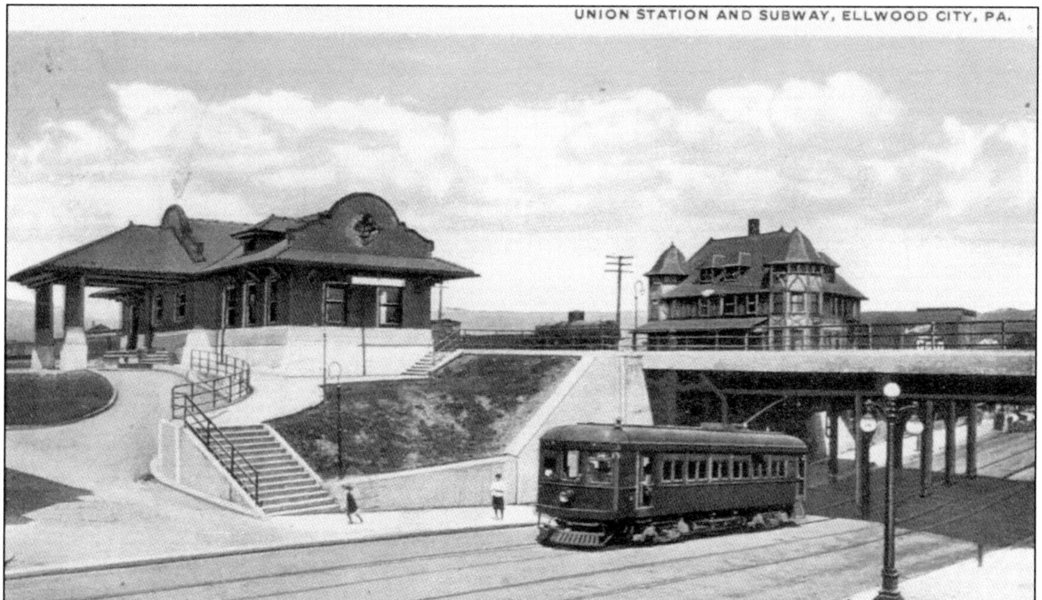

UNION STATION AND SUBWAY, *C.* 1914. The union station on the southeast side of Fifth Street served both the P&LE and the B&O. Convenient to the Park Hotel, it opened in 1912. The underpass on Fifth Street, called the subway, was a convenience for pedestrians and trolleys alike. The Harmony Line cars built to fit under the subway were called "gunboats."

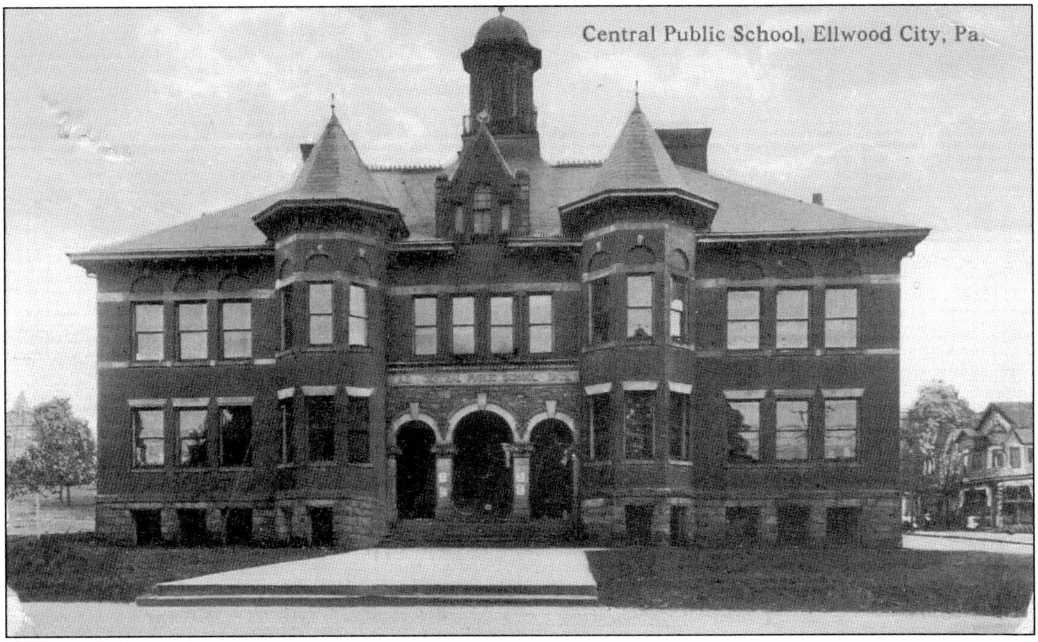

CENTRAL PUBLIC SCHOOL, EARLY 1900S. The third public school in Ellwood City was the Central Public School on the southeast corner of Lawrence Avenue and Sixth Street. Although the school was sold to Ellwood City for use as a city building, the school board rented the building from the city until 1935, when it was razed. The municipal building was constructed in its place.

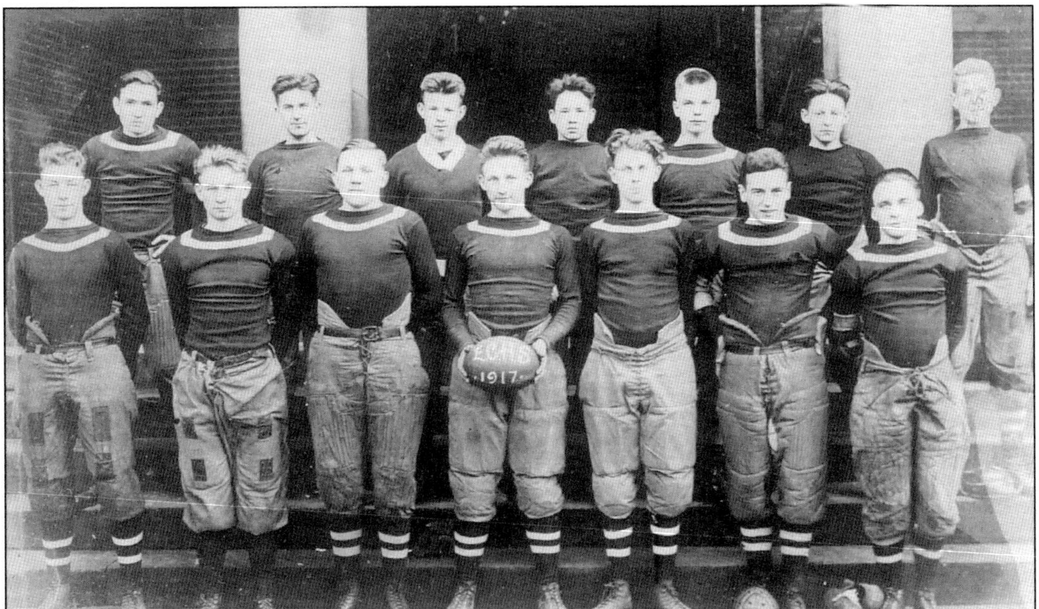

ELLWOOD CITY HIGH SCHOOL FOOTBALL TEAM, 1917. With the growth of industry in Ellwood City, the need for schools increased. Classrooms were crowded, and the Central Public School was not sufficient. By 1917, Ellwood City's high school was in the old Hotel Lawrence, renamed the Lawrence Building. The school board had acquired the hotel and grounds, converting them to classrooms and an athletic field. Note the team jerseys on the young athletes.

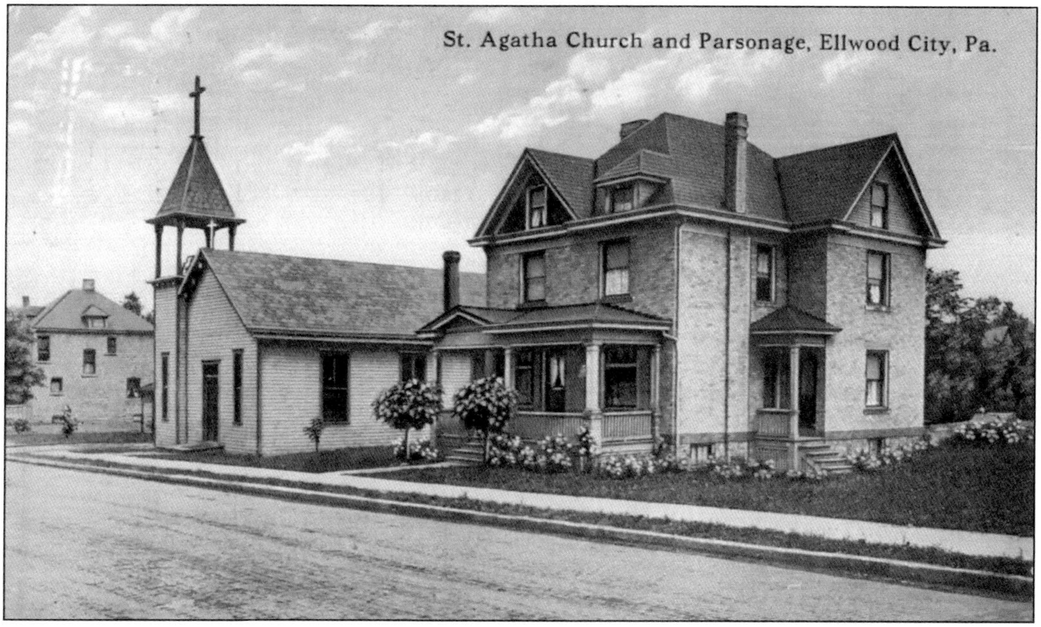

St. Agatha Church and Parsonage, *c.* 1913. Until the St. Agatha parish was founded in 1895, Ellwood City Catholics worshipped in private homes. In 1895, this frame church was built, but by 1914, a new church was needed. The parsonage was retained, and a new church building was dedicated in 1918. In 2000, St. Agatha merged with Purification of the Blessed Virgin Mary to create the new parish of Holy Redeemer.

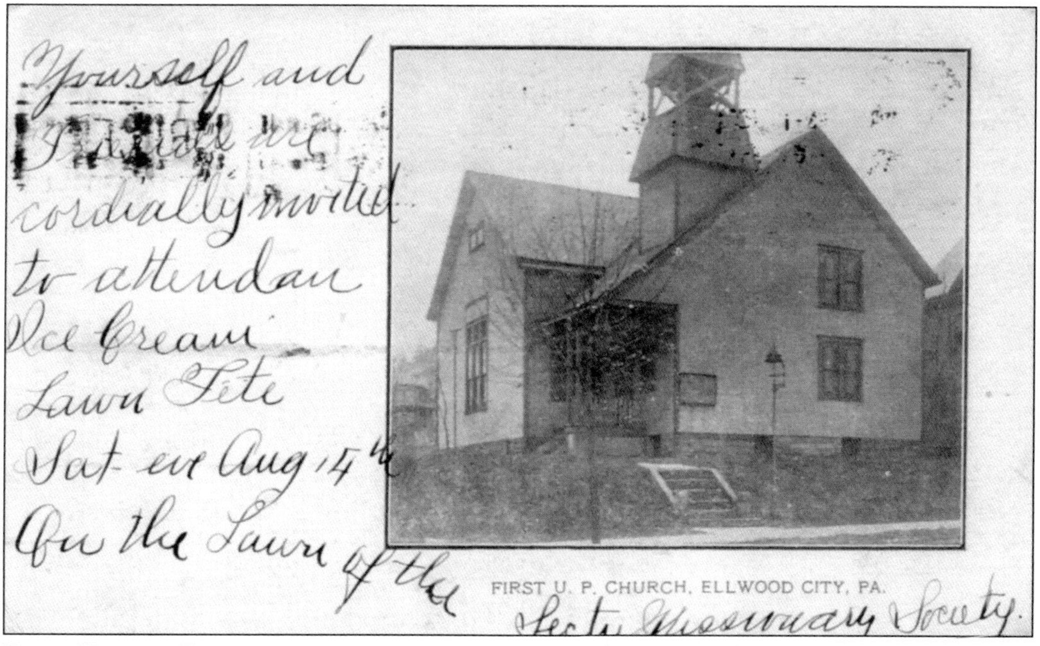

First United Presbyterian Church, *c.* 1909. This simple church building on Crescent Avenue was constructed in 1891 on land donated by the Pittsburgh Company, which was developing Ellwood City. The congregation steadily grew. By 1915, a more elaborate new building on the same site was dedicated.

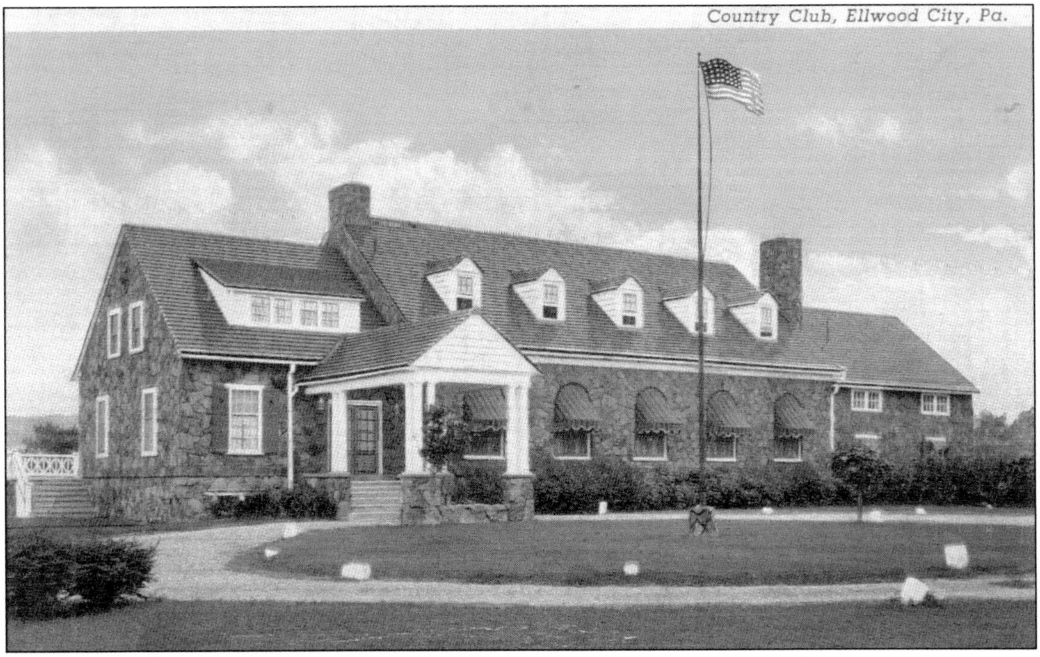

ELLWOOD CITY COUNTRY CLUB, 1920S. The country club was organized in 1917. The original clubhouse, the remodeled mansion of Dr. J. M. Hazen, was within walking distance from a private stop on the Harmony Line. In 1927, this new clubhouse was built about 1,000 feet south of the original club.

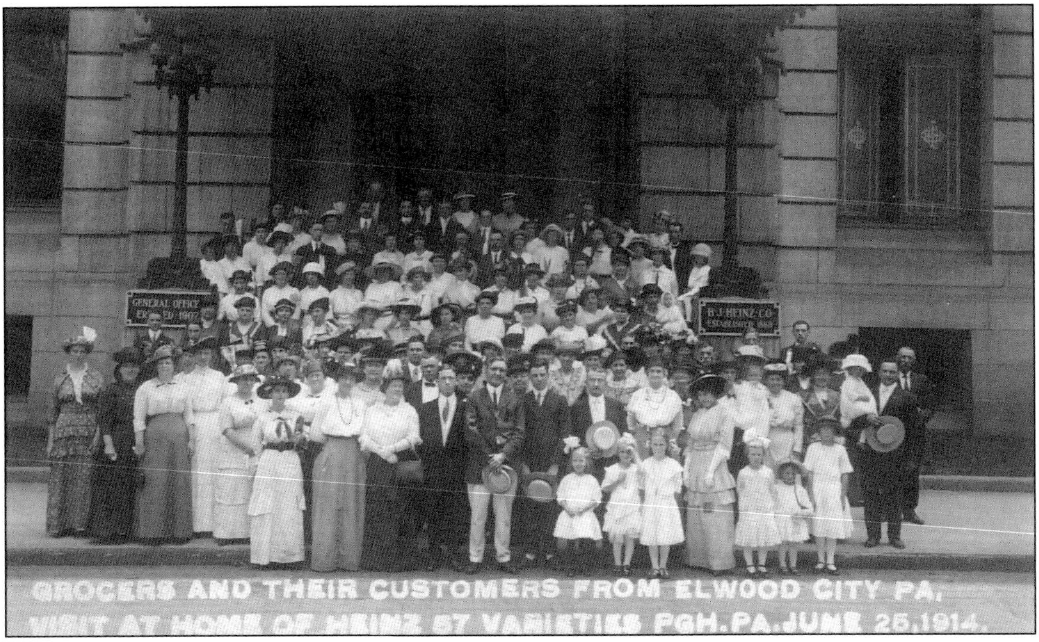

HEINZ 57 VARIETIES PLANT VISIT, 1914. Schoolteachers, clubs, and other groups were frequent visitors at the Heinz Company in Pittsburgh. This group of Ellwood City grocers and their customers posed for a photograph to mark the occasion. Most women who visited the plant, in the style of the day, wore elaborate dresses and hats.

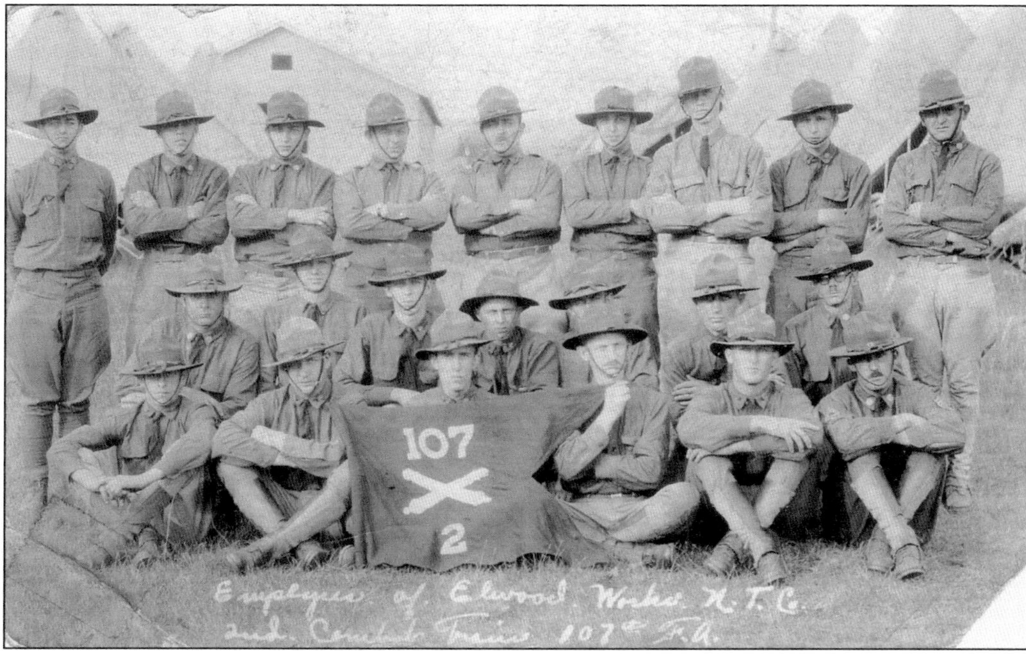

THE 107TH FIELD ARTILLERY, ELLWOOD CITY, *C.* 1918. The inscription on this postcard reads "Employees of Elwood [sic] Works, N. T. Co., 2nd Combat Trainees, 107th F.A." These men represent a National Tube Company unit as part of the mobilization of the Pennsylvania National Guard in World War I. The 107th Field Artillery has a history dating back to the Civil War.

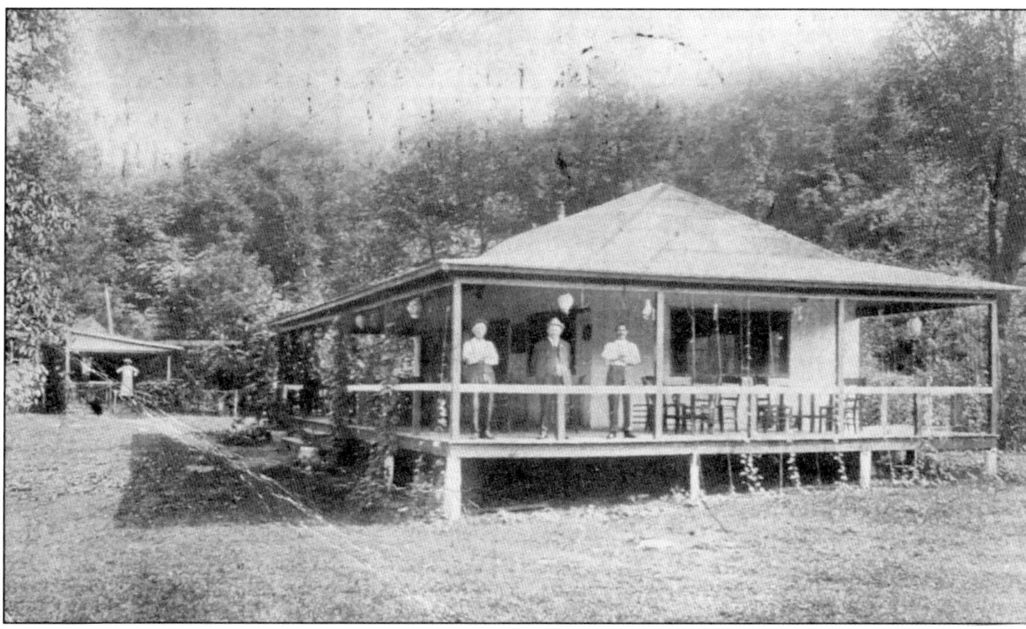

LABOR DAY AT DUCK RUN CAMP, 1912. Duck Run is north of Ellwood City. This postcard, sent to a Mount Jackson address in August 1912, announces that Labor Day would be Men's Day at the camp. The event would feature a chicken and corn roast and "various amusements." The price was $1.

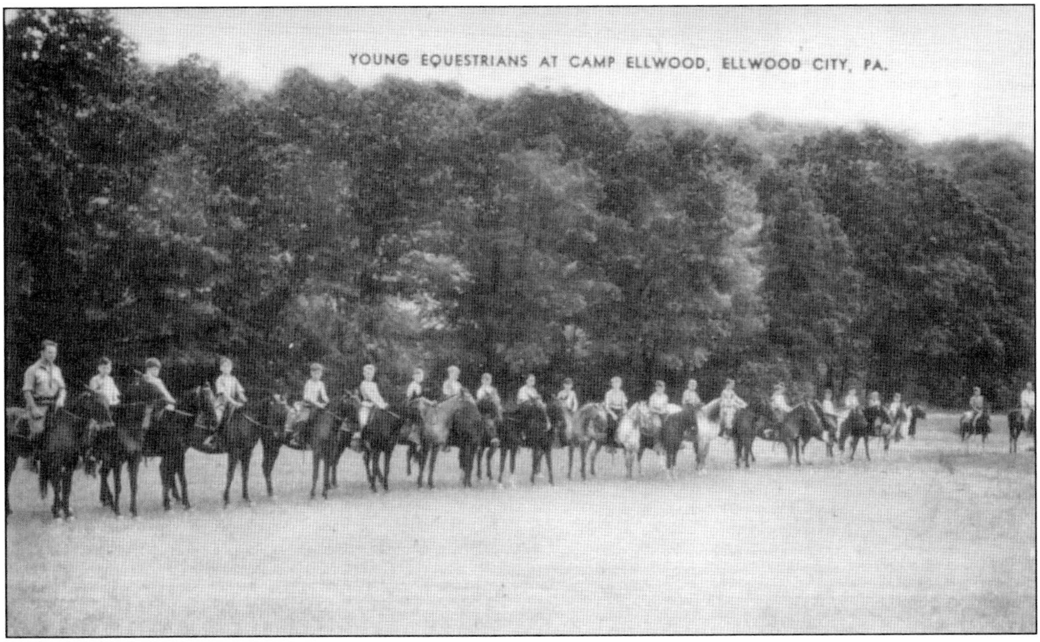

YOUNG EQUESTRIANS AT CAMP ELLWOOD, 1930S. Boys from all over the United States enjoyed boating, swimming, crafts, and other summer programs at this camp on the Slippery Rock Creek northeast of Ellwood City. The boys also learned to ride and care for horses. The camp is now the Salvation Army's Camp Allegheny.

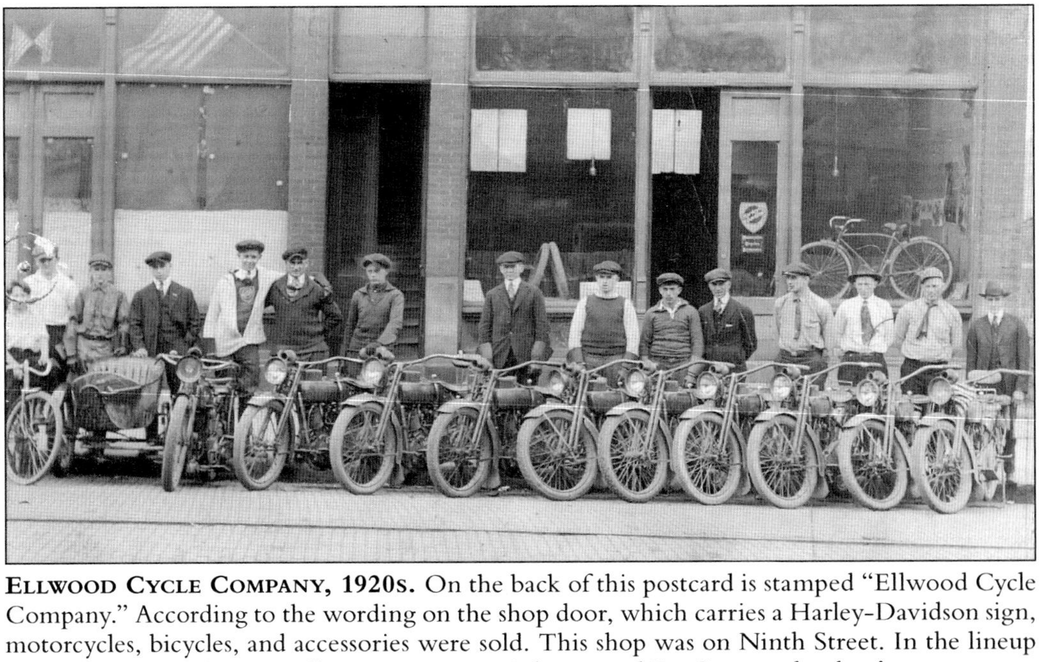

ELLWOOD CYCLE COMPANY, 1920S. On the back of this postcard is stamped "Ellwood Cycle Company." According to the wording on the shop door, which carries a Harley-Davidson sign, motorcycles, bicycles, and accessories were sold. This shop was on Ninth Street. In the lineup of riders are Eli Falconie, Bill McDevitt, Sam Salerno, and Jim Swartz, the shop's owner.

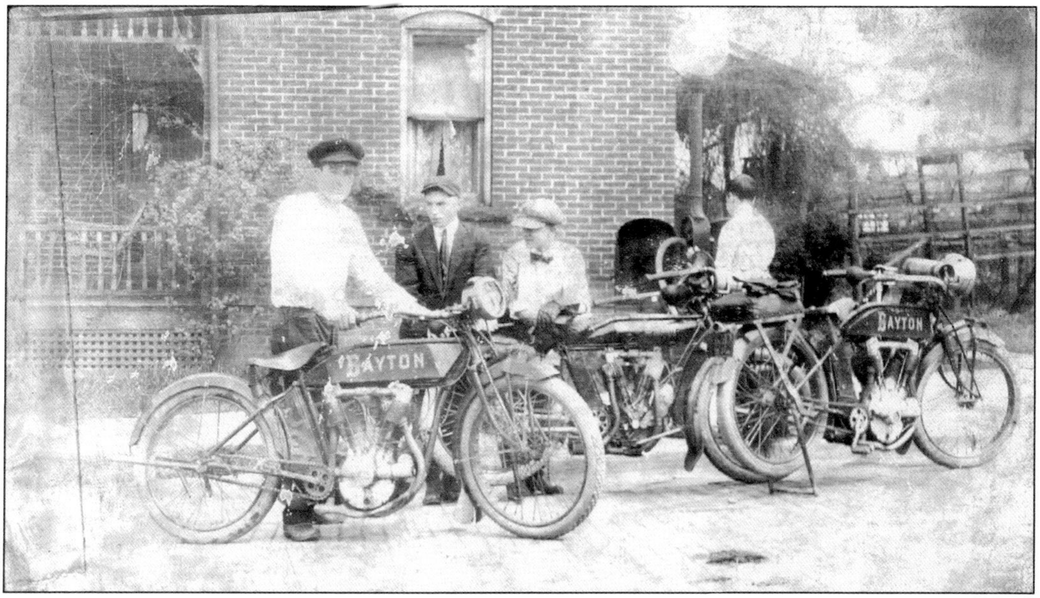

RUNYAN SERVICE STATION, 1920S. According to notations on the back of this postcard, the Runyan Service Station was on Fourth Street across from the old Chevrolet garage. In the picture are bike riders Marian Vescoe, Harvey Hazen, and Herb Daellenbach. In the background is Mrs. Runyan pumping gas.

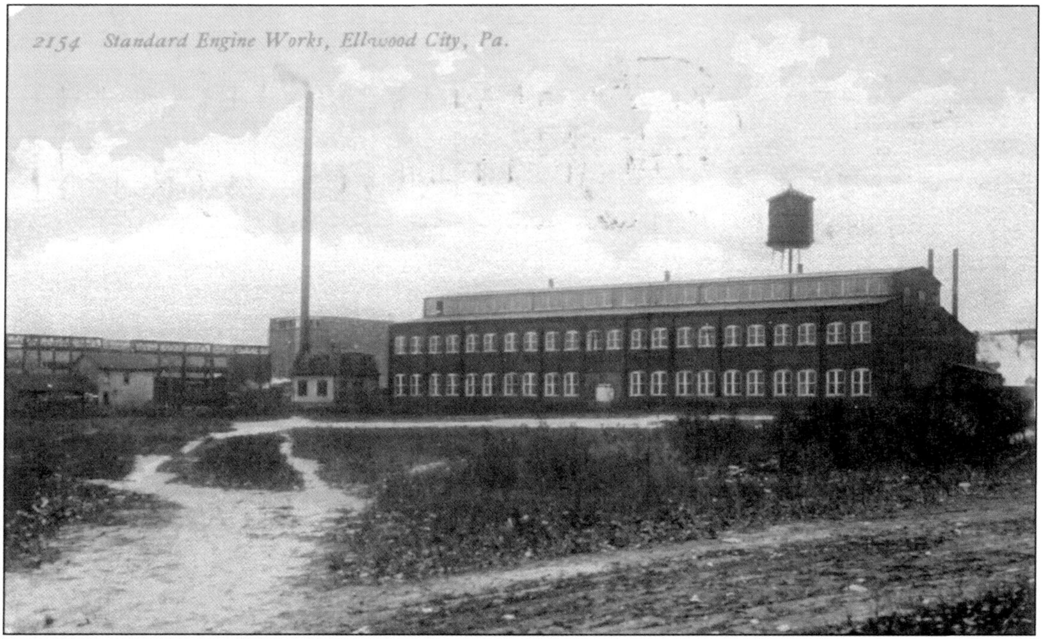

STANDARD ENGINEERING WORKS, *c.* 1913. The Standard Engineering Company merged with the Ellwood City Gas Engine Company and the National Machine and Tool Company of Pittsburgh. The merger combined the building of gas engines and rolling mill machinery with pipe-threading machinery. A plant was built at Park Avenue and Second Street in 1903. The company became part of Aetna Standard Engineering Company in 1926.

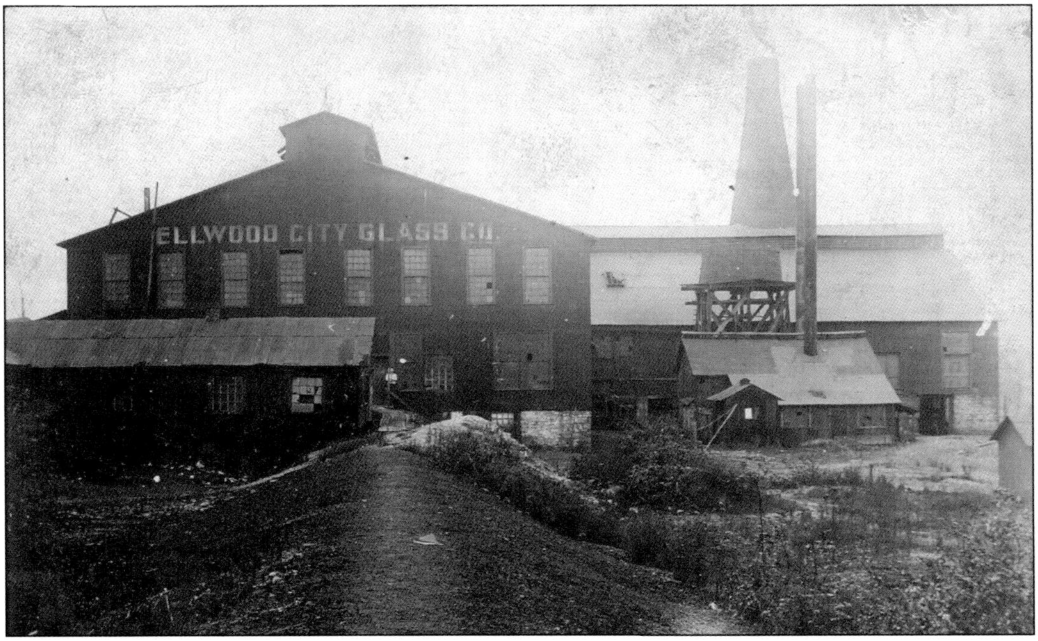

ELLWOOD CITY GLASS, c. 1905. The Northwood Glass Company came to Ellwood City from Ohio in 1892. Located at the north end of Ninth Street, it manufactured fancy household glass. In 1898, American Lamp and Brass Company (the Clark Brothers Glass Company) took over the operation. In 1905, the Clark Brothers Glass Company became the Ellwood City Glass Company.

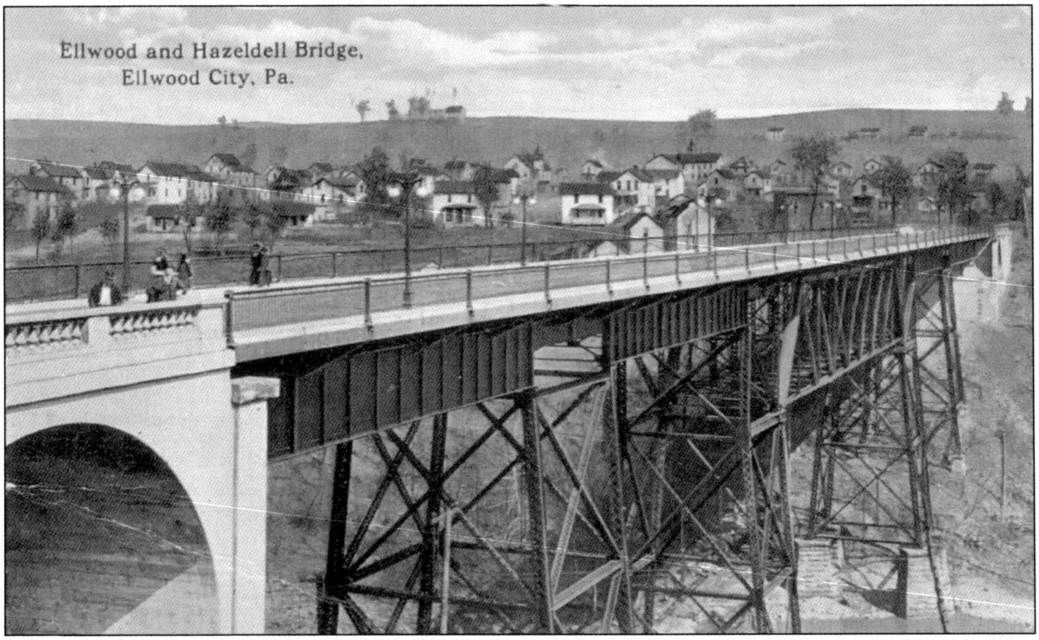

ELLWOOD AND HAZEL DELL BRIDGE, c. 1917. Three early bridges linked Ellwood City and Hazel Dell. First was a covered bridge east of Fifth Street known as the Jones Mill Bridge, or the White Bridge (razed in 1898). A second bridge, a steel bridge built in 1896, linked Sixth Street to College Street in Hazel Dell. The third bridge is the Fifth Street Bridge, shown here, which opened in 1915.

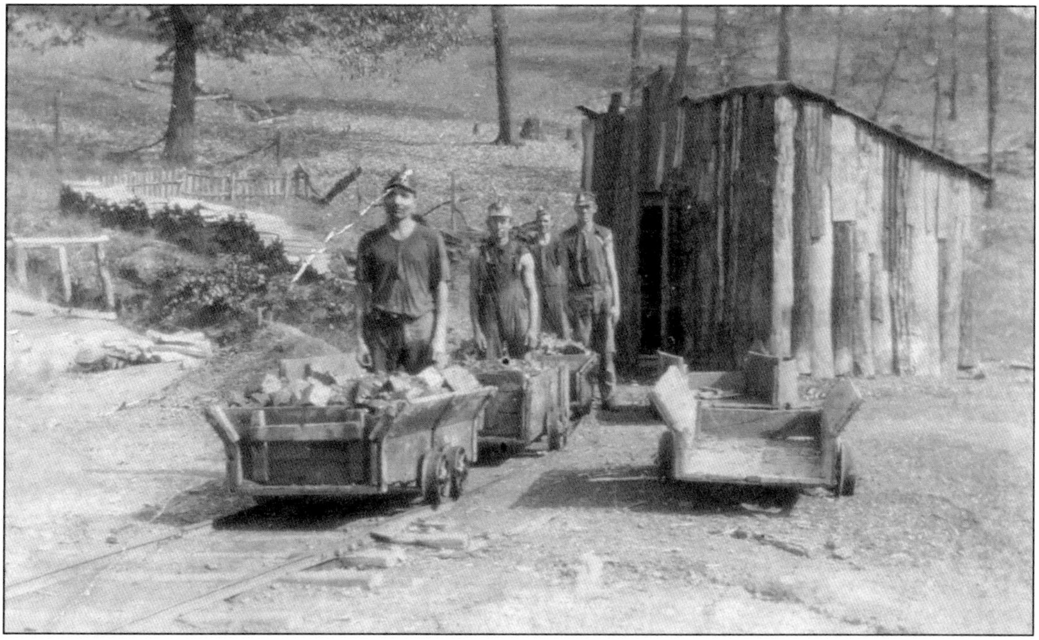

HAZEL DELL COAL MINE, c. 1920. These miners stand at the entrance of one of the many small coal mines found on farms between Hazel Dell and Chewton. The stacks of wood in the background at left are posts used to shore up the ceiling of this mine. The name Charles Majors on the back of the card may indicate the mine's owner or one of the miners.

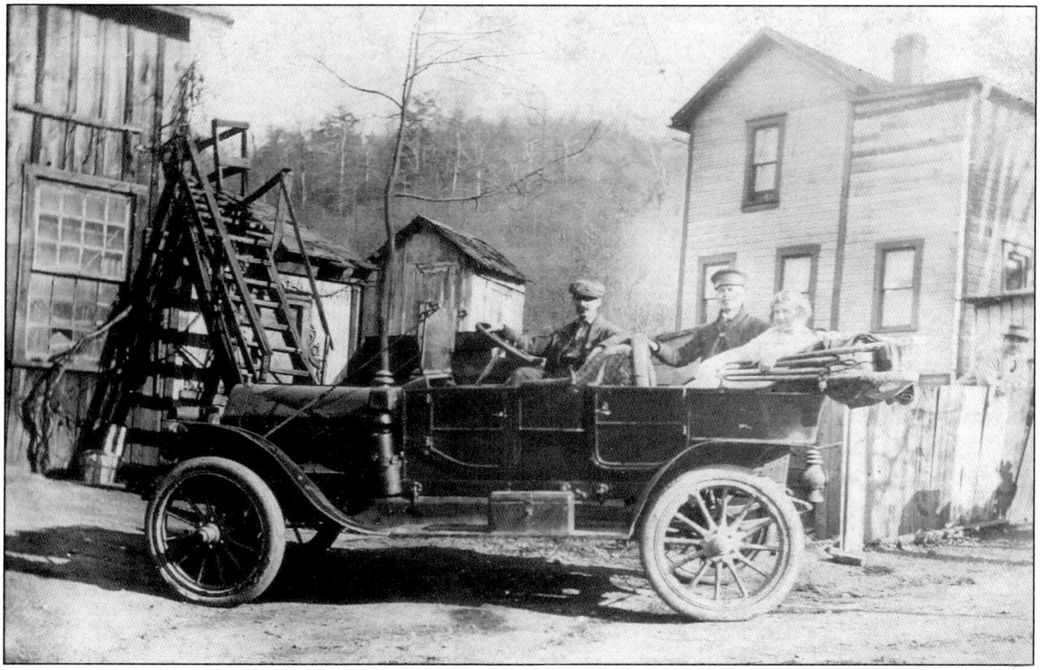

CARL DAELLENBACH GARAGE, PARK GATE, c. 1920. Carl Daellenbach was an automobile builder whose garage was in Park Gate southwest of Ellwood City. This view by the garage shows Daellenbach in the back seat of a car with his daughter Lamia. Seated at the wheel is the owner of the vehicle, Charlie Wineman.

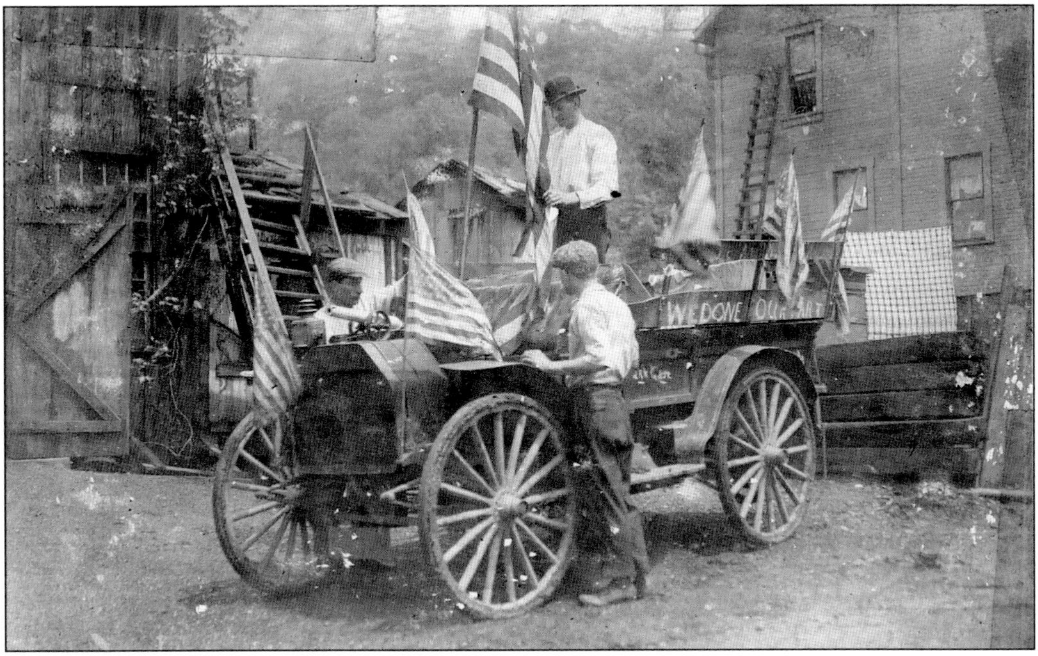

FLAG-DECORATED CAR, DAELLENBACH GARAGE, PARK GATE, *C.* 1918. This postcard shows the Daellenbach Garage and the Cragle brothers and James Gibbons decorating an automobile with American flags. Painted on the side of the vehicle is the slogan "We Done Our Part," probably referring to preparation for World War I.

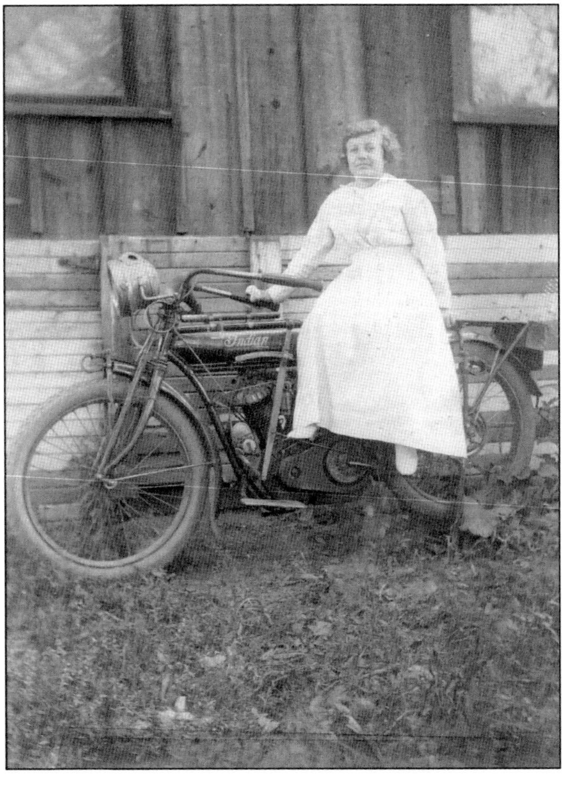

LAMIA DAELLENBACH, DAELLENBACH GARAGE, PARK GATE, *C.* 1920. Posing for a postcard photograph, Lamia Daellenbach, daughter of car builder Carl Daellenbach, is seated on an Indian motocycle (not motorcycle). From 1903, the motocycle competed strongly with Harley-Davidson's motorcycle. The competition was over in 1954 when the Indian was no longer manufactured.

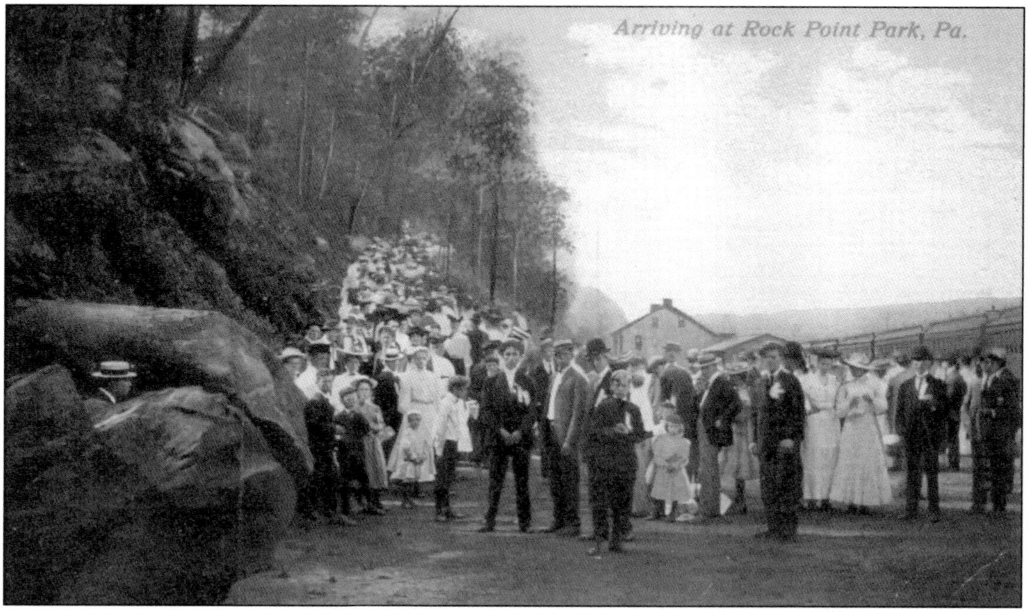

ARRIVING AT ROCK POINT PARK, EARLY 1900S. In 1885, the Pennsylvania Railroad created Rock Point Park as a "railroad park," organizing excursions from Pittsburgh and other towns for the enjoyment of the park's natural beauty and amusements. In this view, a crowd of visitors arrive at the park. The train can be seen in the background on the right. An excursion train often carried 300 or 400 park visitors in one trip.

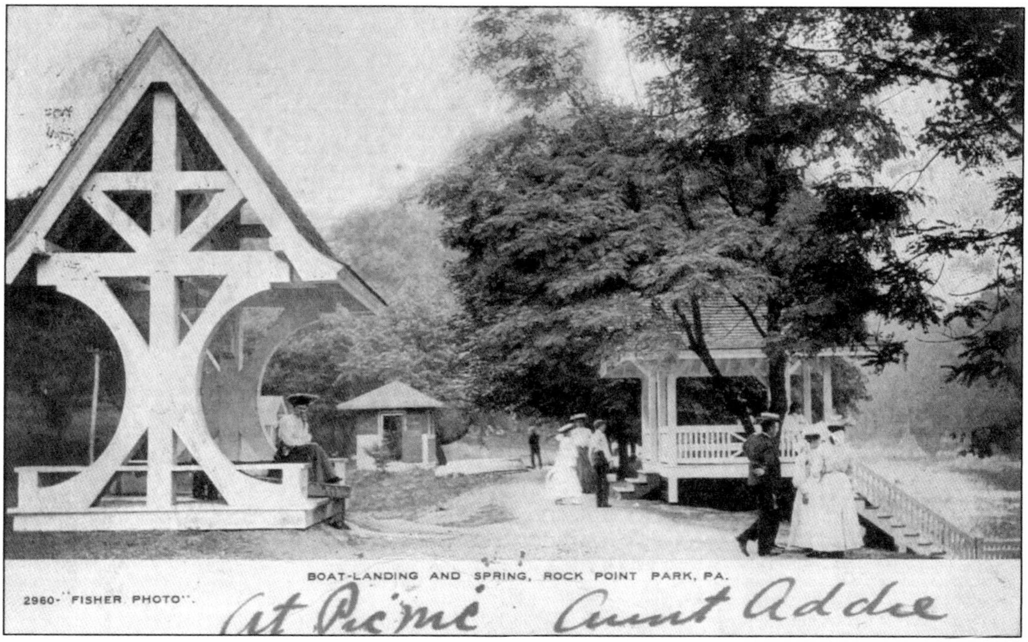

BOAT LANDING AND SPRING, ROCK POINT PARK, *c.* 1906. Scenic Rock Point Park was located three miles west of Ellwood City where the Connoquenessing Creek flows into the Beaver River. Before 1885, when the railroad park was created, Rock Point was a health resort. The park had 13 natural springs, all furnishing clear, cold water.

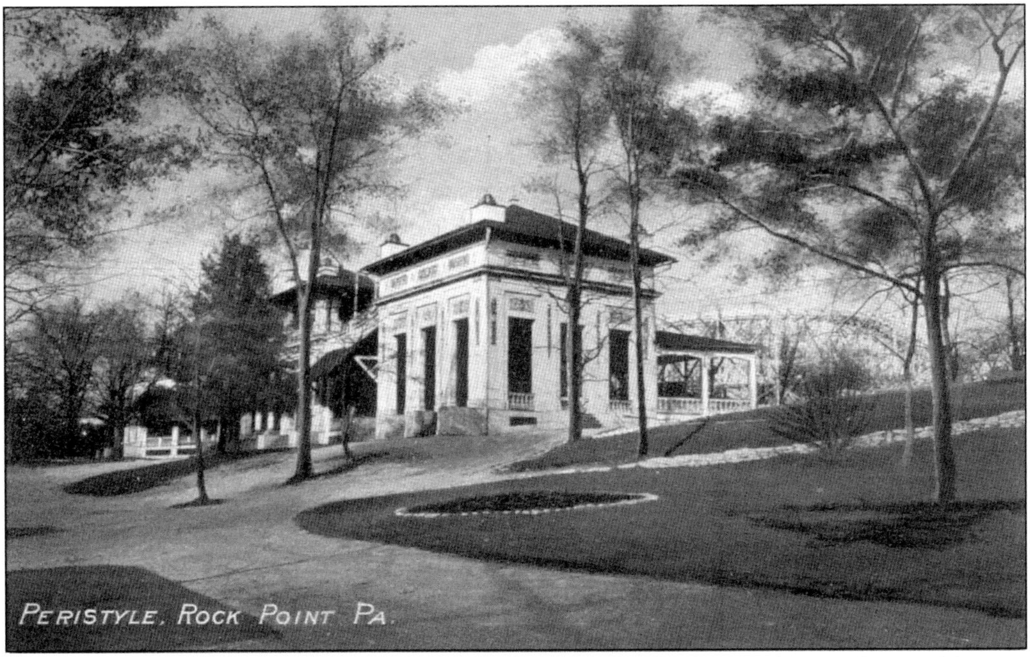

PERISTYLE, ROCK POINT PARK, EARLY 1900S. Rock Point's abundance of natural beauty was accentuated by a number of classic buildings like this peristyle, which is a court or porch surrounded by columns. Greeks and Romans used open-air peristyles as temples, or, in their homes, as a center court for family use.

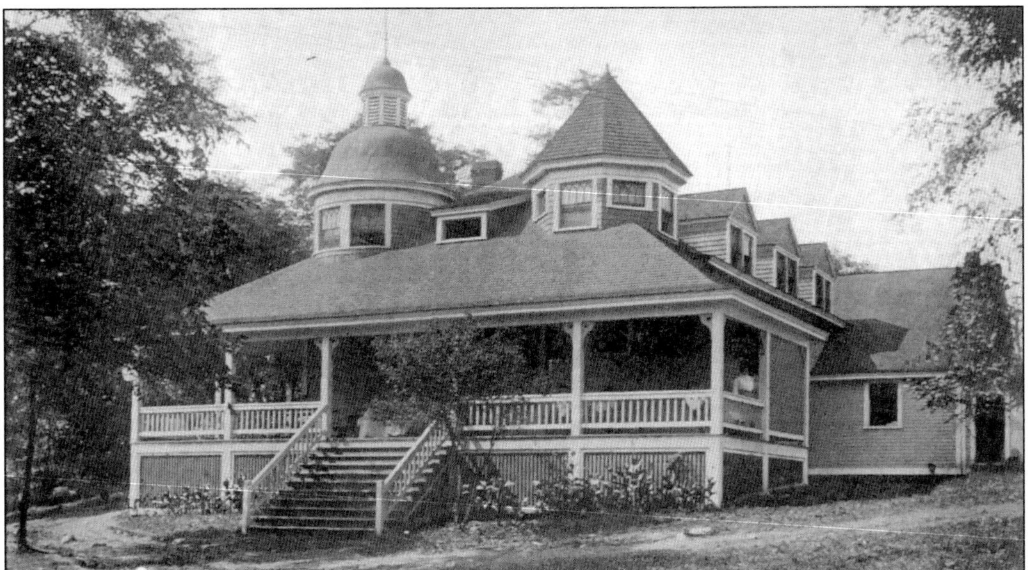

ROCK POINT INN, EARLY 1900S. Metheny's stone tavern, built in 1836 near the Erie-Pittsburgh Canal, was the first inn to house guests at Rock Point. Some of the distinguished visitors there were author James Fenimore Cooper, Pres. James A. Garfield, and Pres. Zachary Taylor. After Rock Point Park opened, the Rock Point Inn, shown here, accommodated overnight guests pouring into the new amusement park and picnic grounds.

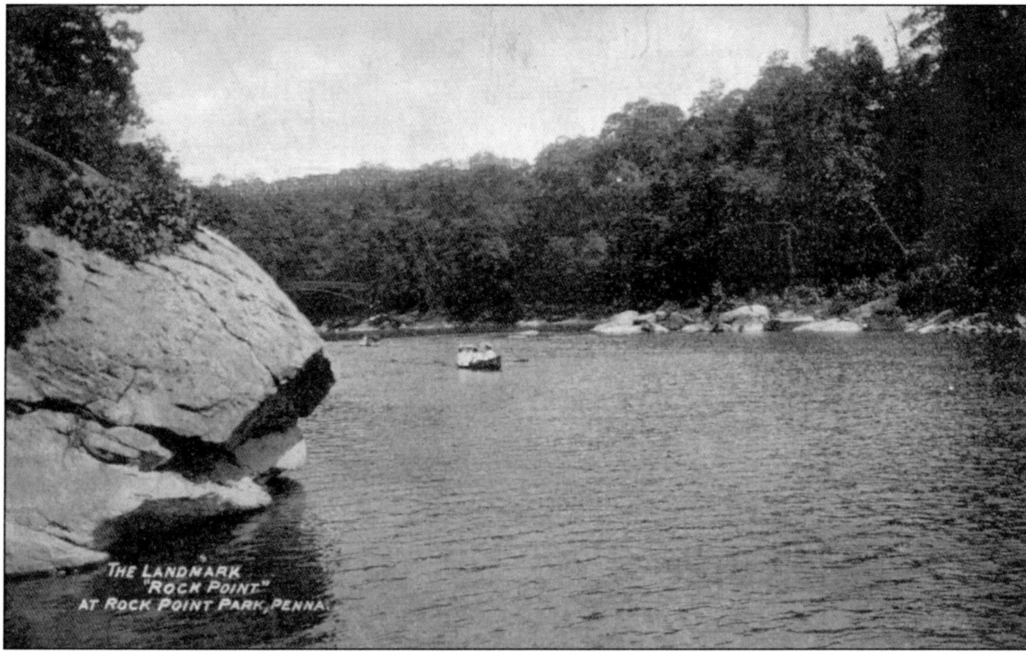

THE LANDMARK AT ROCK POINT. This gigantic rock is near where the old Metheny Tavern stood in Rock Point's early days. The rock gave the spot near the Erie-Pittsburgh Canal its name. The landmark was there many years later when the park was built, so the park adopted its name. The park was abandoned after a fire in 1914 destroyed most of it.

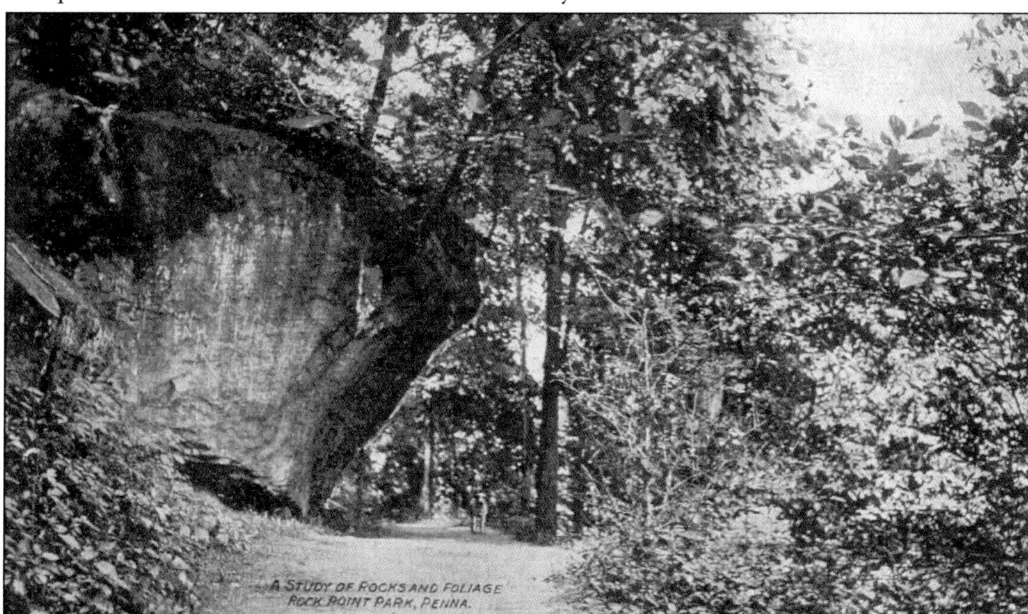

FROGS' INVITATION TO ROCK POINT PARK, 1911. The reverse of this postcard is an invitation to attend the second annual outing of the Frogs at Rock Point Park in July 1911. The Frogs was a social and charitable club for black men in the greater Pittsburgh area. In 1990, it was named the oldest organization of its kind in the United States. "Frogs" is an acronym for "Friendly Rivalry Often Gets Success."

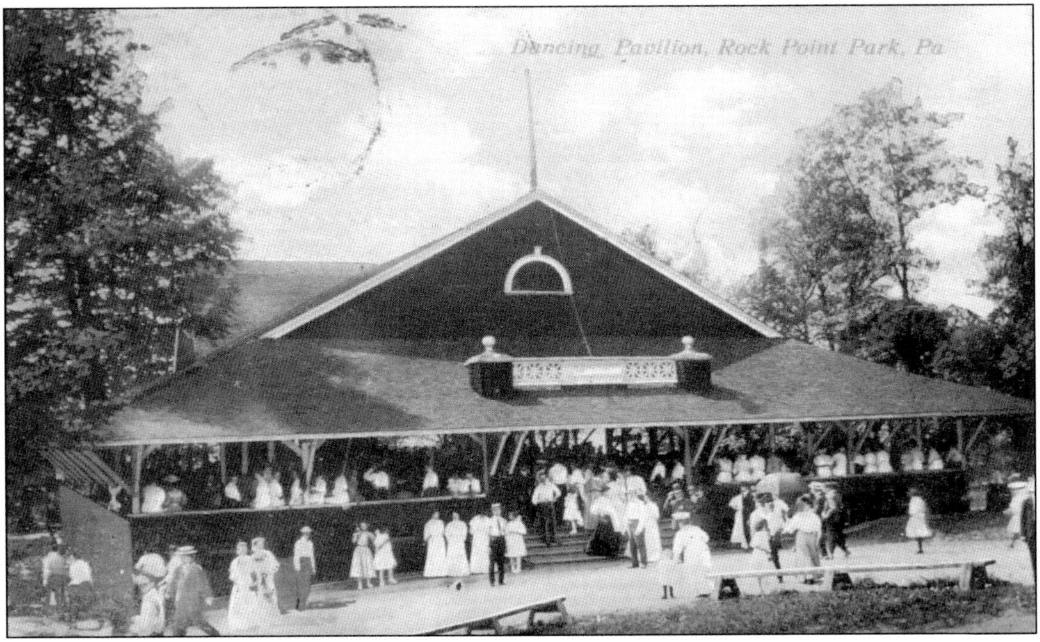

DANCING PAVILION, ROCK POINT PARK, *C.* 1911. What is an amusement park without an open-air dance hall? The music of the early 1900s was ideal for dancing; the ladies could show off their fancy dresses as they waltzed, and children could slide on the dance floor between numbers. Dancing was an all-day affair; one outing at Rock Point advertised dancing from 10:00 a.m. until 9:00 p.m.

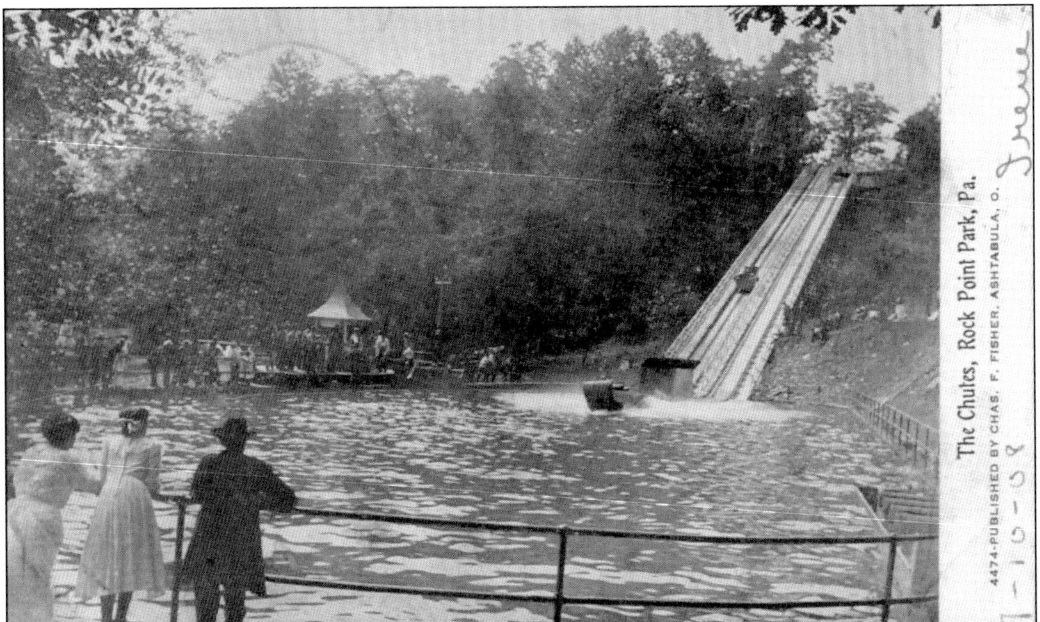

THE CHUTES, ROCK POINT PARK, 1908. The Chutes was a popular ride at Rock Point. The first such ride, called Shoot-the-Chute, was at Sea Lion Park at Coney Island in 1895. A flat-bottomed boat on a guided track rides into the water, skips over the water, and is pulled up the chute to start again. A modern version of this ride can be found at Kennywood Park in Pittsburgh.

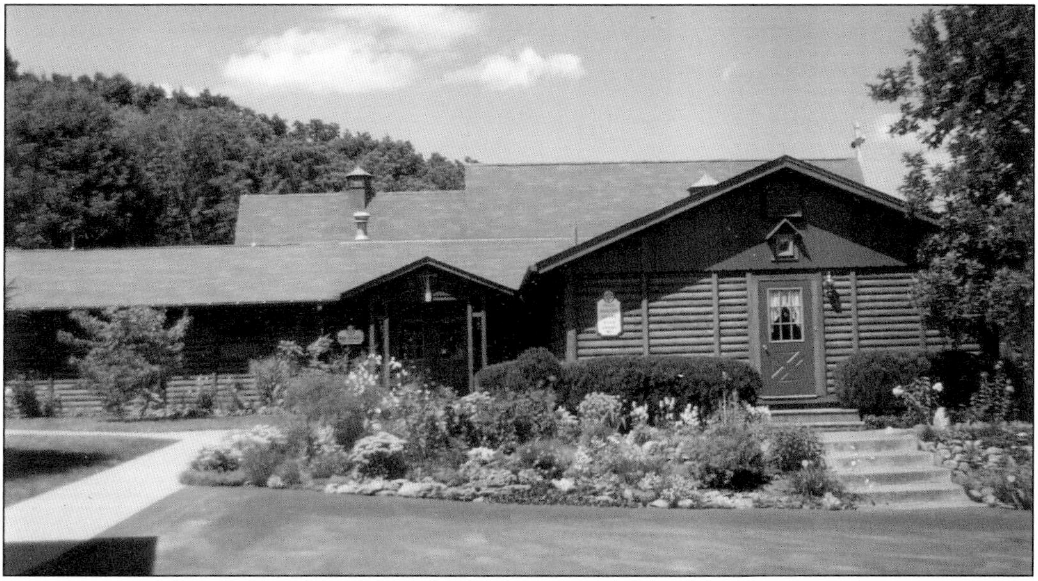

ADMINISTRATION BUILDING, ORTHODOX MONASTERY OF THE TRANSFIGURATION, WURTEMBURG, 2004. The land where Wurtemburg now stands was settled around 1795. In the early 1800s, the community had salt wells and a linseed oil mill. In 1967, Mother Alexandra, the former Princess Illeana of Romania, chose Wurtemburg as the site for a monastery for American orthodox women. The monastery owns 100 acres of land, much of it wooded. (Courtesy of Monastery of the Transfiguration.)

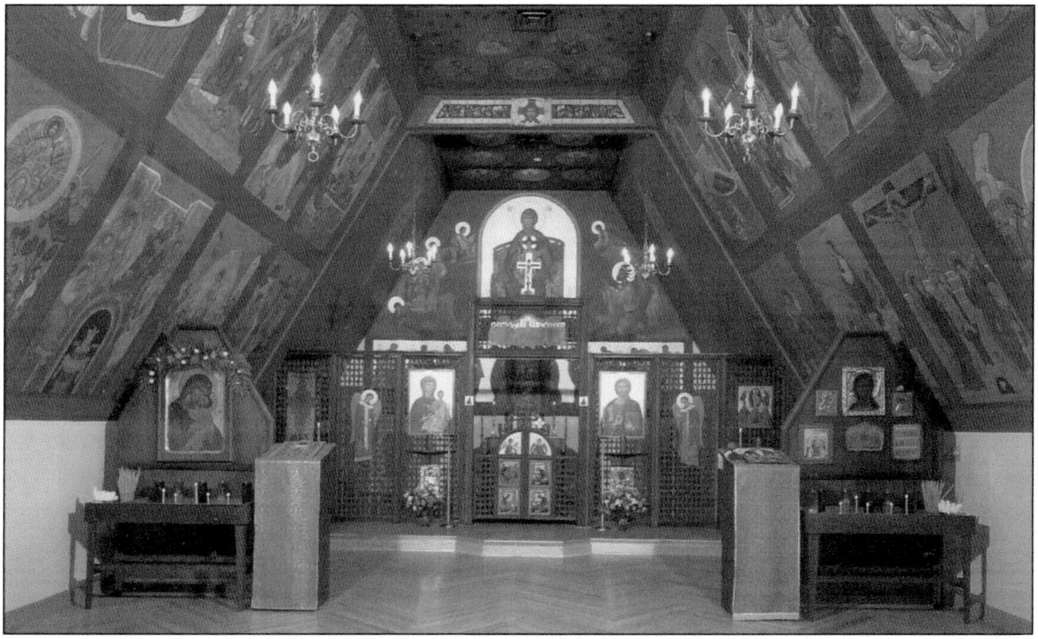

CHAPEL, MONASTERY OF THE TRANSFIGURATION, WURTEMBURG. Bursting with color, the chapel of the Monastery of the Transfiguration is used for morning and evening services as well as private prayer. Artwork and numerous hand-painted icons decorate the walls and ceiling. The chapel was consecrated in 1968 and enlarged in 1993. Services are open to all. (Courtesy of Monastery of the Transfiguration.)

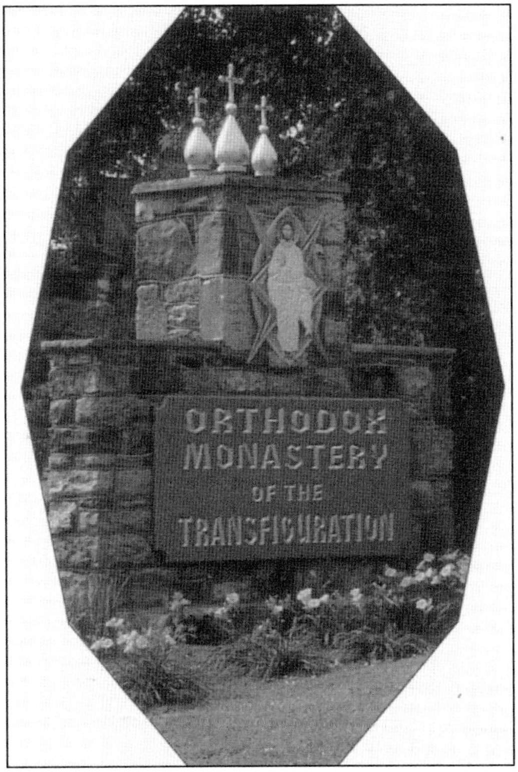

ENTRANCE, MONASTERY OF THE TRANSFIGURATION, WURTEMBURG. Visitors are welcome at the monastery. Two guesthouses are available for overnight stays arranged for in advance. An outdoor pavilion for services and a playhouse for visiting children are also on the grounds. Each year on August 5 and 6, the monastery celebrates the patronal feast day. (Courtesy of Monastery of the Transfiguration.)

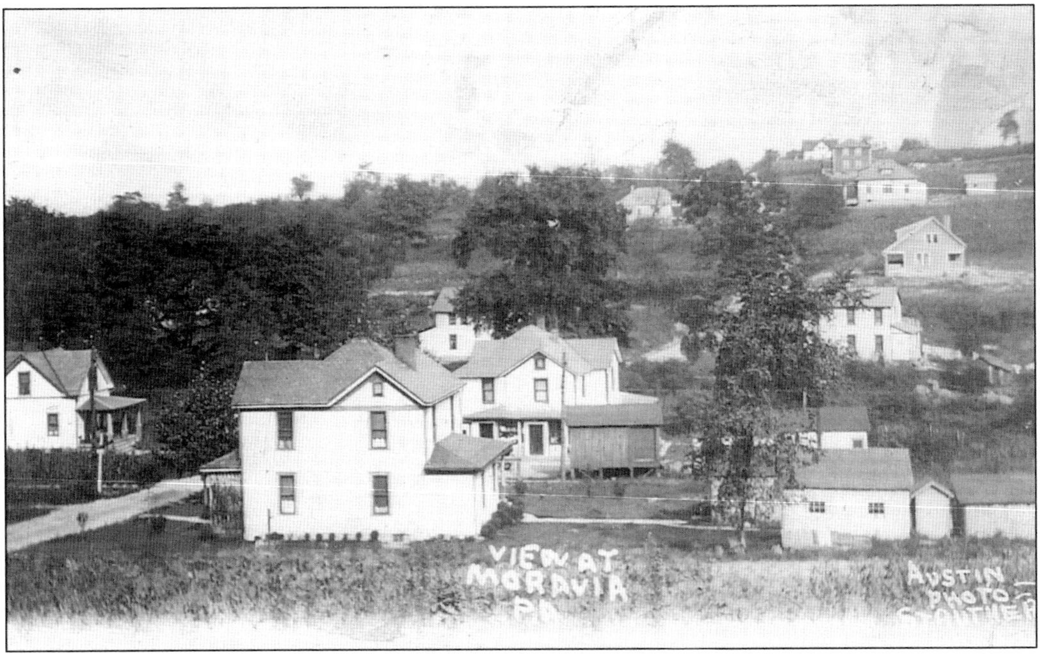

VIEW AT MORAVIA STOP (CASTLEWOOD), EARLY 1900S. The Harmony Line had numerous stops on the road to Ellwood City (now Route 65). One of them, Moravia Stop on Harmony Baptist Road, had the same name as the community called Moravia near West Pittsburg. Eventually the Moravia Stop area became Castlewood. (Courtesy of Wade Kennedy.)

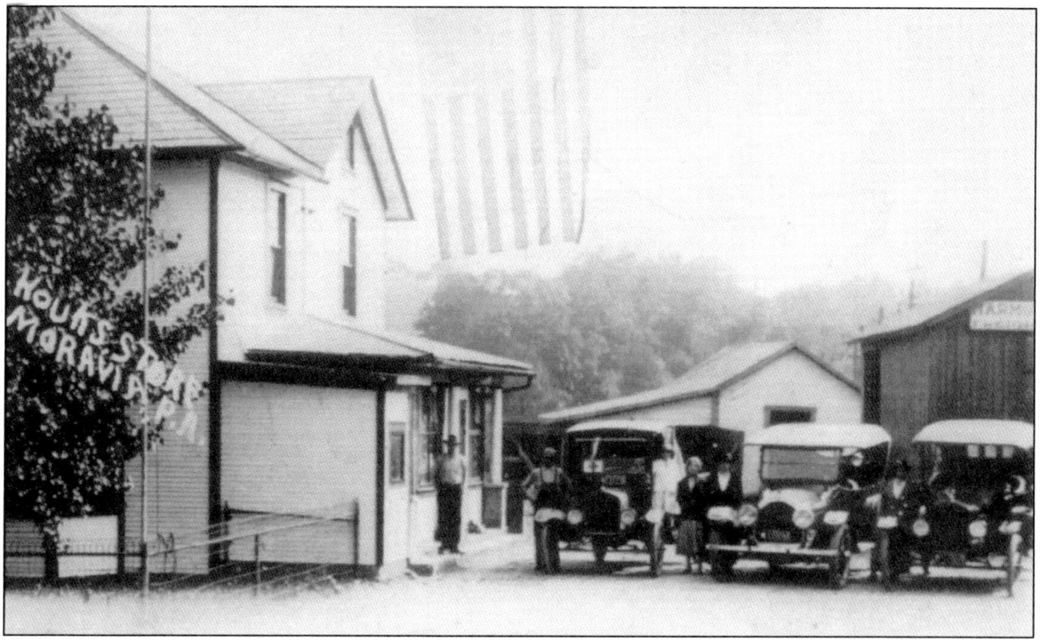

HOUK'S STORE, MORAVIA STOP (CASTLEWOOD), EARLY 1920S. The Harmony Line carried freight as well as passengers. In this photograph, the freight station can be seen in the right background. On the left is Houk's store. The automobiles may be waiting to pick up passengers at Moravia Stop. (Courtesy of Wade Kennedy.)

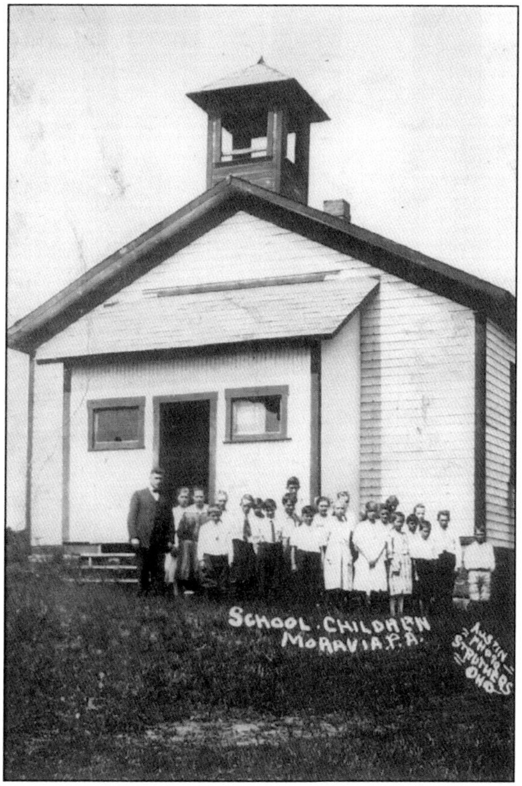

HILL SCHOOL, EARLY 1900S. Before 1915, children in the Castlewood area attended Hill School. A typical suburban school, drinking water and toilets were outdoors, and several grades were in the same room. The boys and girls walked to and from school and went home every day for lunch. A new school was built in 1915. (Courtesy of Wade Kennedy.)

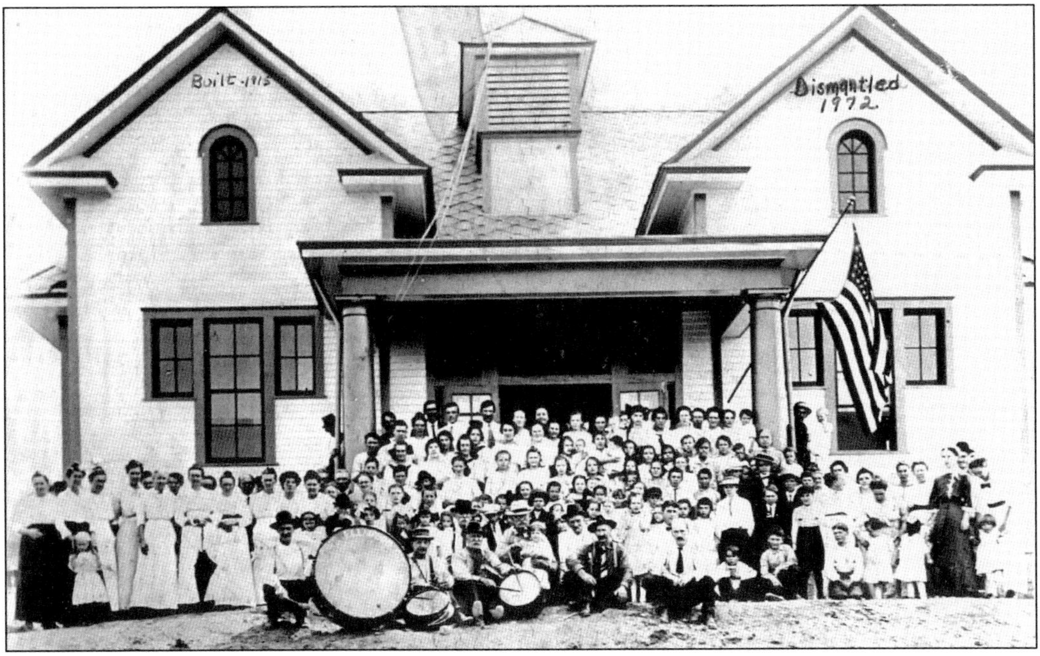

CASTLEWOOD SCHOOL, 1921. This school was built in 1915. No longer in use when children started going to the Shenango Consolidated School, the Castlewood School was dismantled in 1972. In this photograph, the Houk-Newton Band played for an event marking the beginning of the Christian and Missionary Alliance Sunday School. (Courtesy of Wade Kennedy.)

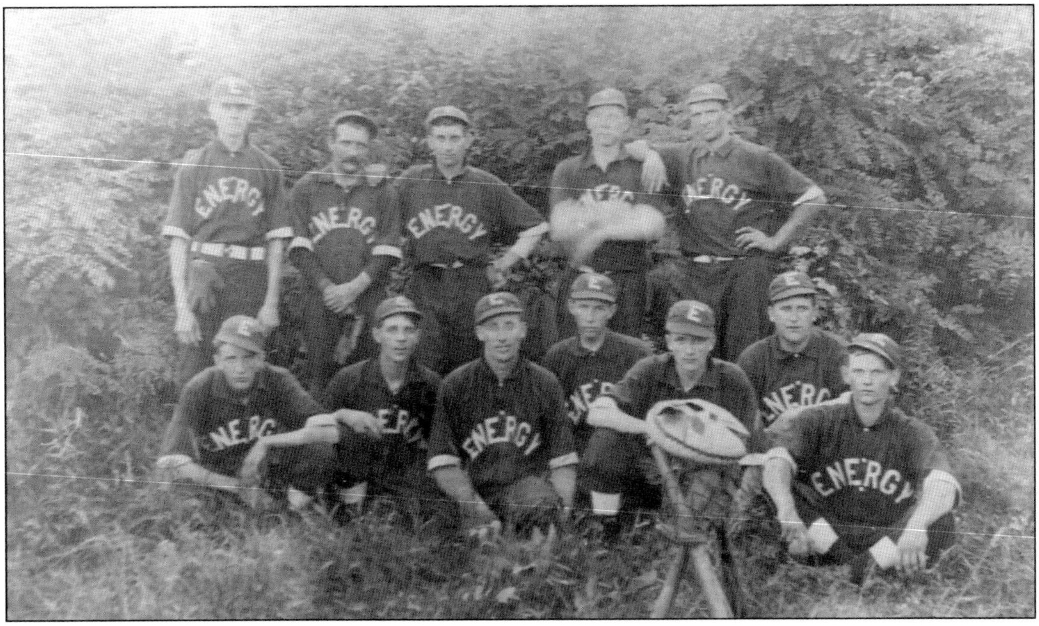

ENERGY BASEBALL TEAM, 1913. Energy was another stop on the Harmony Line between New Castle and Ellwood City. Largely a residential area, it had its own independent baseball team. Pictured from left to right are (first row) C. Henderson, Frank Meyers, ? Wellhausen, unidentified, John Houk, unidentified, and unidentified; (second row) William Newton, Clyde Meyers, Sam Houk, Konrad Houk, and J. Hill. (Courtesy of Wade Kennedy.)

Four

New Castle Area

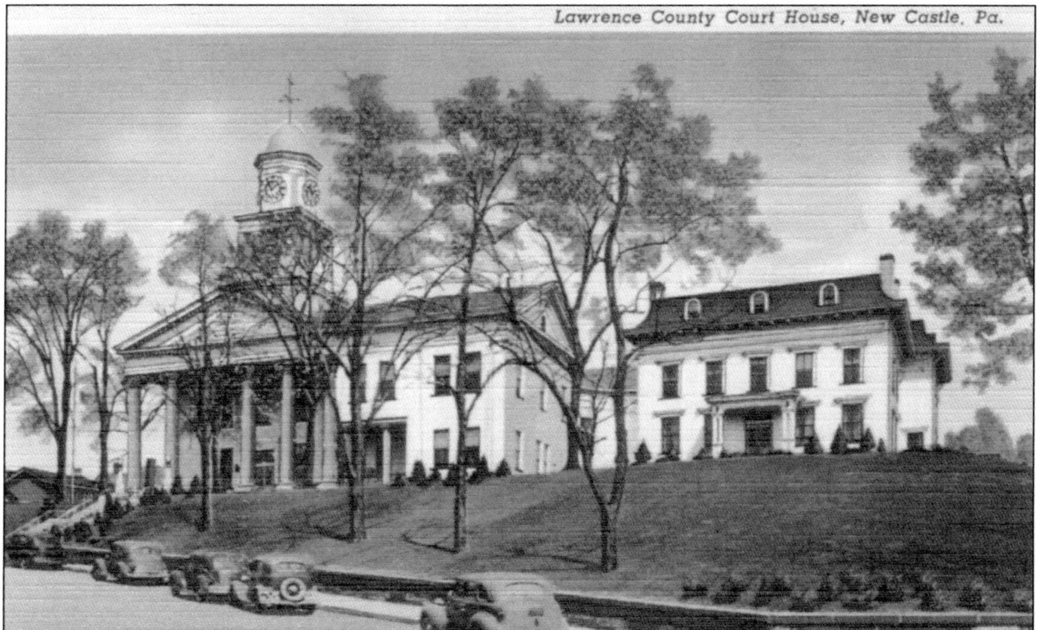

Lawrence County Courthouse, New Castle, 1930s. In 1849, parts of Beaver County and Mercer County were merged to form Lawrence County. New Castle, which had been settled long before, in 1798, became the county seat. The Lawrence County Courthouse opened in 1851. In 1979, the adjacent Lawrence County Government Center was built to provide more office space. The courthouse is on the National Register of Historical Places.

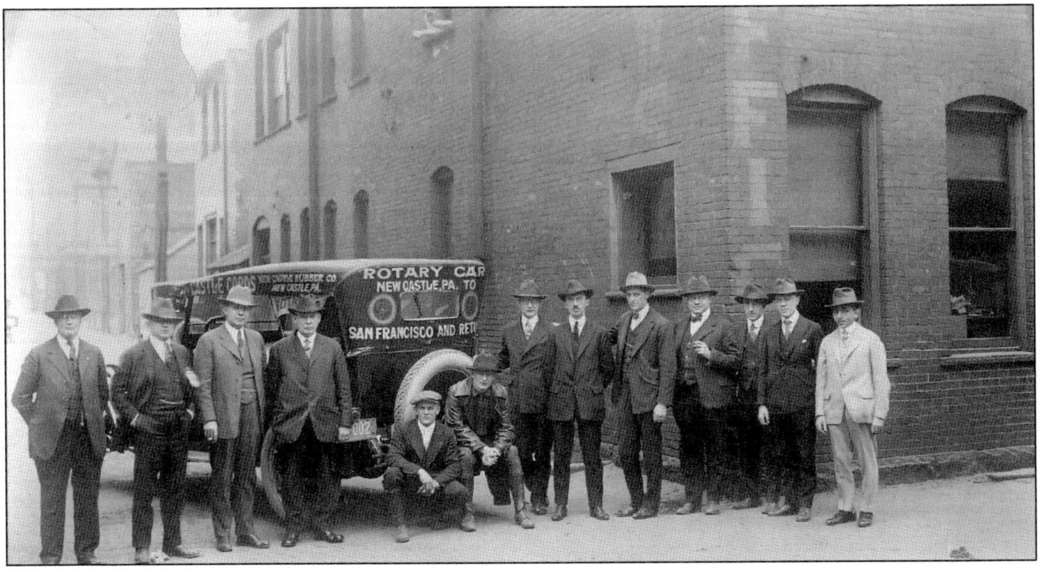

Rotary Club Automobile Race, New Castle, *c.* 1920. Around 1920, the Rotary Club sponsored this car in a race to San Francisco and back. The New Castle Rubber Company is advertised on the driver side of the car, and the license plate is a dealer plate. Here Rotary Club dignitaries pose at Apple Alley and Sycamore Alley behind the New Castle News office. The Temple Building is in the background on the left.

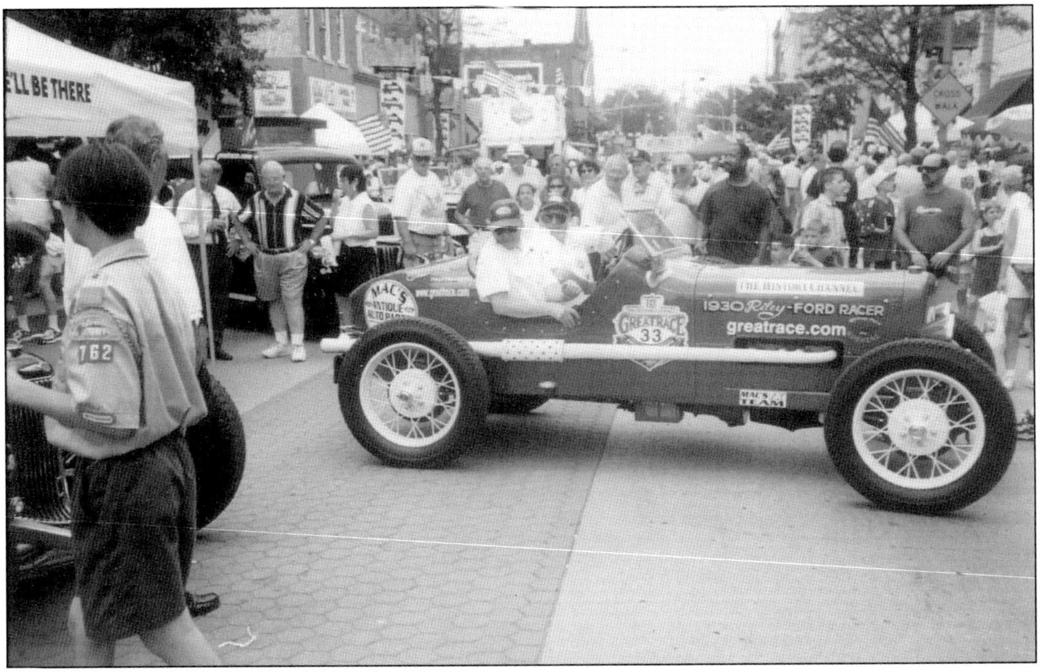

Great Race, New Castle, 1998. Times have not changed much. In 1998, television's History Channel sponsored the Great Race that came through New Castle on its cross-country rally of vintage automobiles. This photograph shows residents examining the cars during the lunchtime stop on Washington Street. A $5,000 prize was awarded to the New Castle Public Library because New Castle offered the best hospitality to car drivers.

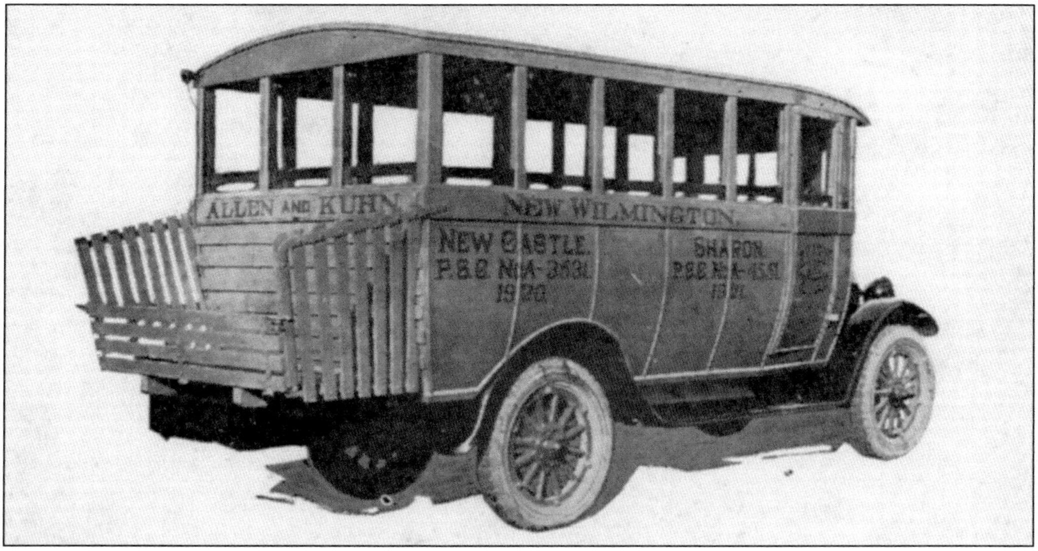

H. A. K. Bus, *c.* 1920. By 1920, automobiles had become a familiar sight on Lawrence County roads. Their increasing numbers served to accelerate the improvement of roads and the disappearance of the horse and buggy. At that time, bus lines began to replace interurban railway lines. This Allen and Kuhn Bus Line traveled between New Castle and Sharon through New Wilmington.

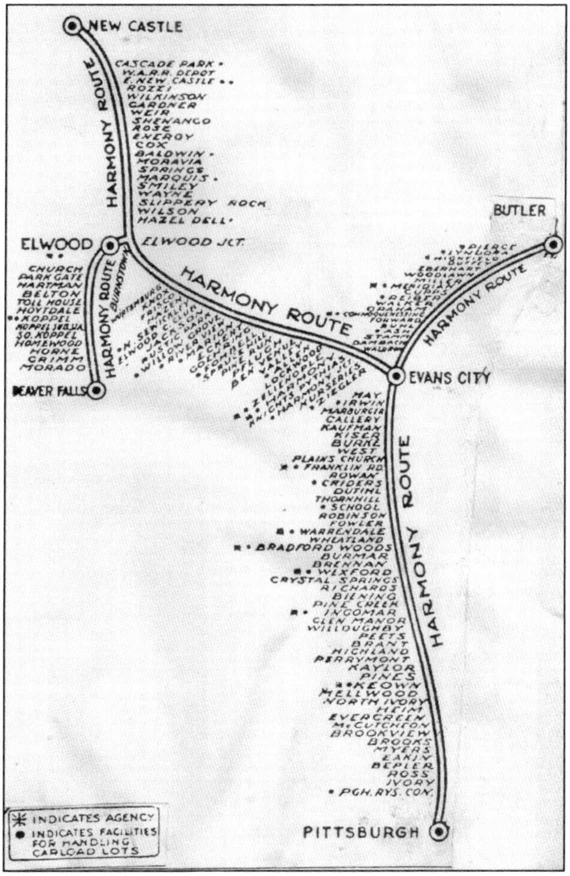

Harmony Line Map. From 1908 to 1931, the Pittsburgh, Harmony, Butler, and New Castle Railway line ran trolleys on a narrow-gauge track, providing small communities with an economical means to travel. In New Castle, the line ran from a car barn on East Washington Street to Pittsburgh, stopping at Cascade Park, Gardner Stop, Shenango Stop, Rose Stop, and other roads in Shenango Township. The roads still carry the names of the Harmony Line stops.

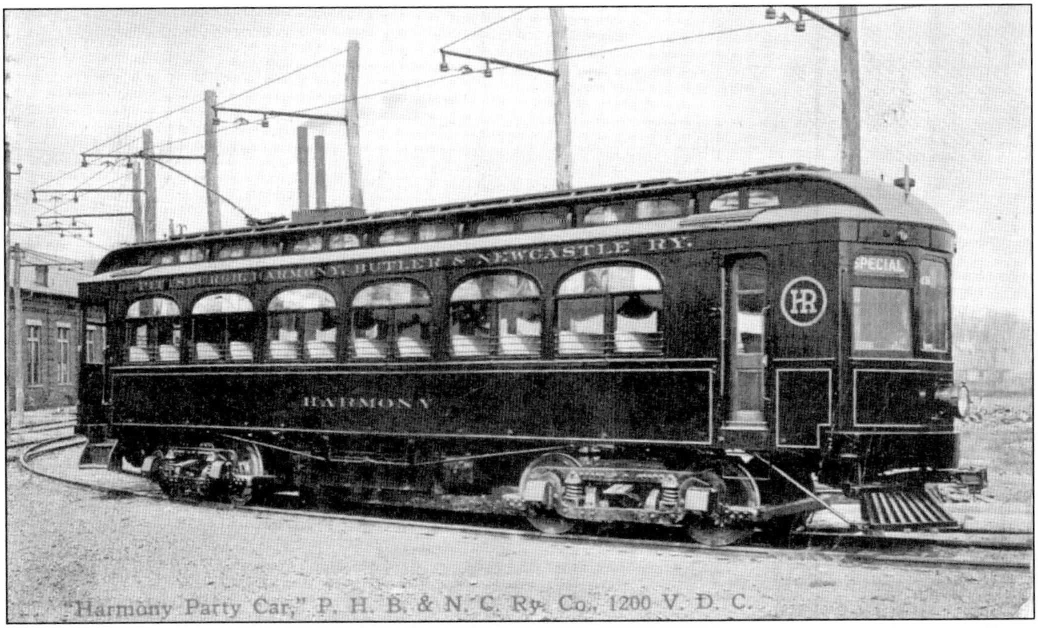

HARMONY LINE PARTY CAR, 1920S. A department store owner in Pittsburgh, Russell H. Boggs started the Harmony Line with his partner Henry Buhl. Boggs was from Evans City and understood the value of a commuter line for those who lived north of the big city. The railway ran on the Harmony Line's 1,200-volt direct current. Party cars like this one could be rented for $55 a day.

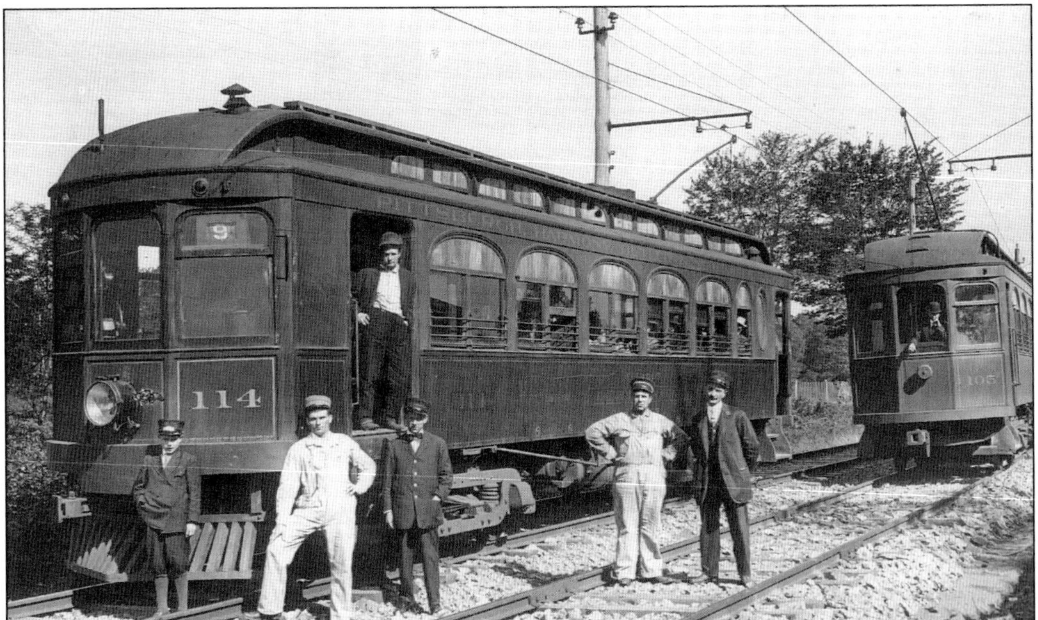

HARMONY LINE CREW, 1920S. Here the Harmony Line personnel pose in front of one of the handsome maroon-and-gold trolley cars. In addition to bringing travel opportunities to isolated communities, the Harmony Line provided electricity to some rural homes for the first time. The last run for the railway in New Castle was in 1931 at Taylor and East Washington Streets.

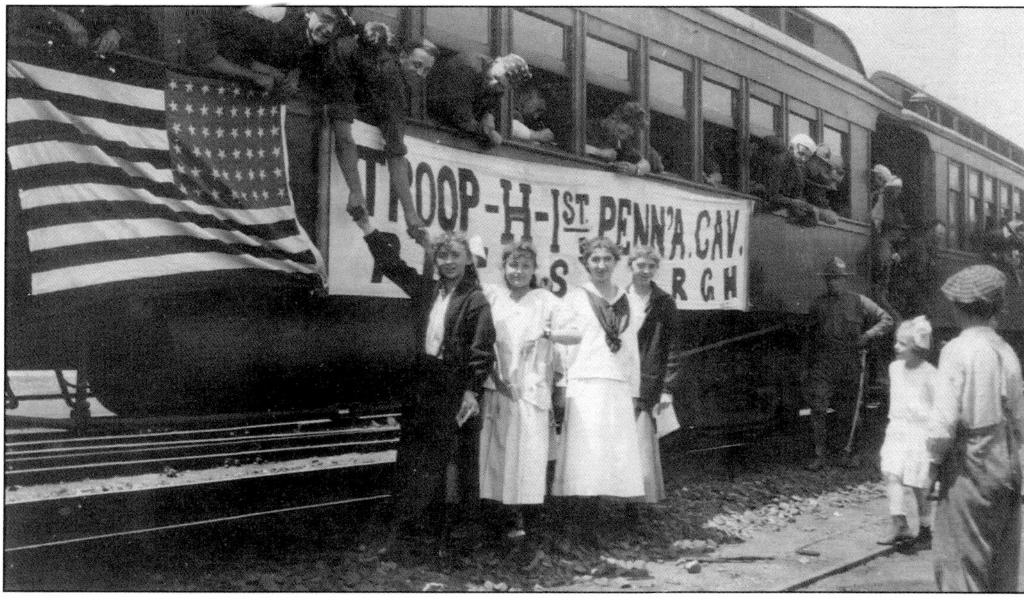

TROOP H, 1ST PENNSYLVANIA CAVALRY, C. 1918. Troop H of the 1st Pennsylvania Cavalry greets well-wishers. During World War II, Troop F of the 1st Pennsylvania Cavalry trained with horses kept at Deshon Annex. Later the horses were moved to a 100-acre area in Union Township near Madonna Church Cemetery where Troop K trained. Lawrence County sent 3,820 men to World War I and 12,561 men to World War II.

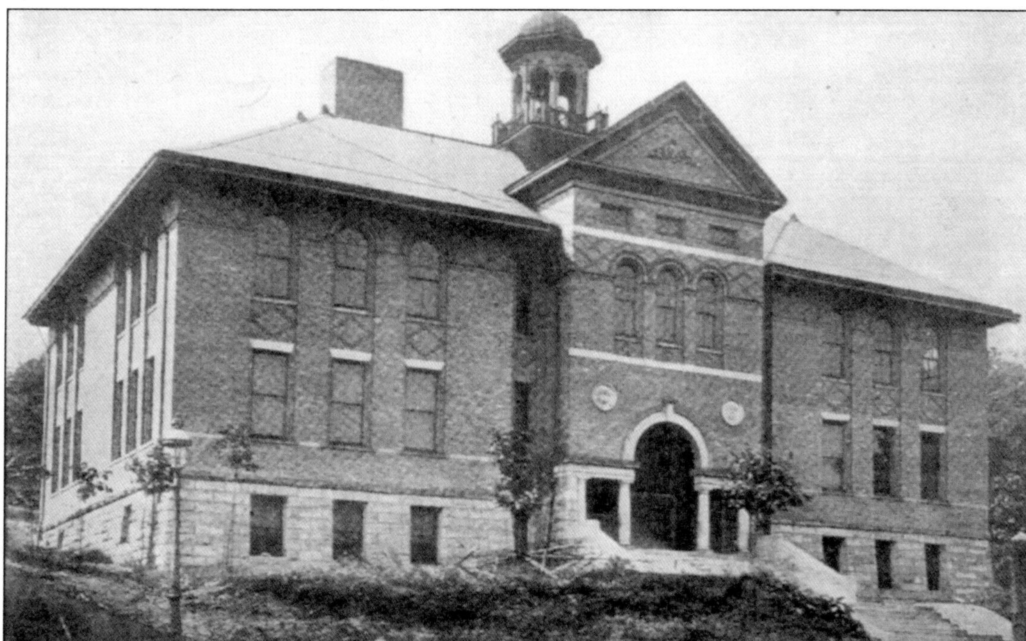

LAWRENCE SCHOOL, EARLY 1900S. The Lawrence School was built around 1900 in the southern part of New Castle called "Tube Town," which was close to Mahoningtown. It was built to accommodate children of families who lived within walking distance of the rapidly growing industries in that area such as the New Castle Tube Company, the tin mill, and the New Castle Stamping Company. The school closed in the early 1930s.

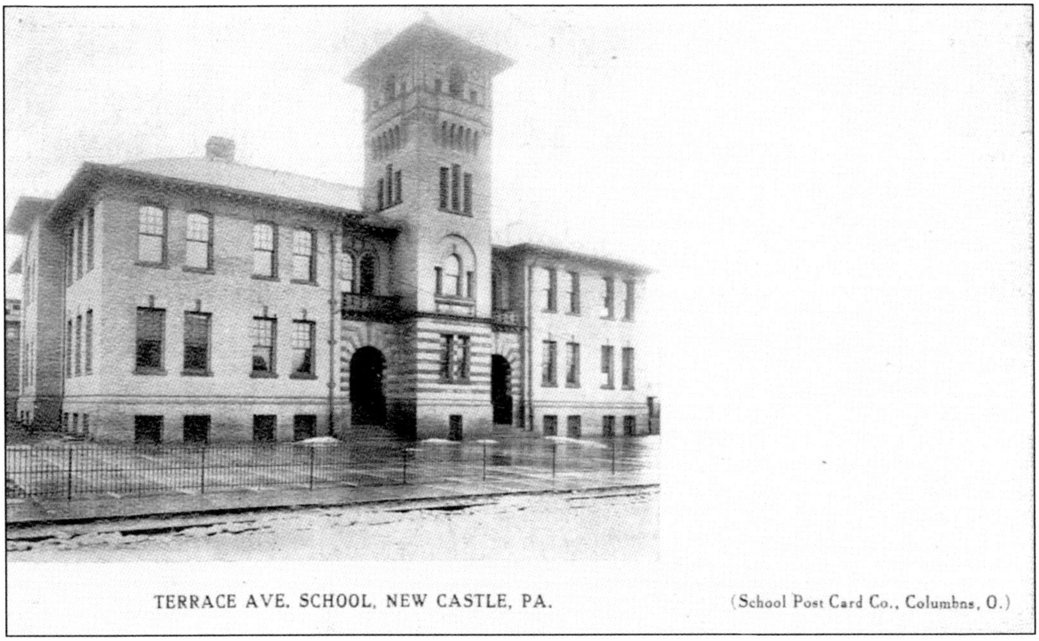

TERRACE AVENUE SCHOOL, EARLY 1900S. When the Lawrence and Terrace Avenue Schools were built, New Castle's population was doubling. New neighborhoods were forming, and industries were hiring. The Terrace Avenue School was for the children of the growing number of families living on Sheep Hill. In the 1940s, the school building was bought by SS. Phillip and James Church, and it first became a vocational school, then a parochial school.

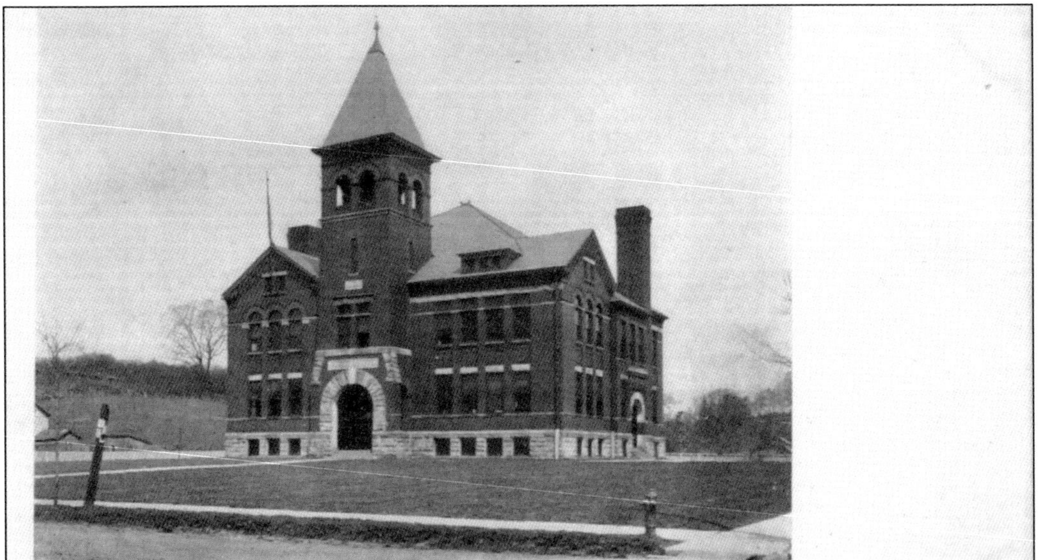

CHESTNUT STREET SCHOOL, *C.* 1897. It is believed that the Chestnut Street School and Oak Street School were one and the same. Both streets are on the east side of New Castle, a block apart. At the time, school construction was accelerated because of the rapid rise in numbers of school-age children, and if there were two schools, it is likely that their architecture was similar.

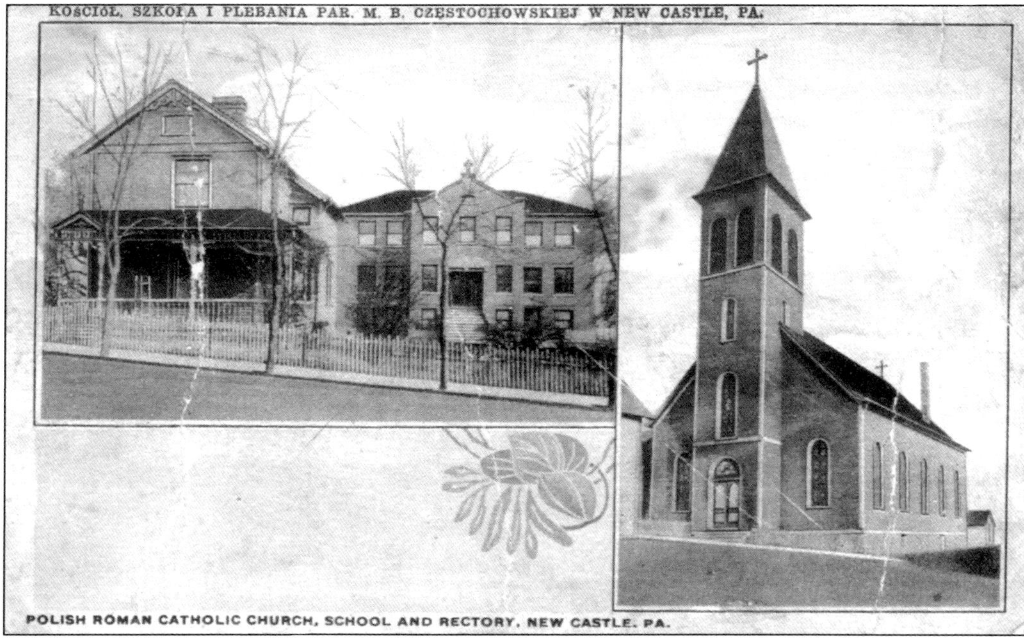

MADONNA CHURCH, SCHOOL, AND RECTORY, EARLY 1900S. Madonna of Czestochowa parish was founded as an ethnic church in 1902 for the Polish people in the Oakland district. By 1909 the parish had a one-room parochial school, but more classrooms were needed. A new school was built, and it opened in 1913.

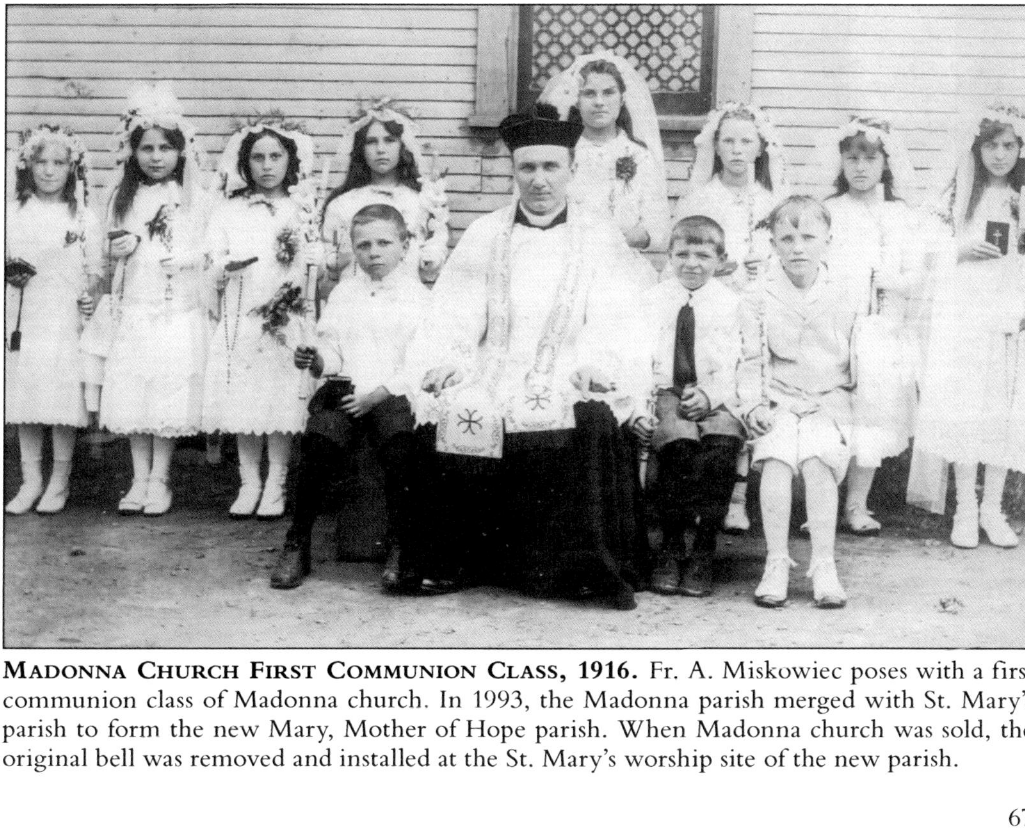

MADONNA CHURCH FIRST COMMUNION CLASS, 1916. Fr. A. Miskowiec poses with a first communion class of Madonna church. In 1993, the Madonna parish merged with St. Mary's parish to form the new Mary, Mother of Hope parish. When Madonna church was sold, the original bell was removed and installed at the St. Mary's worship site of the new parish.

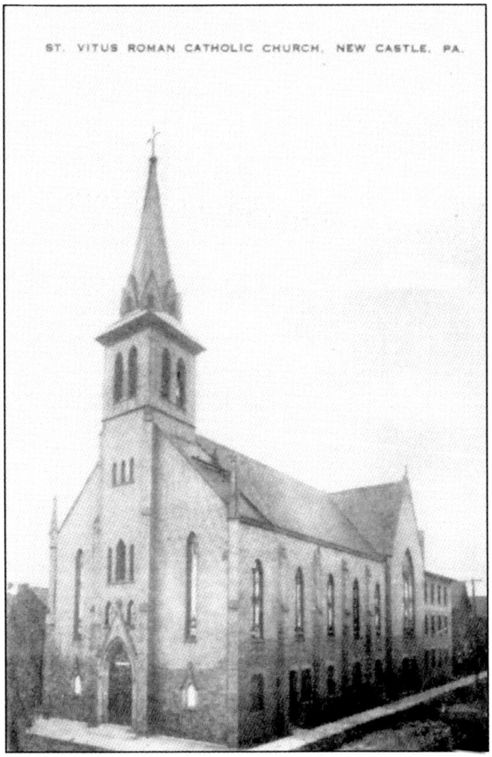

ST. VITUS CHURCH, *C.* 1907. In 1900, Italian-speaking residents on the south side of New Castle bought the first St. Vitus church building from the Maitland Memorial Primitive Methodist congregation. In 1905, Fr. Nicholas DeMita was assigned to New Castle and the St. Vitus congregation of 400 families, and by 1907, a second church, pictured here, was newly built and dedicated. The third (and present) St. Vitus church building was dedicated in 1963.

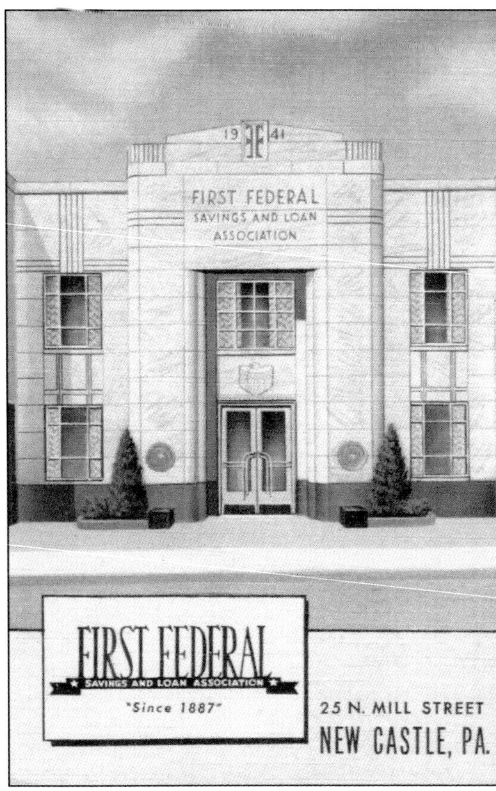

FIRST FEDERAL SAVINGS AND LOAN ASSOCIATION, 1940S. In 1887, this financial institution was known as the New Castle Mutual Building and Loan Association. It became the First Federal Savings and Loan Association in 1940, located on East Street across from the police department. In 1941, it moved into this striking new building on North Mill Street. The building was replaced in 1957 when First Federal Plaza was built on the same site.

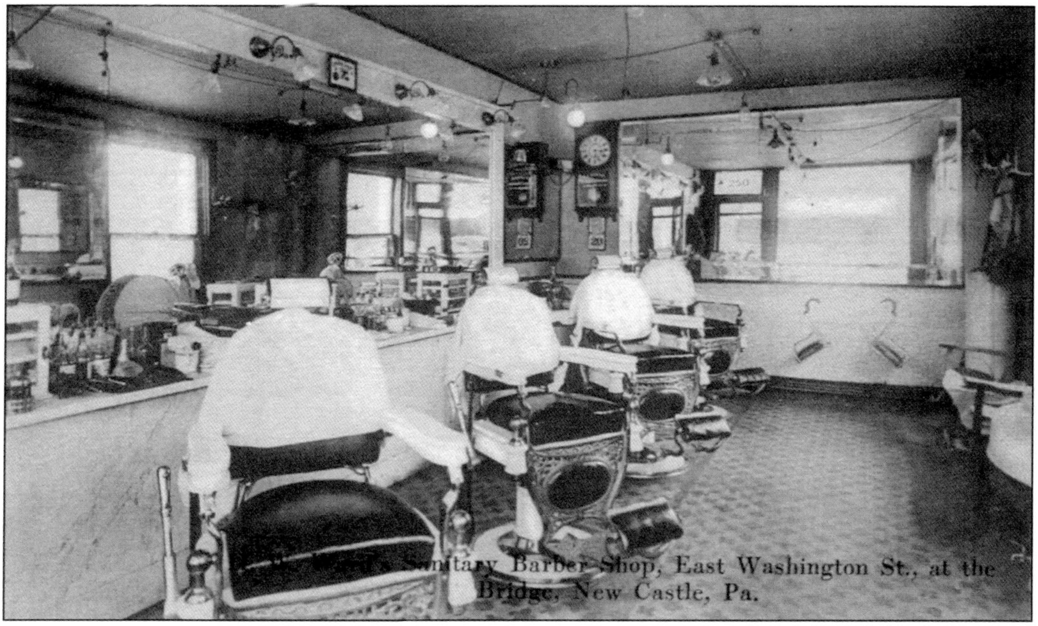

WARD'S BARBER SHOP, *c.* 1915. Howard Ward ran his barbershop for a short time, but this shop will be remembered most often as Zach Allerton's. It was across from the New Castle Dry Goods store on East Washington Street. In the 1970s, New Castle historian Bart Richards, reminiscing about barbers he fondly remembered, mentioned Reed Newell, Frank Turner, Ollie Rodenbaugh, Griff Lewis, Frank "Sully" Sullivan, Bill Gardner, and Sol Davies.

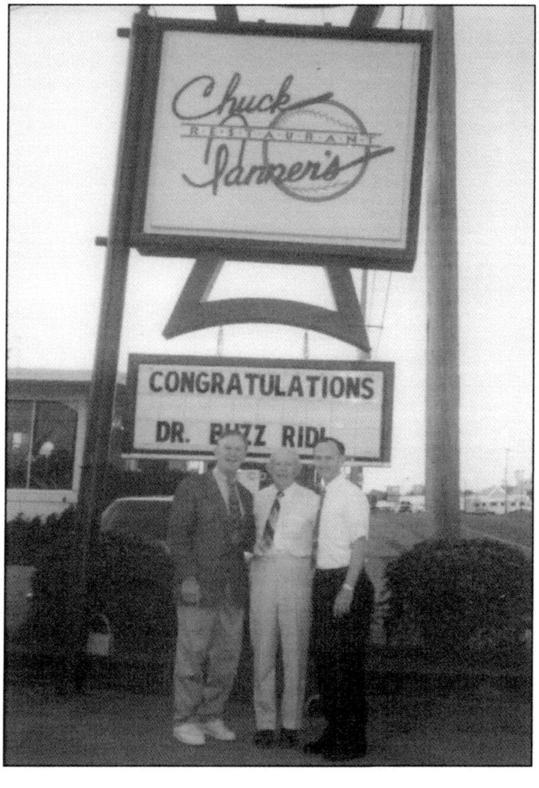

CHUCK TANNER'S RESTAURANT, NESHANNOCK TOWNSHIP, 1980S. Neshannock Township was a rural area in the 1800s. In the 1900s, it became increasingly residential and commercial. Here Chuck Tanner, noted former Pittsburgh Pirate manager, poses with coaching friends in front of Tanner's restaurant in Neshannock Township where the Little Chef Restaurant and the Castle Motel stood in the 1950s. Today Tanner's is owned by Gus Papazekos. (Courtesy of Gus Papazekos.)

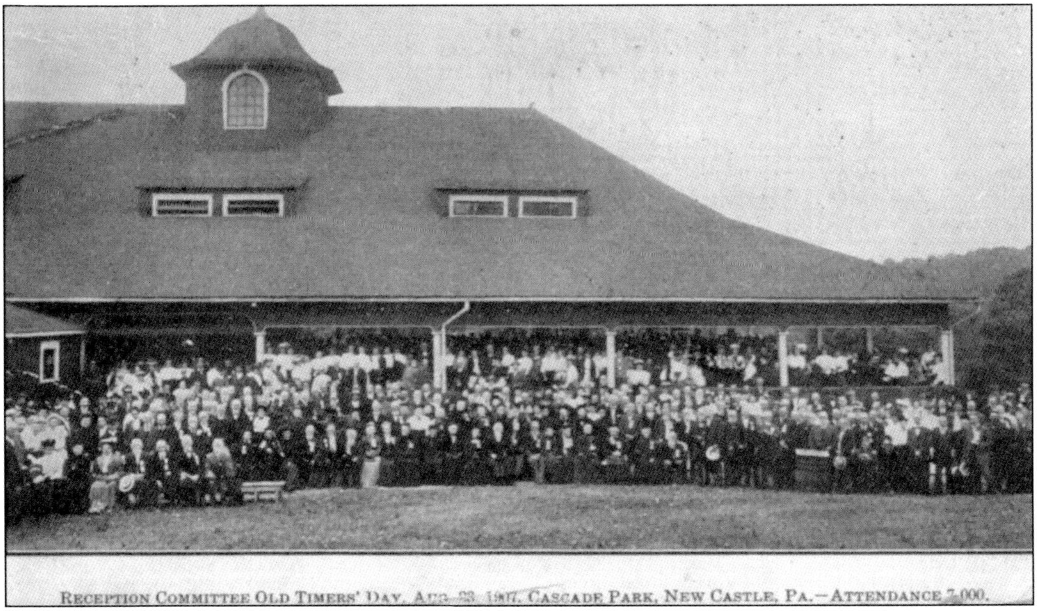

FIRST OLD TIMERS' DAY, CASCADE PARK, 1907. Old Timers' Day has been an annual event at Cascade Park since 1907. According to this postcard, 7,000 people attended the first Old Timers' Day, and the second one was to be held on August 20, 1908. The message on the back of the card reads "Residents of New Castle and immediate vicinity previous to 1861, with their families, their descendents and their families, are invited."

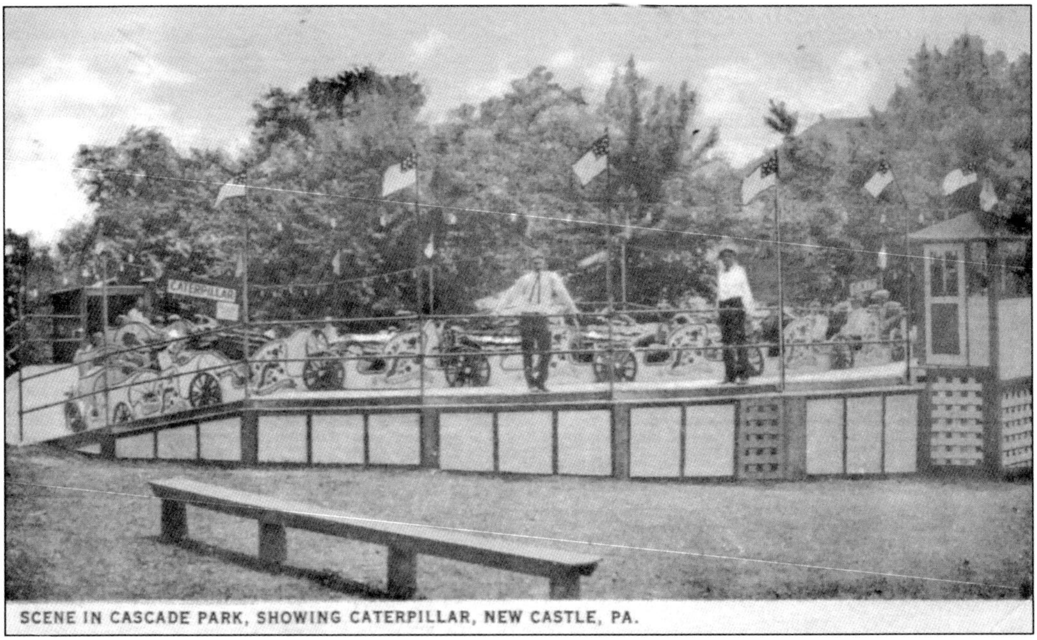

CATERPILLAR RIDE AT CASCADE PARK, 1920S. The Caterpillar ride at Cascade Park was installed by the Standen and Sinclair Company around 1922. The ride was a series of cars on an undulating track. While the cars circled, a canopy would come down over the riders so that to onlookers the ride appeared to be a huge caterpillar in motion. By 1925, this popular scenic park had 17 rides.

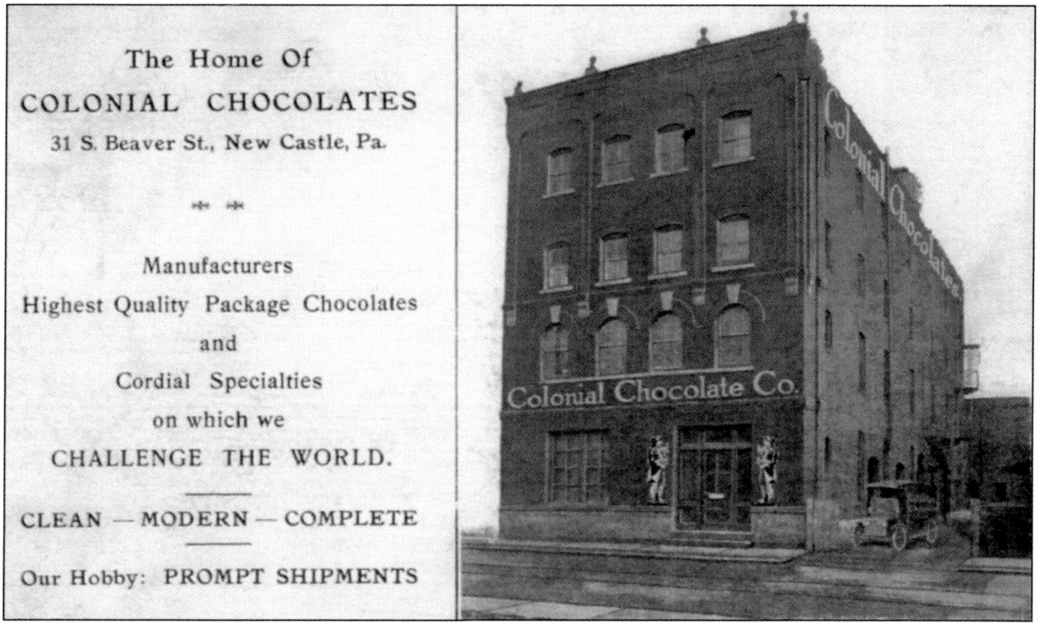

COLONIAL CHOCOLATES, NEW CASTLE, *c.* 1915. New Castle loved sweets. This candy store was on South Beaver Street. New Castle residents also bought candy from the Sotus Company, which was founded in 1890, and the Caizza Candy Company, started in the 1920s. Then there were the Chocolate Shop, the Palace Confectionery, the Sweet Shoppe, and Jameson's. How sweet it was.

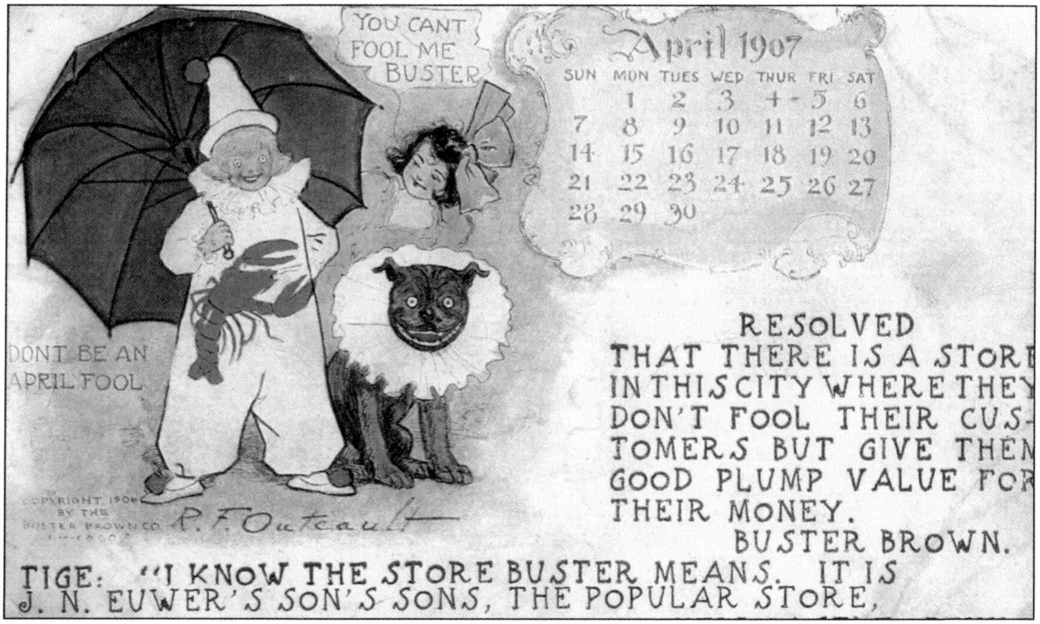

ADVERTISING CARD, EUWER'S STORE, *c.* 1907. Euwer's was a department store established in 1834, continuing business for three generations. Its building on East Washington Street near North Mill Street had five floors. Another building was around the corner on North Mill Street at Water Street, just before the bridge. The Buster Brown cartoon character and Buster Brown shoes have been around for more than 100 years.

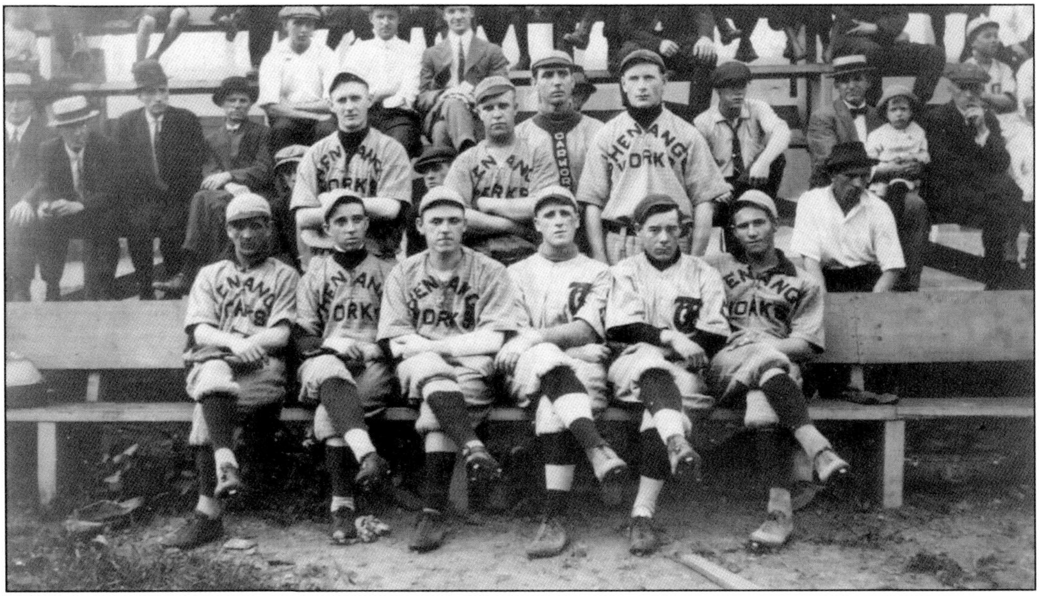

SHENANGO WORKS BASEBALL TEAM, *c.* 1919. This picture postcard was taken after World War I. The Shenango Works was part of the tin mill. Team members are, from left to right, (first row) unidentified, Daniel Jenkins, John Jones, Stan Jones, unidentified, and unidentified; (second row) Harry Glover, unidentified, unidentified, and unidentified. In the background, seated in the center among the spectators, is Arthur W. Howell of Ellwood City.

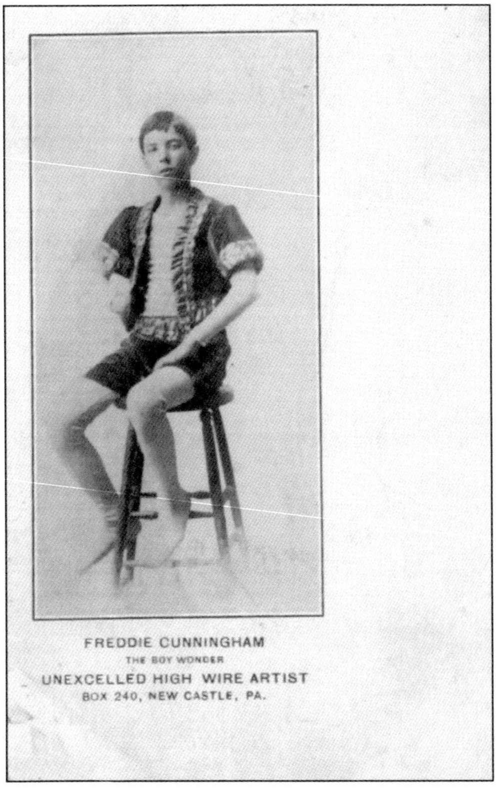

ADVERTISING CARD, FREDDIE CUNNINGHAM, *c.* 1910. This high-wire artist performed at the 1910 Independence Day Celebration in downtown New Castle. He entertained the crowd (said to be 70,000 people for the weekend) with an exhibition on a high wire stretched over the Neshannock Creek between the Dean and Rohrer Buildings.

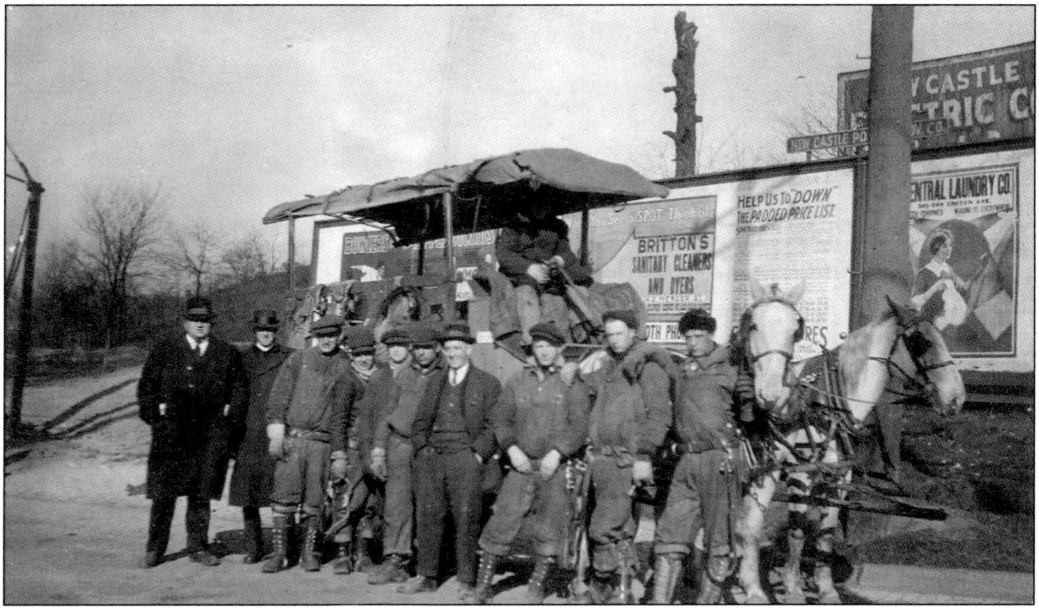

NEW CASTLE ELECTRIC COMPANY CREW, *c.* 1918. The New Castle Electric Company provided electricity to the city until 1928 when the Mercer and Lawrence County power companies merged to form the Penn Power Company. This group is standing on Cochran Way at East Washington Street. The billboard signs in the background advertise a bowling alley, Britton's Cleaners, and the Central Laundry Company.

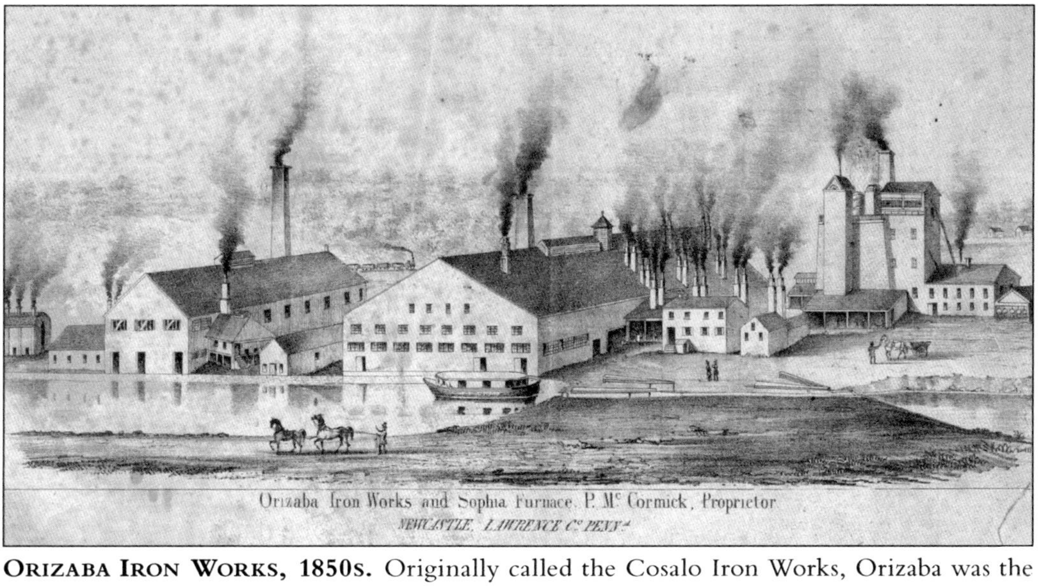

ORIZABA IRON WORKS, 1850S. Originally called the Cosalo Iron Works, Orizaba was the name chosen by new owners in 1853 when they built the Sophia Furnace. Later Orizaba became the Shenango Iron Works. This operation was on the Erie Extension Canal near the south bank of the Neshannock Creek across from the end of North Mercer Street. Note the canal boat and stone walls of the canal.

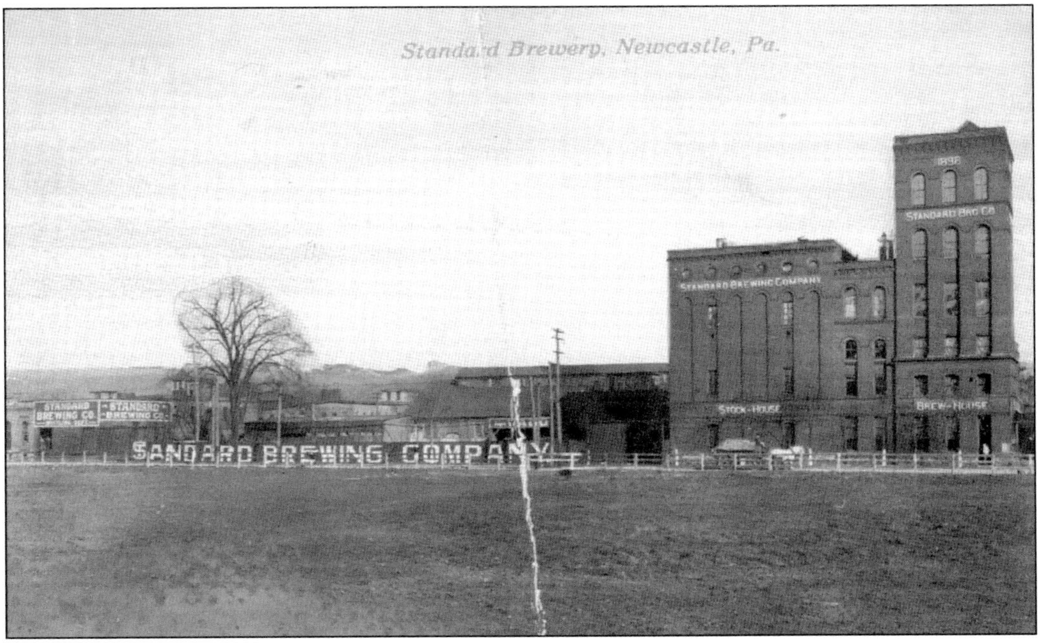

STANDARD BREWERY, EARLY 1900S. This building went up in 1898 on Sampson Street along the Shenango River. It was considered the latest in breweries with ice-making and bottling facilities. Water was drawn from an artesian well on the premises. Eventually this building was acquired by the Union Brewing Company.

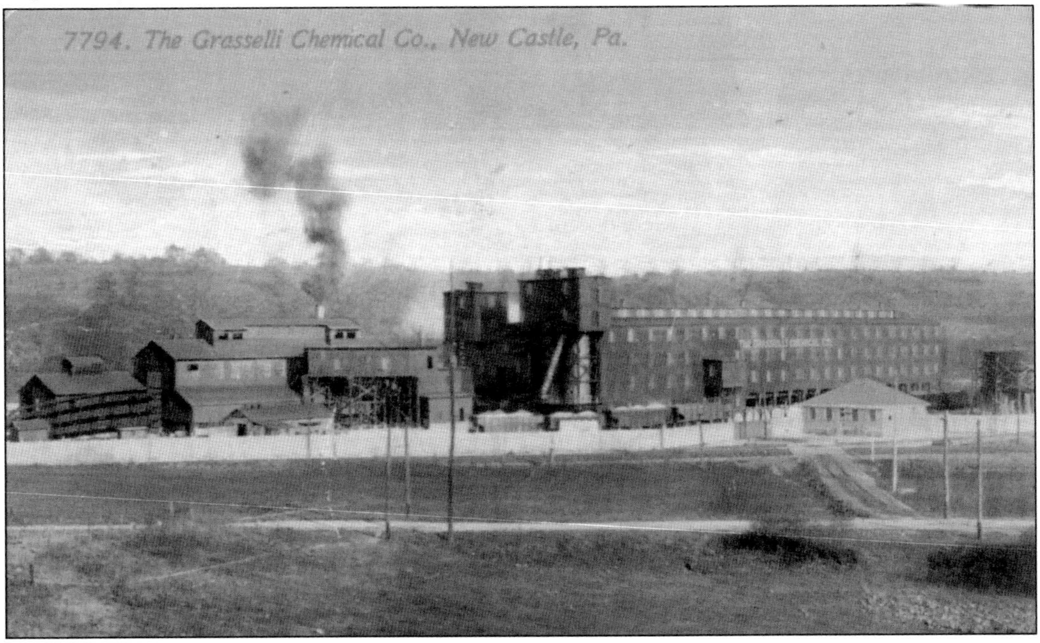

GRASSELLI CHEMICAL COMPANY, EARLY 1900S. This company was established in 1839 on the west bank of the Shenango River near Sampson Street. It produced explosives, dyestuffs, zinc, and other chemical products. The company continued until the mid-1930s, when it became the Grasselli department of the E. I. Dupont de Nemours Corporation in Delaware. The New Castle Chemical Company was in that location in the 1950s.

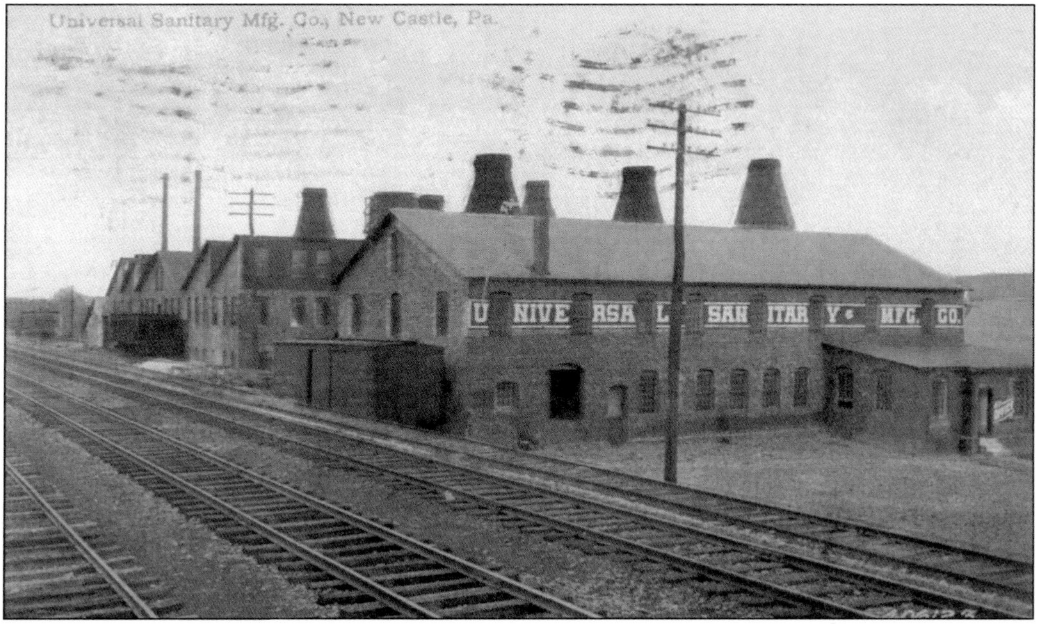

UNIVERSAL SANITARY MANUFACTURING COMPANY, EARLY 1900S. This company was incorporated in 1901. Its six buildings were near Mahoningtown and New Castle Junction. About 125 people manufactured vitreous ceramic plumbing fixtures. Founder Charles J. Kirk revolutionized the ceramic industry by using a tunnel kiln instead of a beehive kiln. The company merged with the Rundle Corporation in 1948 and is now known as the Universal Rundle Corporation.

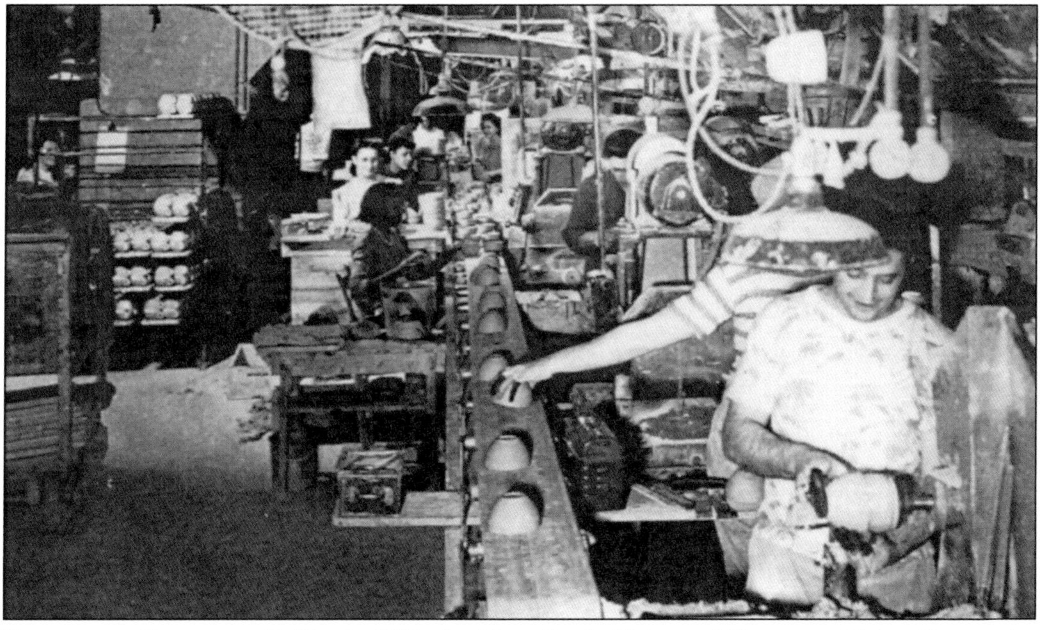

SHENANGO POTTERY, 1940S. In 1901, the New Castle China and Shenango China Companies incorporated with plants on the west side of New Castle. In 1913, James M. Smith consolidated the companies and started producing china for hotels, restaurants, and institutions such as military facilities. In the 1940s, the plant produced fine Castleton and Haviland china. The company changed hands several times in the years before 1991, when the plant closed.

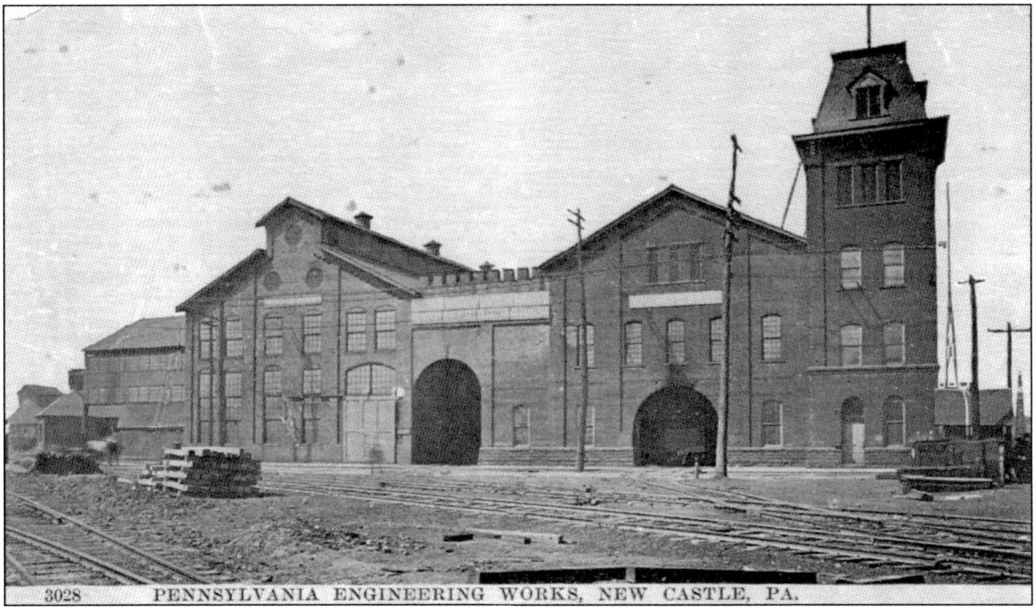

PENNSYLVANIA ENGINEERING WORKS, LATE 1890S. This building was first owned by J. P. Witherow, who in 1886 manufactured blast furnaces, boilers, and other mill machinery. In 1899, William Patterson bought the plant and established the Pennsylvania Engineering Works, which constructed heavy manufacturing equipment. The company operated until the 1980s, earning national and international reputations for its products. The building is now occupied by the Barletto Equipment Company.

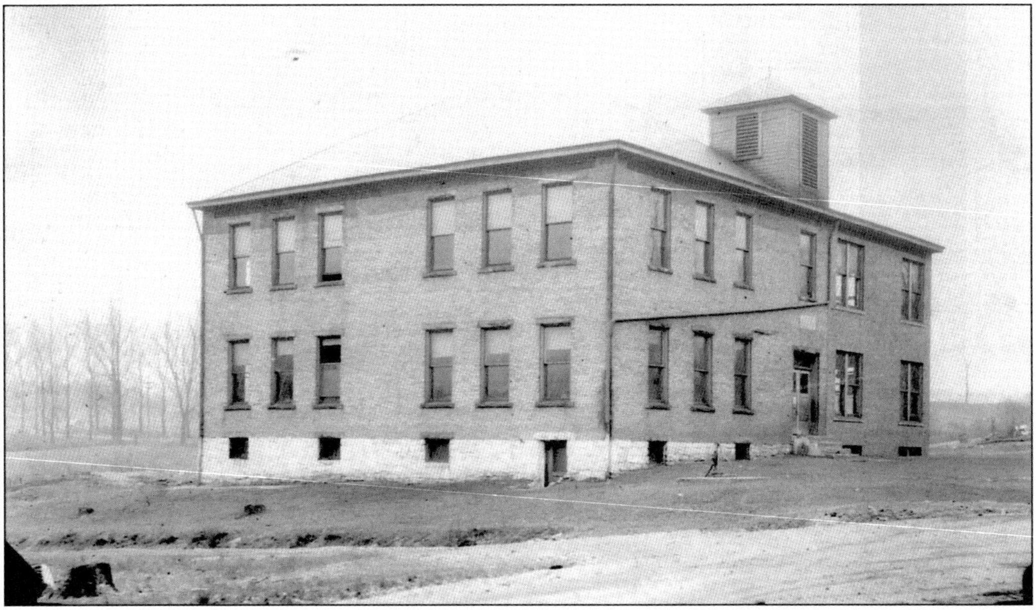

J. P. BYERS SCHOOL, SOUTH NEW CASTLE BOROUGH, 1930S. J. P. Byers was a banker who, in 1896, bought and laid out the 113 acres now called South New Castle Borough and Sheep Hill. This school was near the Rigby Post Office, named for Charles Rigby, an influential businessman. Among the postmasters (not postmistresses) were Harriet Sweet and Bella Walczak. The Rigby Post Office closed in 1944. (Courtesy of Josephine Dec.)

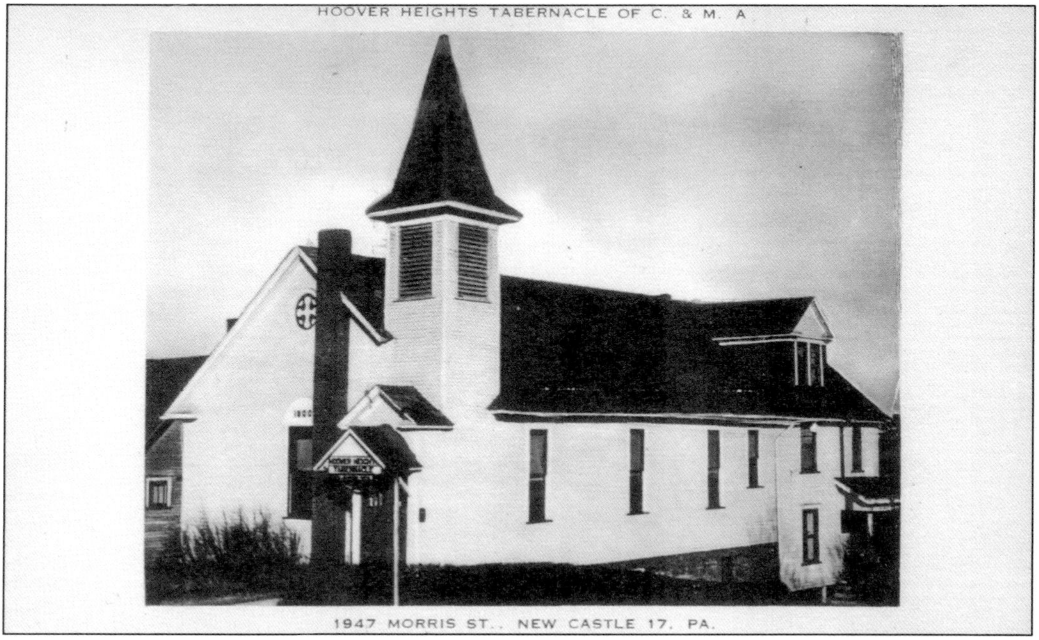

HOOVER HEIGHTS TABERNACLE, SOUTH NEW CASTLE BOROUGH, EARLY 1900S. The congregation of this church formed one of the largest branches of the Christian and Missionary Alliance (C&MA) in Lawrence County. Built around 1900, it is still standing in what is called the Hoover Heights District of South New Castle Borough. With other C&MA churches on Pearson Street and in Castlewood, the denomination dates back to 1887.

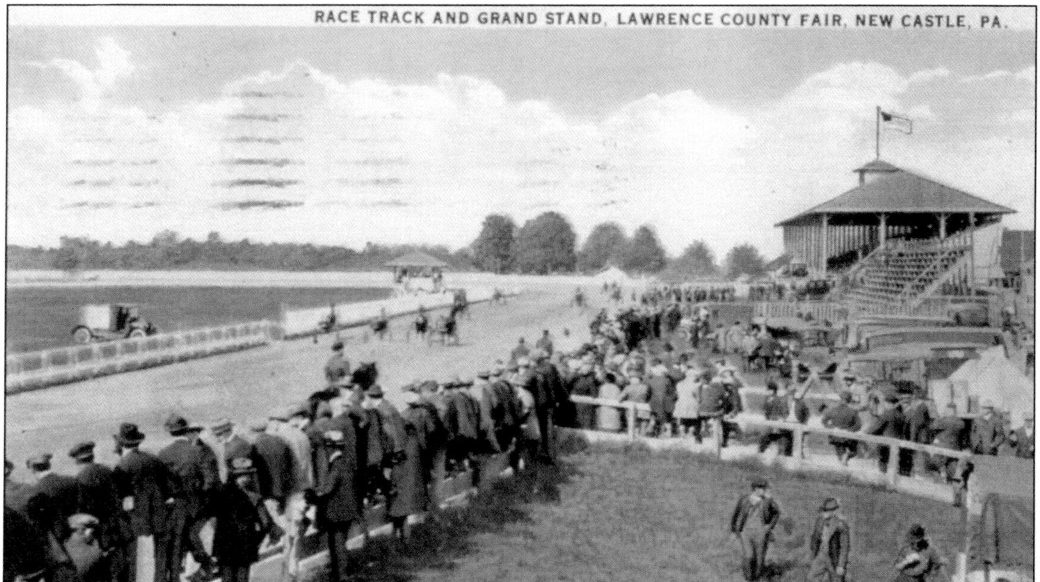

LAWRENCE COUNTY FAIRGROUNDS, 1920S. Agriculture remained strong during the industrial heyday in New Castle. To promote rural life, land on Harlansburg Road was bought for exhibition buildings, barns, a half-mile racetrack, and grandstands, and the New Castle Fair was established. The yearly event stopped in 1941, but in the 1950s, a county commission bought the Rick farm in Laurel and set up the Lawrence County Fair as an annual event.

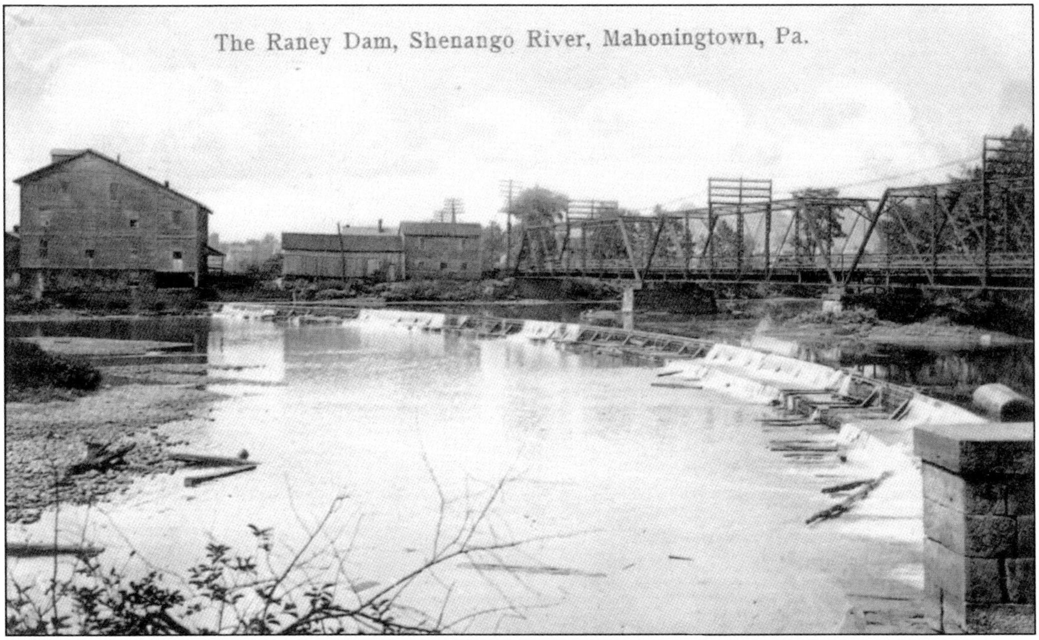

RANEY DAM, SHENANGO RIVER, MAHONINGTOWN, *C.* 1910. This postcard shows James Raney's flour mill and dam, which was on the south side of East Cherry Street. The location of the mill, which produced 100 barrels of flour a day, was convenient to both the B&O and Pennsylvania Railroad.

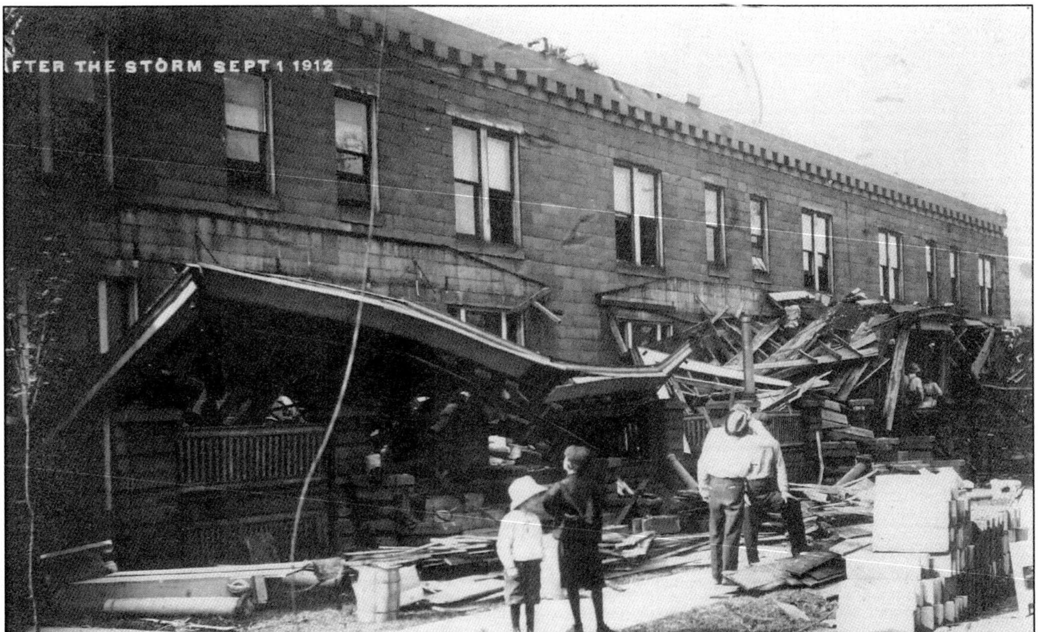

MAHONINGTOWN WIND STORM, 1912. On September 1, 1912, a violent storm tore the roof off the Gardner Apartments on South Lafayette Street in Mahoningtown. Wires fell to the ground, porches were destroyed, and rain drenched the occupants of the six apartments. The wind carried timbers and wreckage to a house across the street, which also suffered damage.

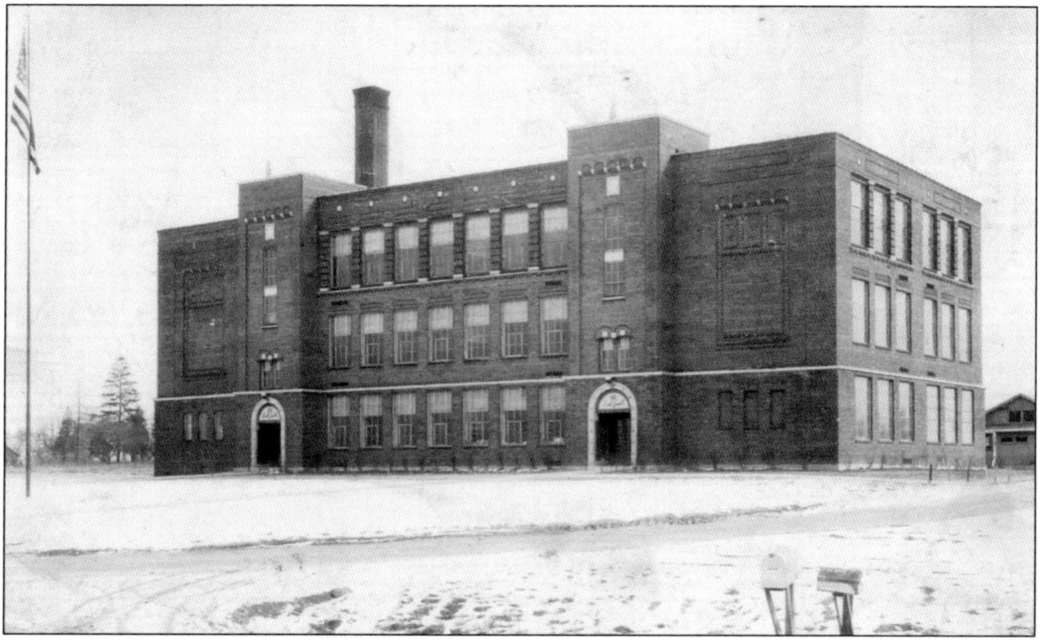

SHENANGO HIGH SCHOOL, *C.* 1930. In 1926, all of the schools in Shenango Township, such as J. P. Byers and Castlewood, were brought together as the Shenango Consolidated School. The new building was not ready for the fall opening, so students met in a church. The building shown in this postcard was designed by Thayer Architects, and it served all 12 grades.

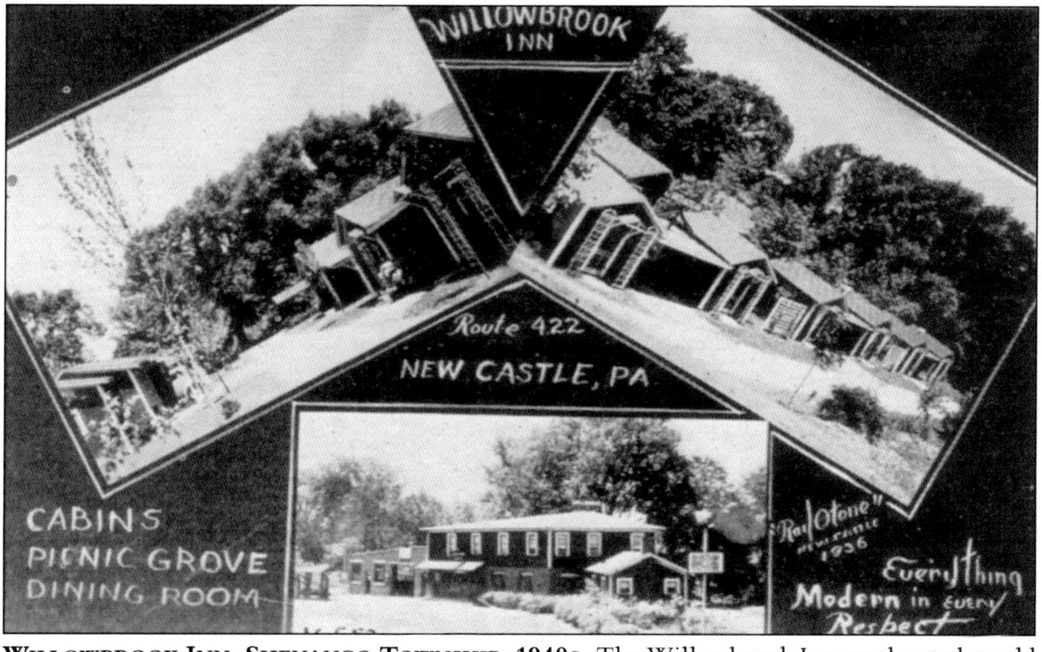

WILLOWBROOK INN, SHENANGO TOWNSHIP, 1940S. The Willowbrook Inn was located on old Butler Road in the Willowbrook area of Shenango Township. It offered a number of amenities, such as tourist cabins, dancing, and fine dining, to increasing numbers of post–World War II travelers. Some local residents found it a convenient stop for a drink of beer.

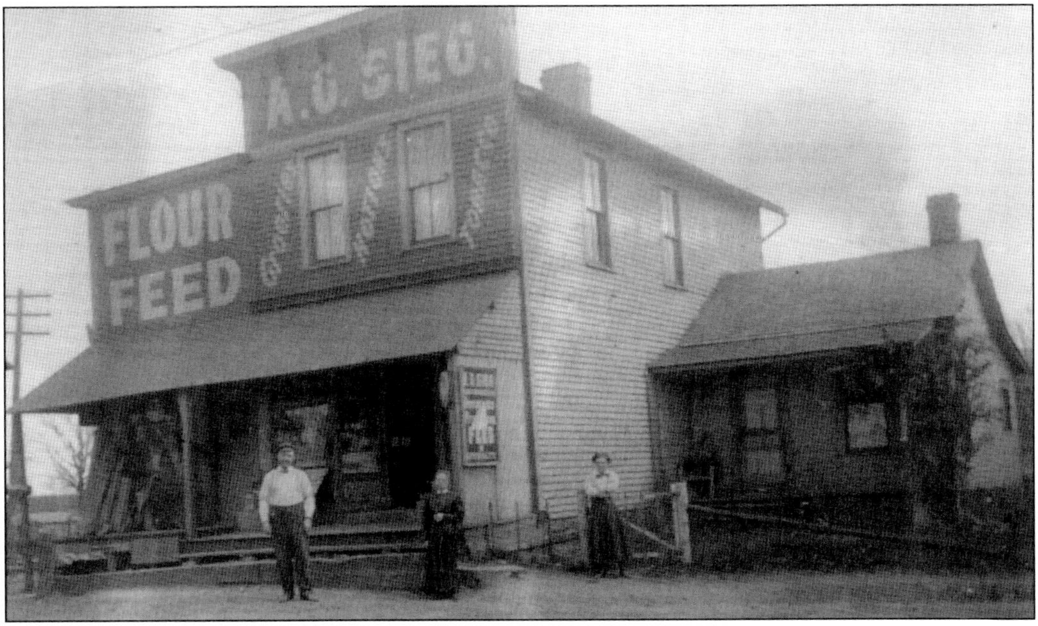

General Store, Joyce, Shenango Township, 1911. A. G. Sieg's general store was also a post office for the community of East New Castle, once called Punkintown. The store was located at what was the fork of Old Pittsburgh Road and East Washington Street. Sieg named the post office Joyce for his daughter (center), and the area came to be called Joyce. The name now appears on maps of the area. (Courtesy of LCHS, Hitch Collection.)

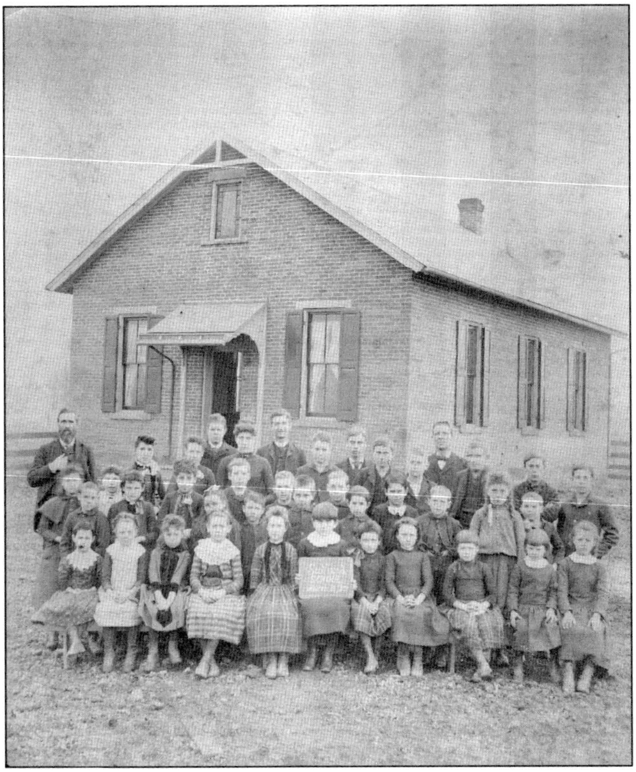

Scotland School, Union Township, 1889. This sturdy brick school may have been built in the 1860s. It stood at the corner of Scotland Lane and State Street until it closed in the 1950s. When it closed, two grades were attending, the first grade sitting on one side of the stove and the second grade sitting on the other. The children used outdoor toilets behind the school. (Courtesy of Jane Santini.)

Five

New Wilmington and Pulaski Area

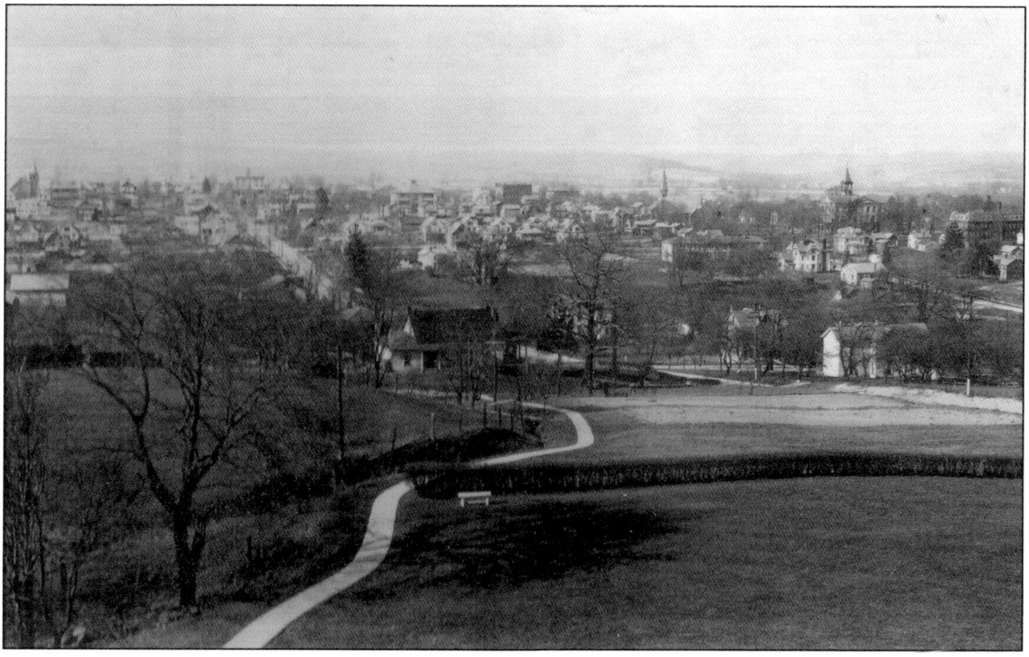

View of New Wilmington. This panoramic view of New Wilmington was taken from the hill of Overlook health care facility. In the distance, center right, can be seen the steeple of Westminster College's Old Main, which burned down in 1927. In the distance at center left is Vine Street School. (Courtesy of New Castle Public Library.)

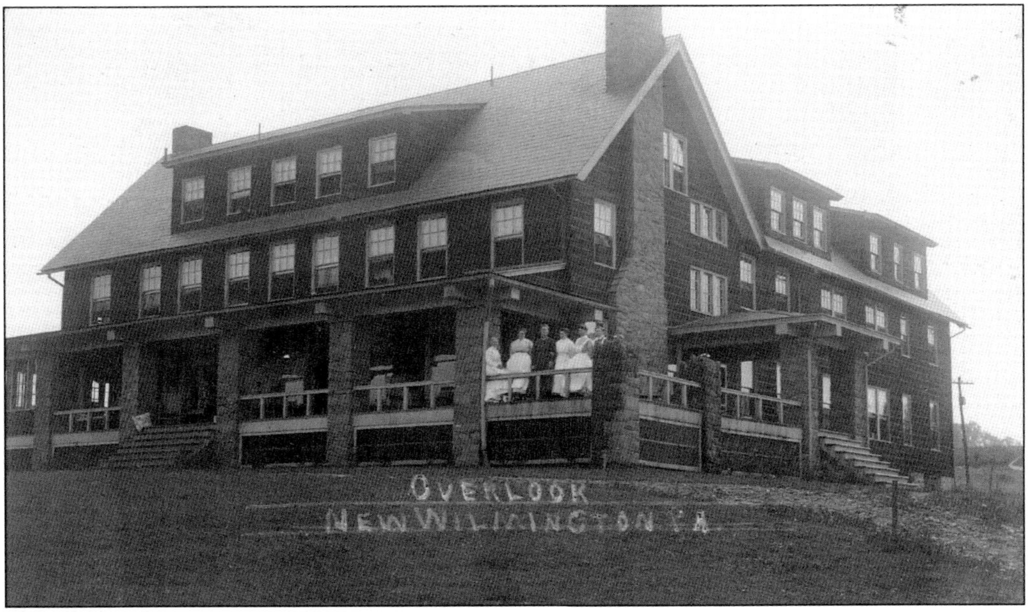

OVERLOOK SANITARIUM, NEW WILMINGTON, 1920S. In 1911, Dr. Elizabeth McLaughry founded Overlook on the family farm located on Furnace Hill. With her brother and sister, she created and directed a sanitarium for "nervous" patients. Many people traveled a distance for Overlook's restful and healing treatment. Today it is a nursing home offering extended care. It is eligible for listing as a national registered historic site.

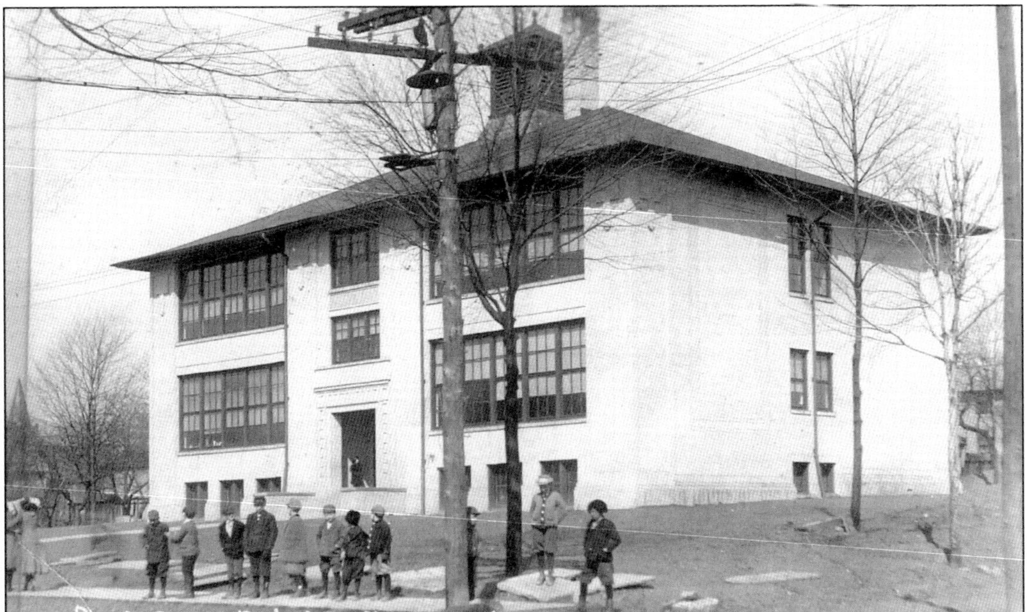

VINE STREET SCHOOL BUILDING, NEW WILMINGTON. The first school in New Wilmington was a log schoolhouse built around 1810 about a quarter of a mile west of town. Later schools were either log or frame buildings, then in 1868, a redbrick school went up on Vine Street. It was replaced in 1909 by the public school pictured here. Four classrooms were added to this building in the 1930s. Now an apartment building, it still stands on Vine Street.

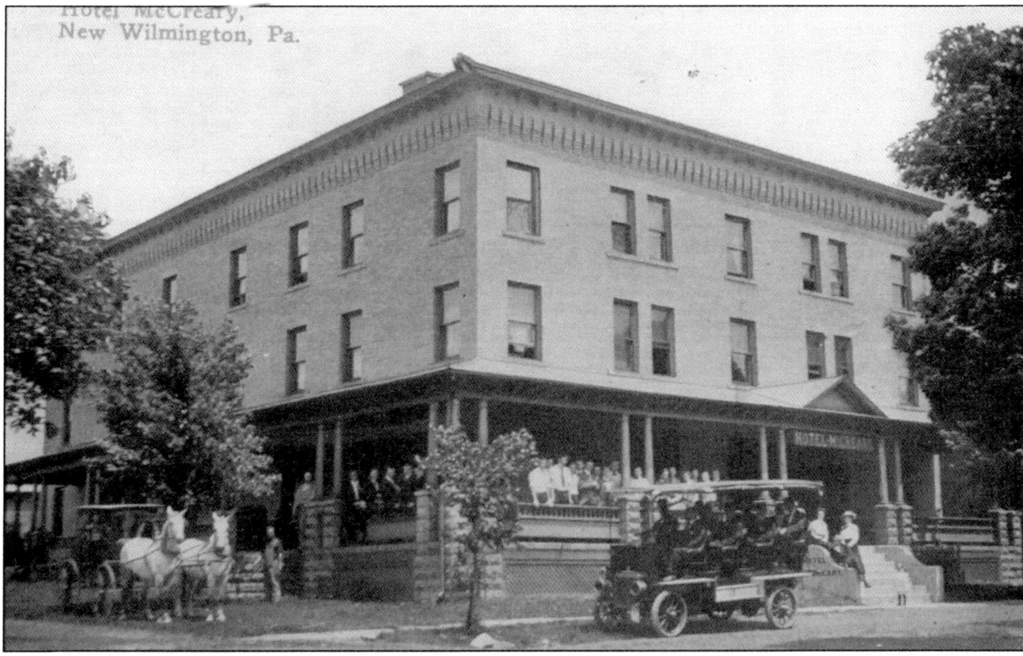

HOTEL McCREARY, NEW WILMINGTON, *c.* 1911. This building has stood at the corner of Neshannock Avenue and New Castle Street since 1904. In 1918, it was used to house U.S. Army trainees, and in 1943, it became a recreation center for servicemen. Over time, it has been a drugstore, a health clinic, a real estate office, an antique shop, and a variety of other businesses. It is now an apartment building.

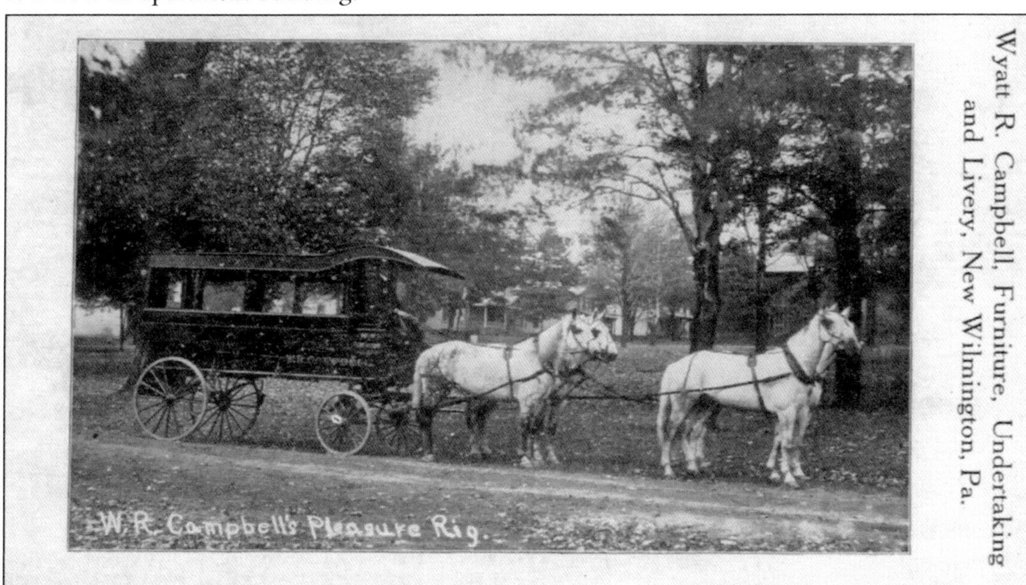

W. R. CAMPBELL PLEASURE RIG, EARLY 1900S. Wyatt R. Campbell's business combined furniture sales, undertaking, and livery services such as the elaborate pleasure rig seen here. A team of four horses and a closed carriage would have been the height of luxury for tourists, courting couples, or a family outing. For safety, horses were limited to a gait speed of six miles per hour, a speed limit established in 1892.

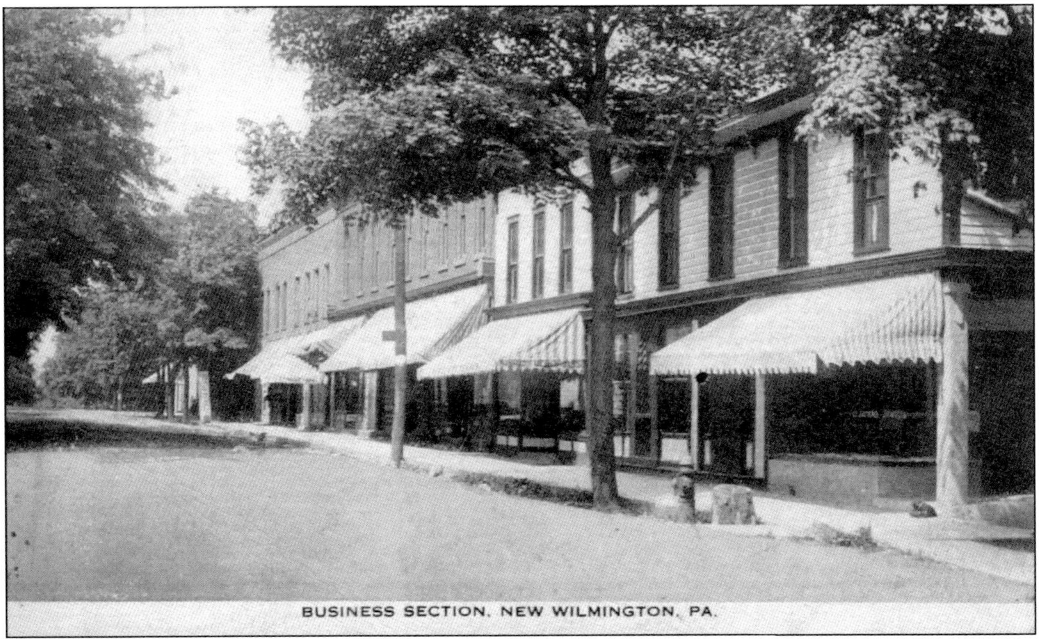

BUSINESS SECTION, NEW WILMINGTON, *c.* 1919. One tree remains in this block on the east side of Market Street. This is "Isaly's corner," looking north from Vine Street. The facades of these storefronts have been changed over the years, but the buildings are recognizable. Today the tree is gone and parked cars line the street in front of the stores.

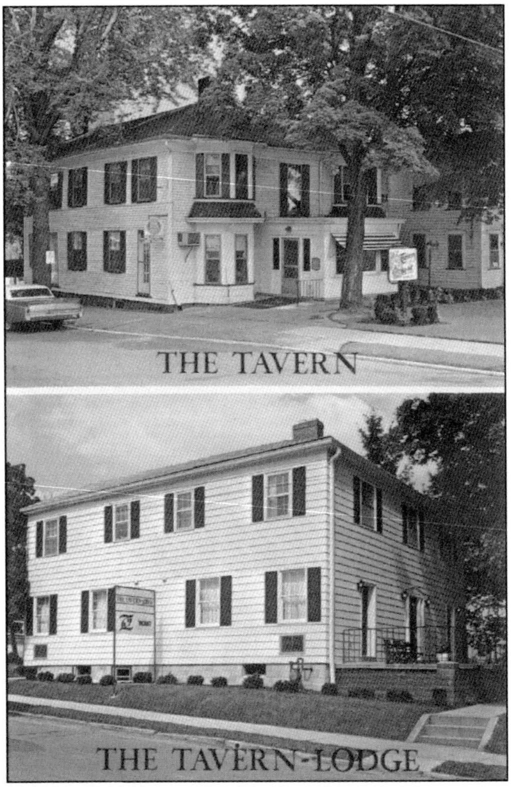

THE TAVERN, NEW WILMINGTON. This house was built in the 1840s as a residence for Dr. Seth Poppino and his family. It likely was used as a stop on the Underground Railroad during the Civil War. When Cora and Ernie Durrast opened the Tavern as a restaurant in the 1930s, they preserved the historic aspects of the building while earning an outstanding reputation for the dining room.

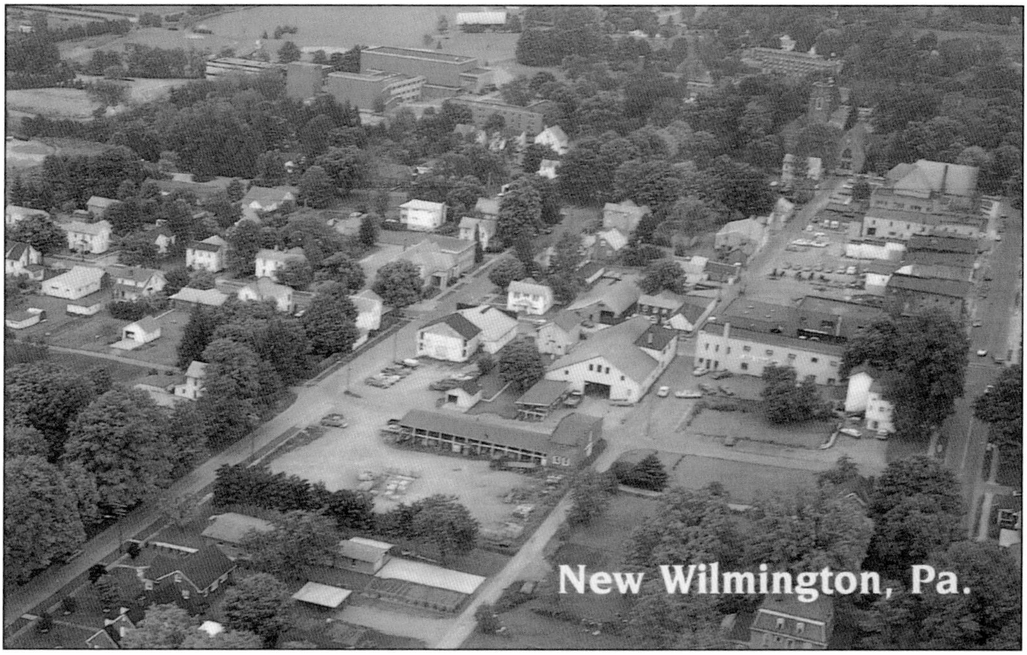

BIRD'S-EYE VIEW OF NEW WILMINGTON, 1980S. Looking south, this view shows Mercer Street on the left, Chestnut Street in the center, and Market Street to the right. At right center, the white building nestling in the trees is the Tavern. In the background is the New Wilmington Presbyterian Church and the Westminster College campus.

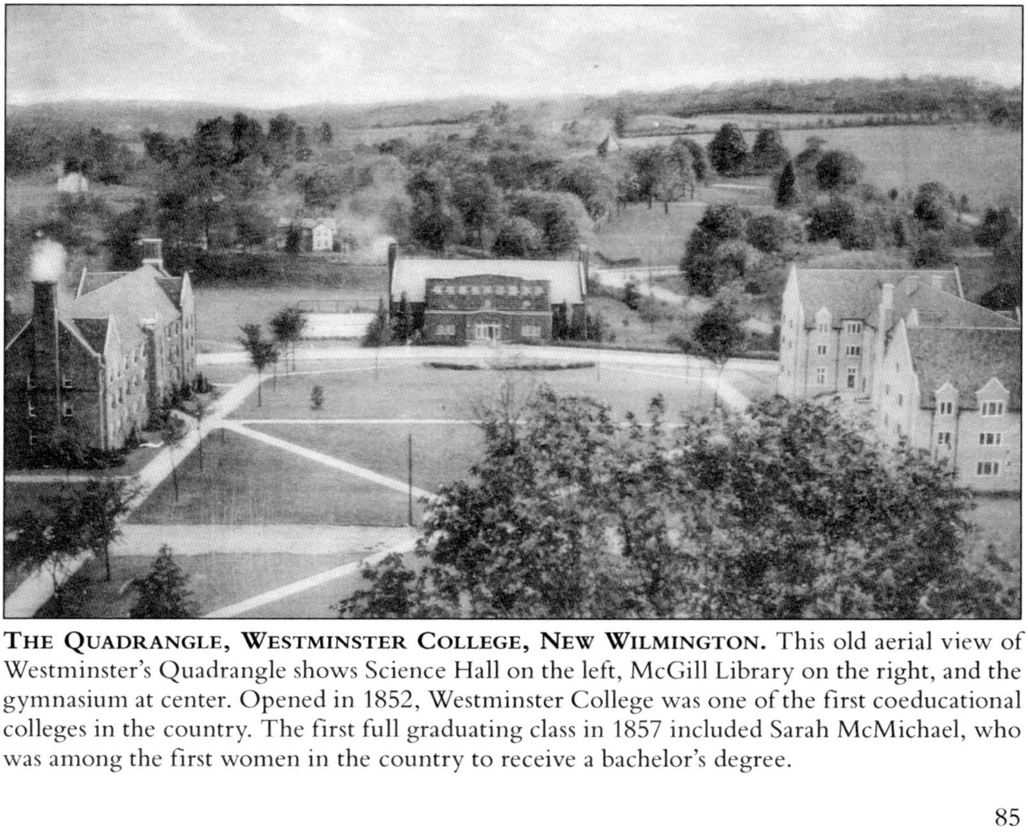

THE QUADRANGLE, WESTMINSTER COLLEGE, NEW WILMINGTON. This old aerial view of Westminster's Quadrangle shows Science Hall on the left, McGill Library on the right, and the gymnasium at center. Opened in 1852, Westminster College was one of the first coeducational colleges in the country. The first full graduating class in 1857 included Sarah McMichael, who was among the first women in the country to receive a bachelor's degree.

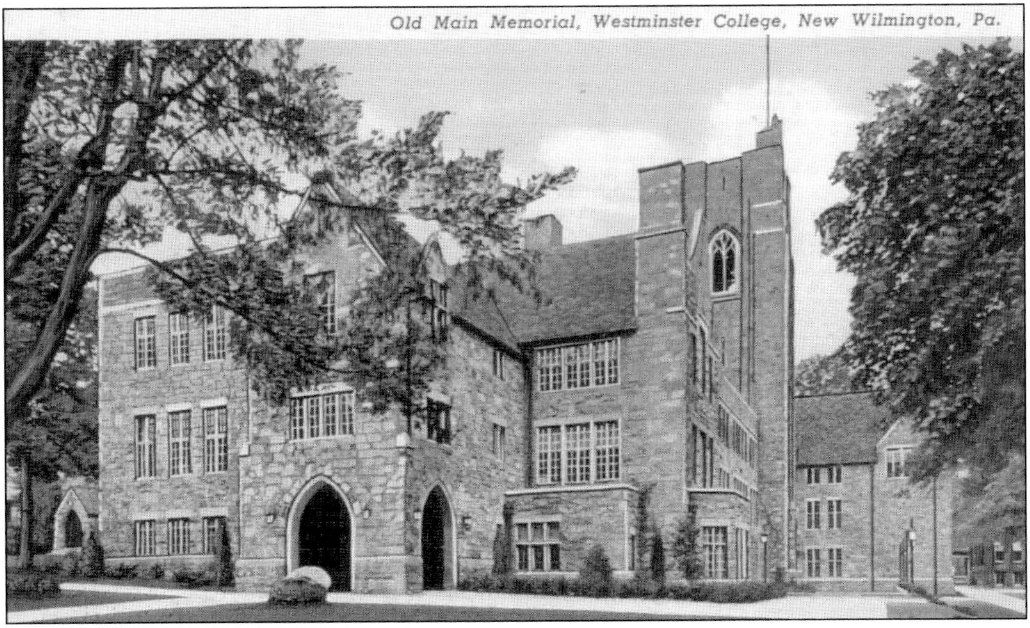

OLD MAIN MEMORIAL, WESTMINSTER COLLEGE, NEW WILMINGTON. Westminster's first main building opened in 1855, three years after the college opened. The building burned down six years later. A second main building, called Old Main, stood from 1862 to 1927, when it too burned down. The building pictured here, in an architectural style called Collegiate Gothic, replaced Old Main in 1929.

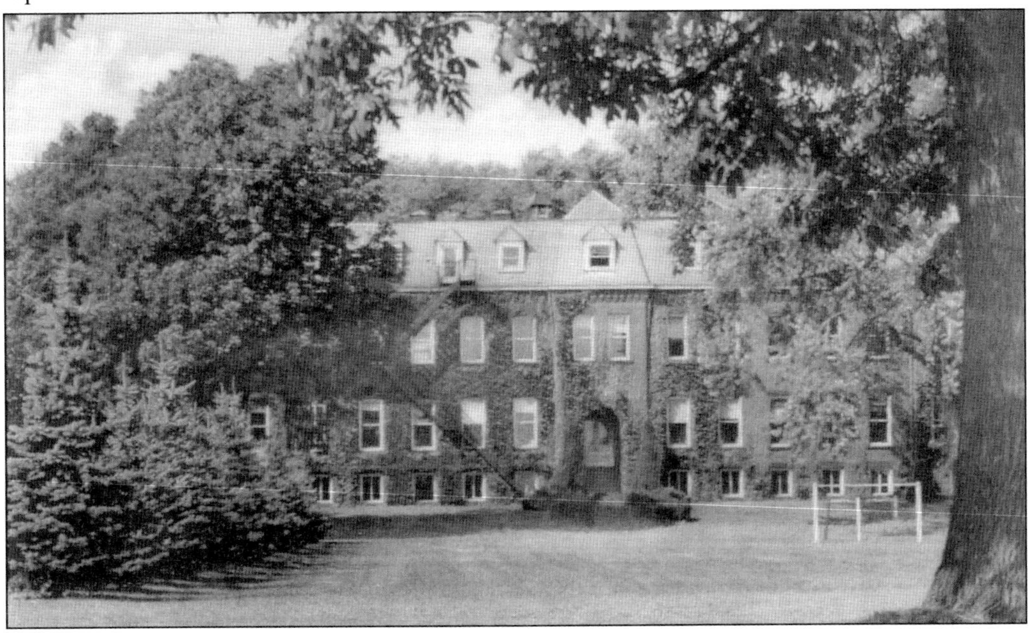

SCIENCE HALL, WESTMINSTER COLLEGE. Thompson Science Hall, named for Westminster graduate and professor Samuel R. Thompson, was built in 1893. Thompson, a physics and botany professor, established a scientific course that emphasized the natural sciences. He funded construction of the new building and developed hands-on laboratory approaches to instruction in the sciences. The building is listed on the National Register of Historic Places.

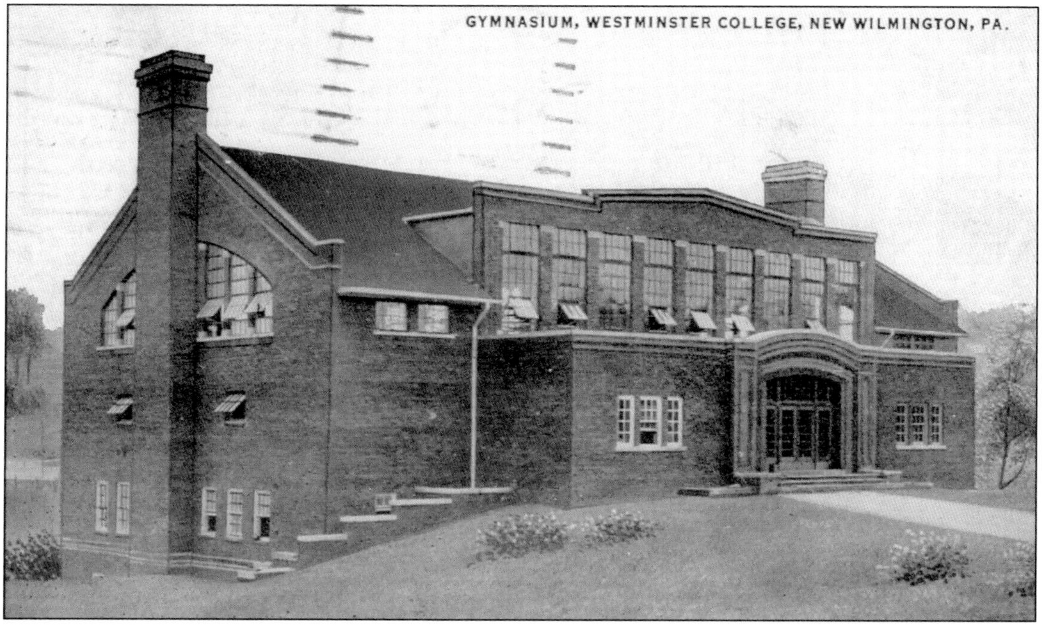

GYMNASIUM, WESTMINSTER COLLEGE, C. 1936. In 1917, college enrollment dropped because of World War I, so Westminster's students went out to high schools to recruit prospective students. Enrollment numbers went up, and the administration responded with a new gymnasium in 1921. This building, now called Old 77 for the basketball team's 77 straight home games won there, still stands. Basketball is now played in the Memorial Field House built in 1951.

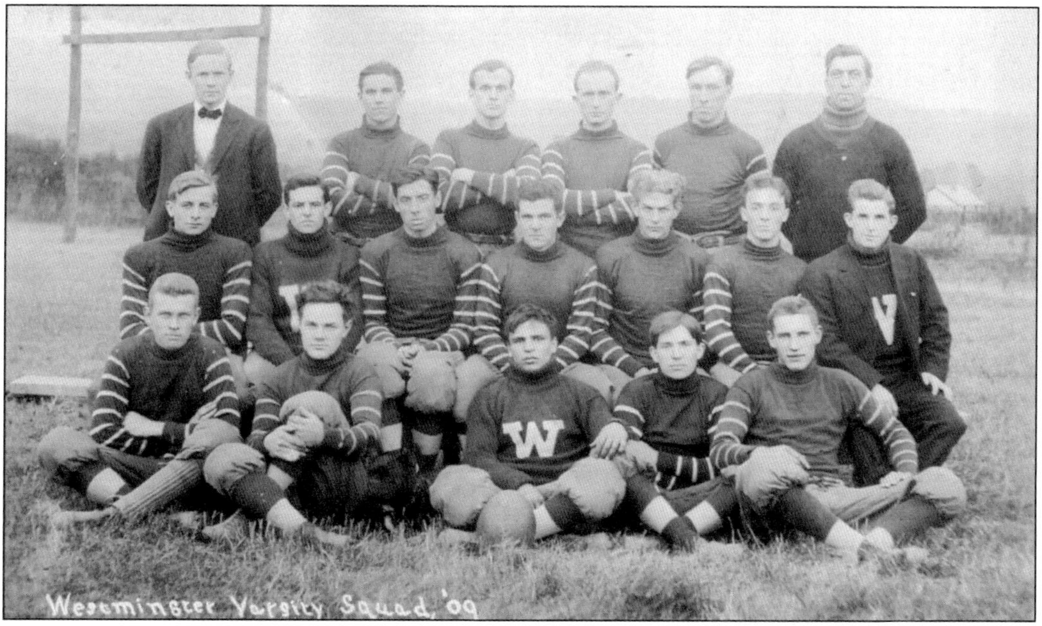

WESTMINSTER VARSITY SQUAD, 1909. Historically Westminster's football teams had undistinguished records, with one winning season in 33 years. Harold Burry stepped into the football program in 1952 and transformed the Titans. Joe Fusco followed Burry in the 1970s, and between the two of them, they coached the Titans to five national championships and a number of undefeated seasons.

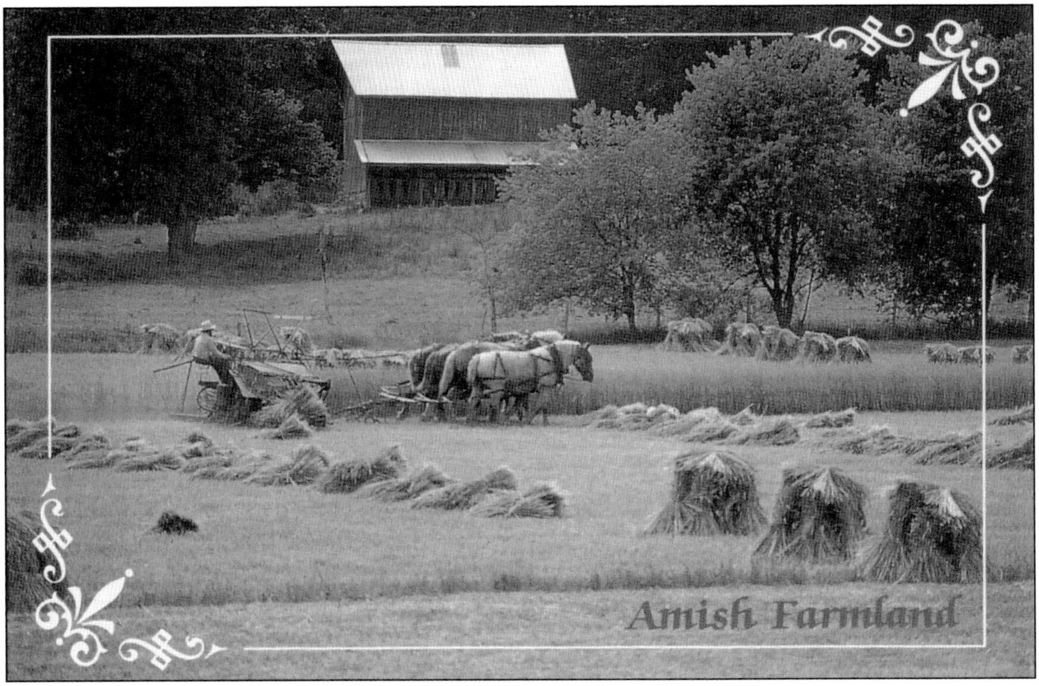

AMISH FARMERS WORKING THE FIELDS. Like generations before them, these farmers use teams of horses to work their fields. The binder shown in the top postcard would be obsolete on a modern farm, but Amish farmers rely on manual labor and traditional machinery. Lawrence County's Amish community was founded by Abraham Zook, who bought land in Mercer County in 1847. Two years later, his land became part of Lawrence County when the county was established. Zook's followers migrated from eastern Pennsylvania, one community settling in northern Lawrence County (Pulaski, Hickory, Wilmington, and Neshannock Townships) and another near Enon Valley. Modern Amish men no longer support their families by farming only. Today they supplement their incomes with carpentry, construction, harness and buggy making, cabinetry, and other trades. Some Amish women contribute to the household income by selling traditional foods and crafts such as quilts.

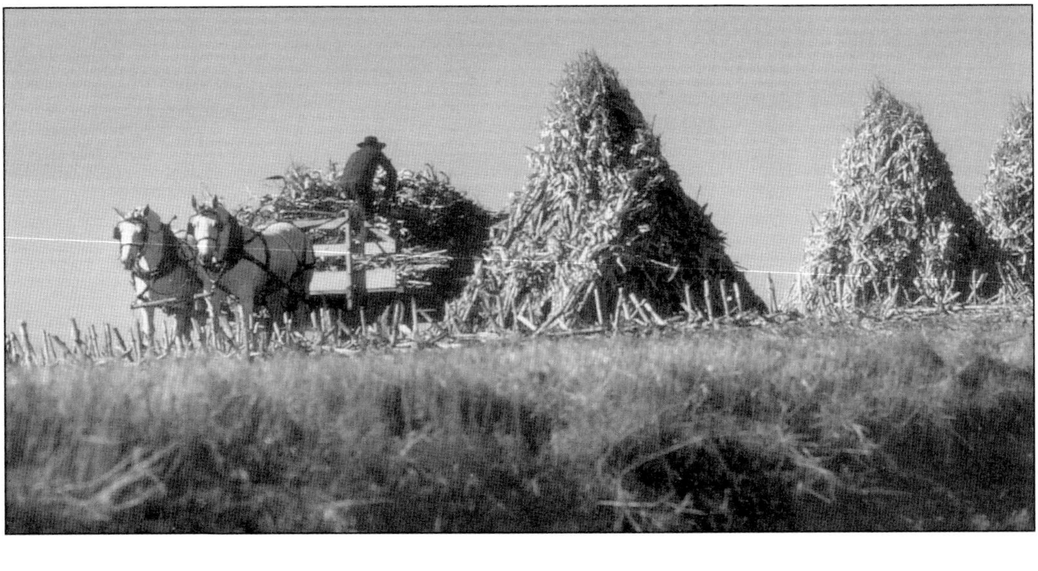

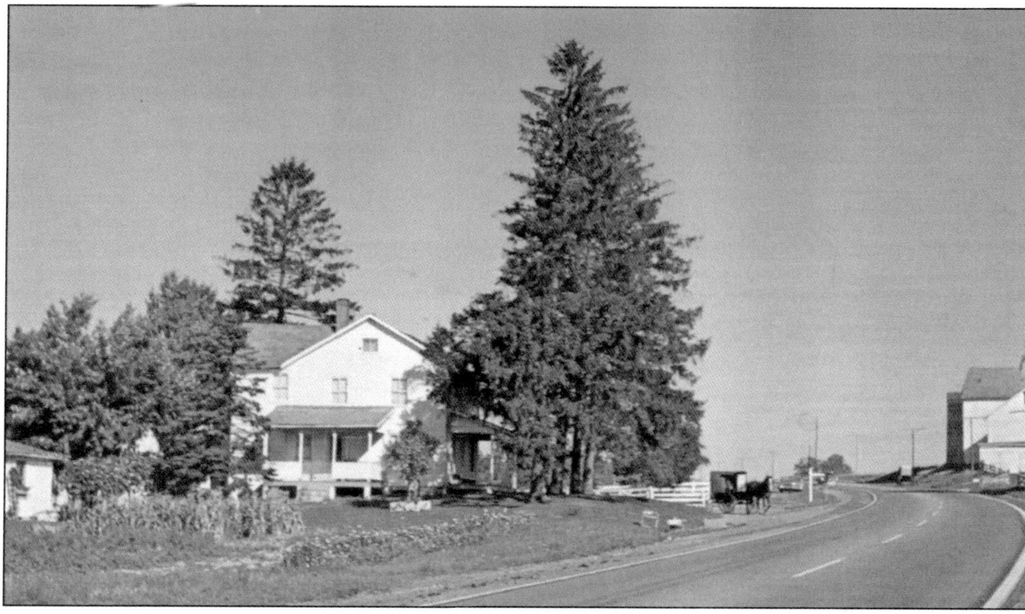

AMISH FARMHOUSE. Unlike the "English," who tend to equip their homes with the most modern conveniences, the Amish buy a new house and remove plumbing, electrical wiring, and telephones. There is no attempt to "keep up with the Joneses" because the Ordnung dictates a plain utilitarian lifestyle including travel by horse and buggy, traditional farming techniques, and homemade clothing in solid dark colors.

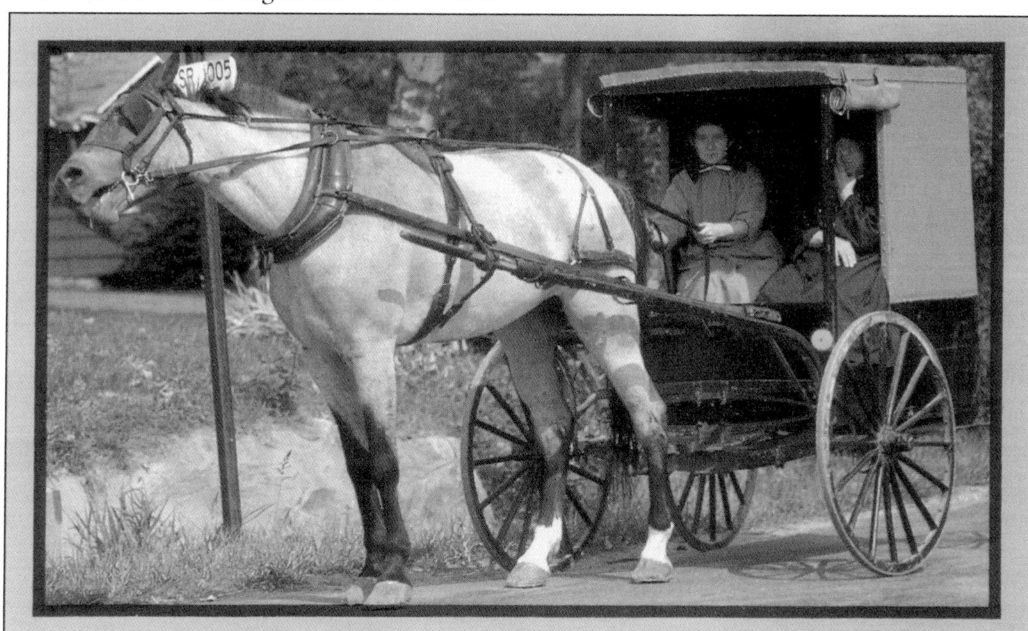

AMISH WOMEN ON THEIR WAY TO MARKET. Amish women and children are allowed to handle the horses and buggies that are familiar sights on the roads around New Wilmington and Pulaski. These women are hiding in the shadow of their buggy because the Amish do not allow their faces to be shown in photographs. They consider such pictures to be the "making of a graven image."

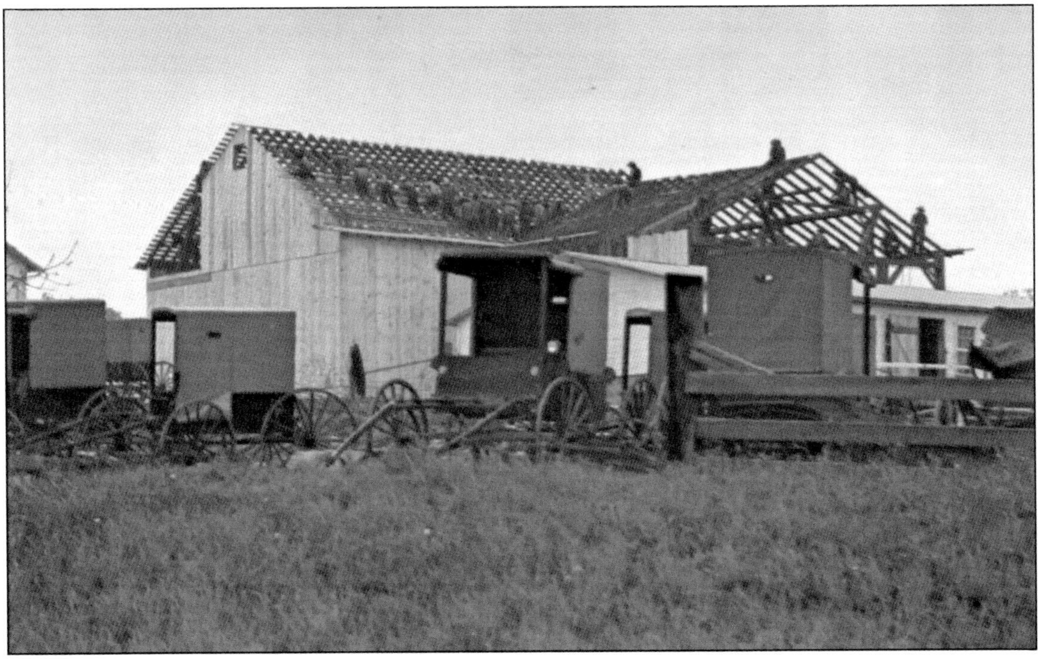

AN AMISH BARN RAISING. A typical barn raising can be accomplished in one day if enough men are available. It is an important event, perhaps for newlyweds starting their own farm. While the men work, the women prepare the food and do needlework. The Amish believe in taking care of their own; working as a community is an important part of their culture.

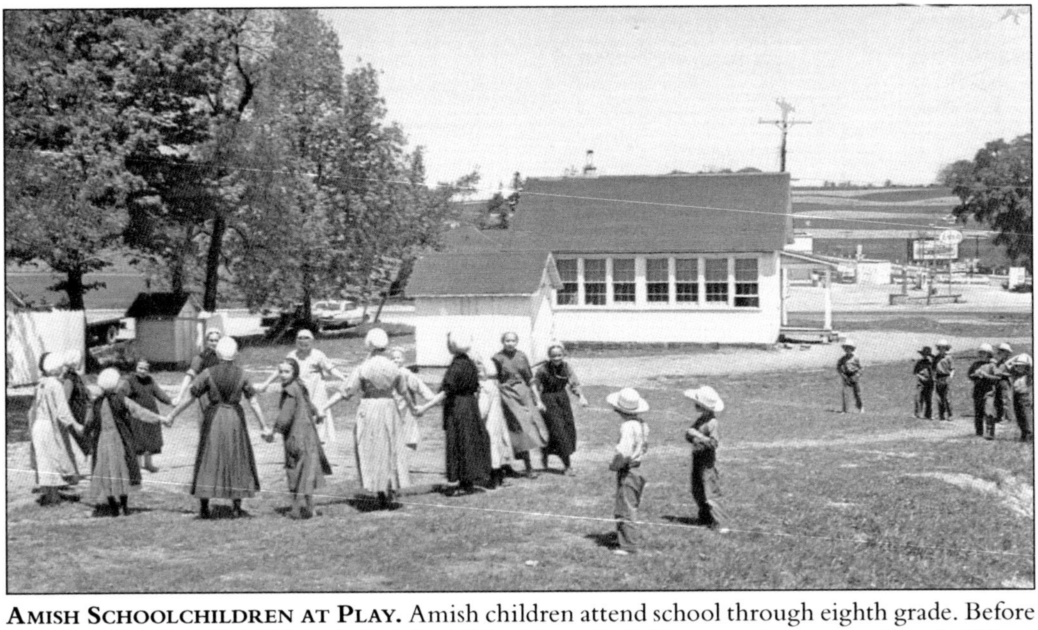

AMISH SCHOOLCHILDREN AT PLAY. Amish children attend school through eighth grade. Before the 1950s, both "English" and Amish children attended the same one-room schools. When the English children began to attend consolidated schools in the 1950s, the Amish established parochial schools staffed by members of the community. These teachers complete eighth-grade schooling but also receive some in-service training and work with materials prepared by the Mennonite Publishing House.

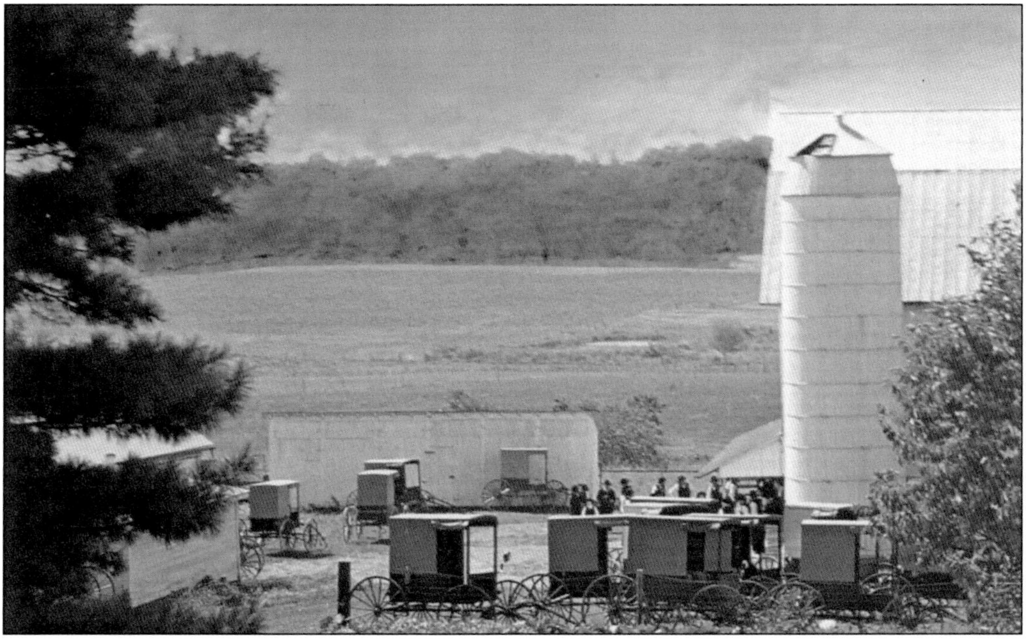

AMISH BUGGIES AT A SUNDAY GATHERING. The Old Order Amish in the community around New Wilmington are called "house Amish" because they meet for worship in their own homes. Their worship and rules of their faith are based on the teachings of Menno Simon, who lived in the Netherlands in the 1500s. The 25 or 30 families who make up a church observe Christian teaching and live by the Ten Commandments.

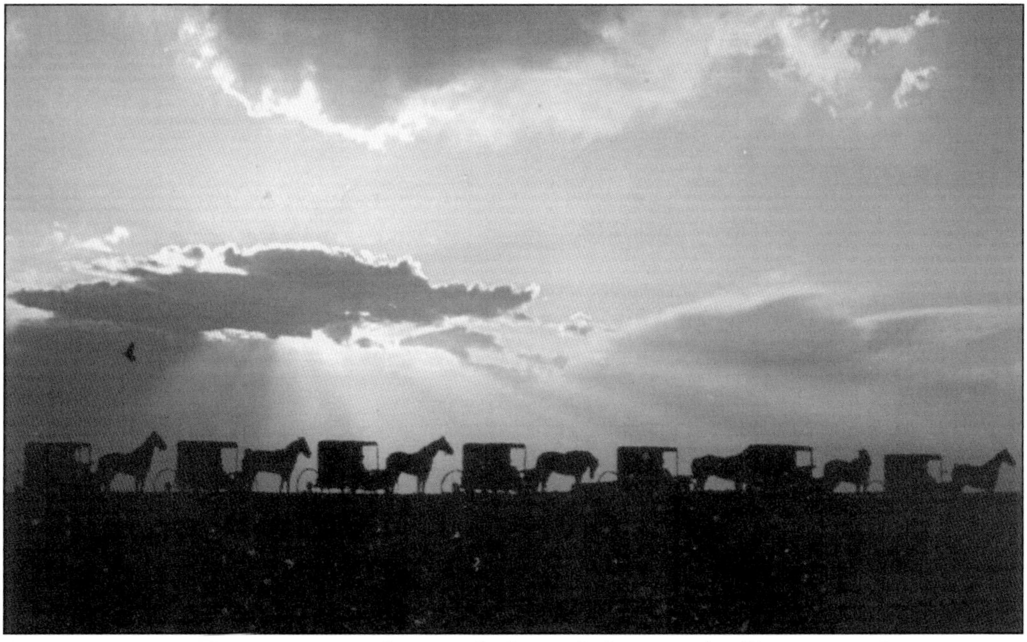

AMISH FUNERAL PROCESSION. The Amish do not believe in the "laying up of treasures on earth" so when calamity, illness, or adversity strikes, they have no insurance to ease the situation. Instead families and communities pool their resources for the welfare of those in need.

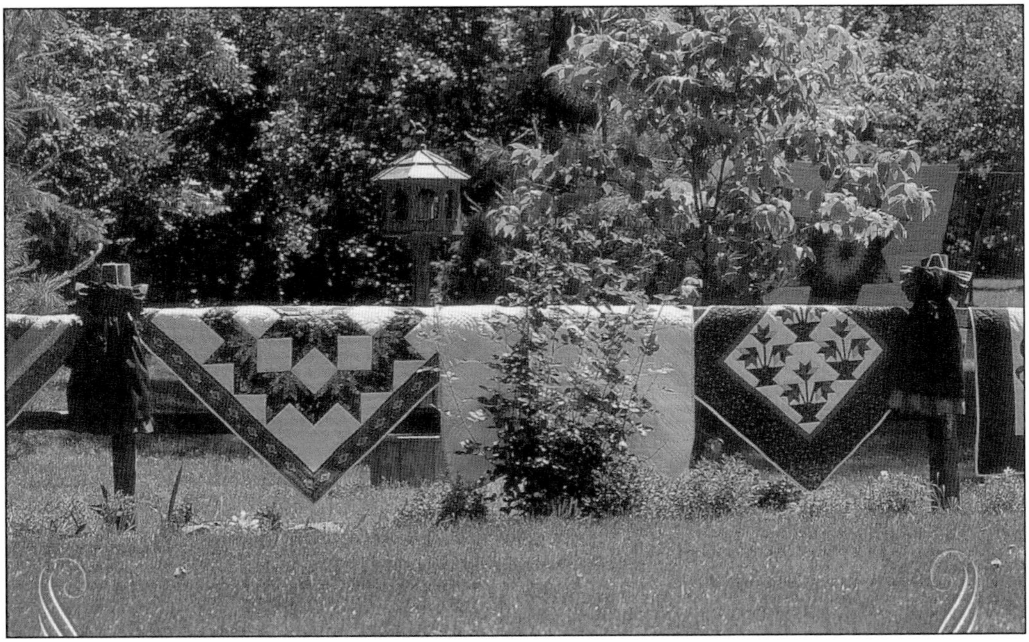

AMISH COUNTRY QUILTS. Although Amish homes and clothing are quite plain, the quilts created by Amish women can be eye-catching and colorful. Prized by the "English," the patterns of these handmade quilts can be genuine works of art. The quilts are utilitarian for the makers and their families.

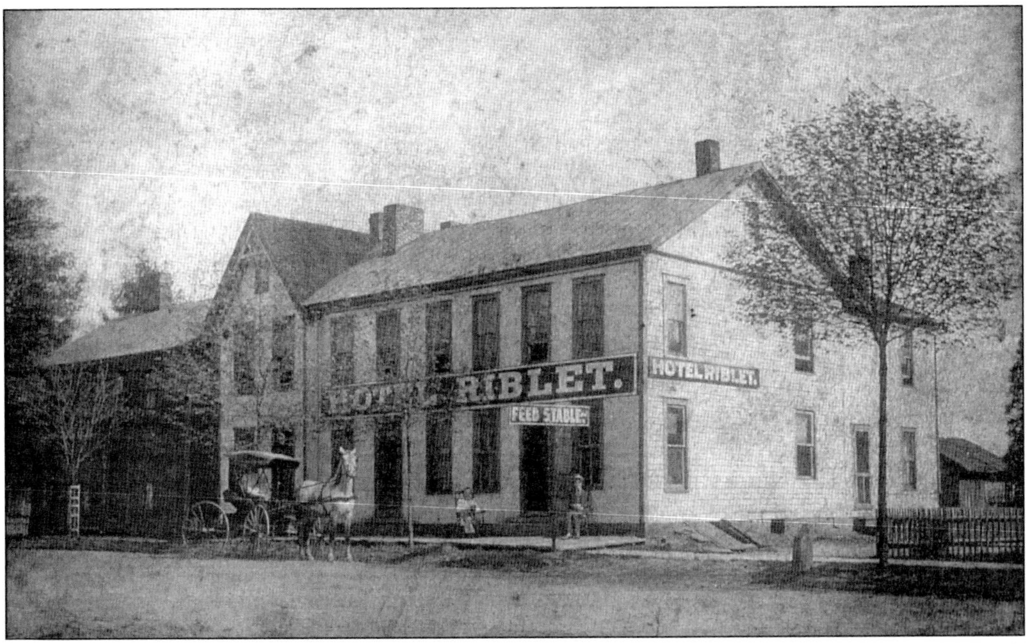

HOTEL RIBLET, PULASKI, EARLY 1900S. Hotel Riblet, Jackson House, and the sanitarium, all on the main street, accommodated Pulaski's many visitors. Pulaski was easy to get to with two railroads. Many out-of-towners flocked to the village not only for the mineral water, which was said to account for the long lives of Pulaski's citizens, but for Pulaski's other attractions such as Nancy's Island. (Courtesy of Pulaski Historical Society.)

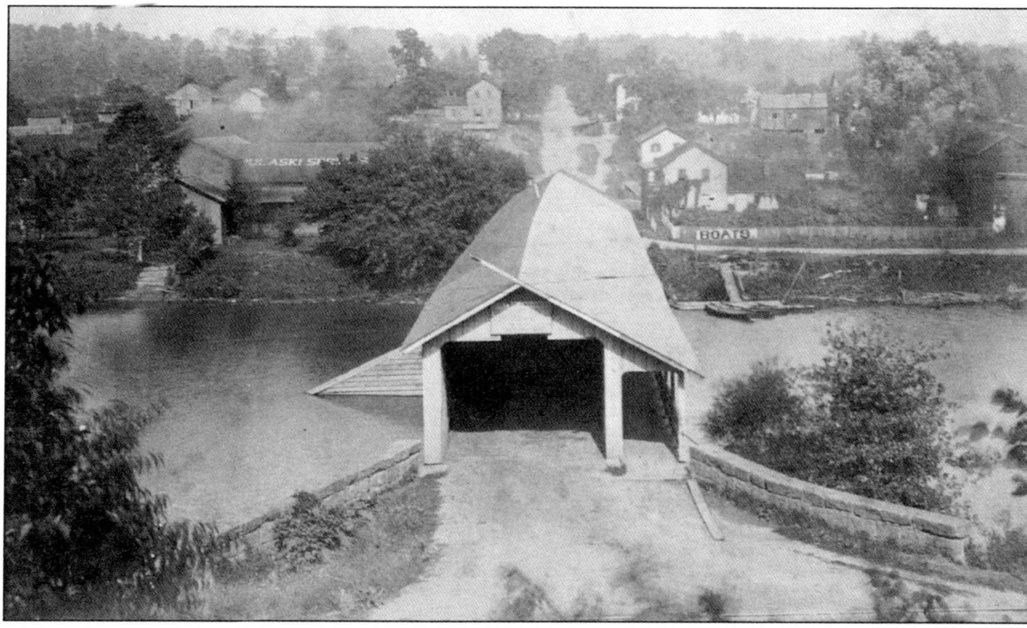

BIRD'S-EYE VIEWS OF PULASKI, LOOKING EAST, 1890S. The village that was to become Pulaski was laid out in 1832; it was named Pulaski when it became a township in 1848. Why the town carries the name of Gen. Casimir Pulaski is uncertain. The military hero came from Poland in 1777 and organized the American cavalry in the Revolutionary War. These views of the town of Pulaski look east. A covered bridge crosses the Shenango River, and the Disciples of Christ Church is in the center in the distance. In the view above, Pulaski Springs spa is at left, and the boat rental at right, with Jackson House Hotel next to it. In the view below, taken a few years later, the town is more densely populated. Pulaski Springs has been replaced by the sanitarium, and on the right, a livery stable is three buildings up from the river. (Courtesy of Tom Walczak.)

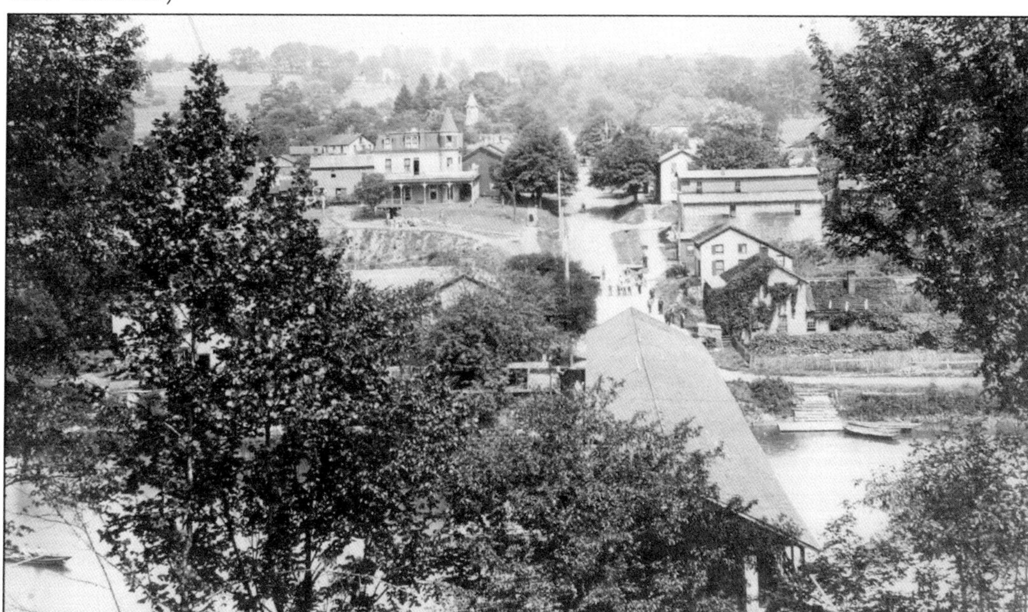

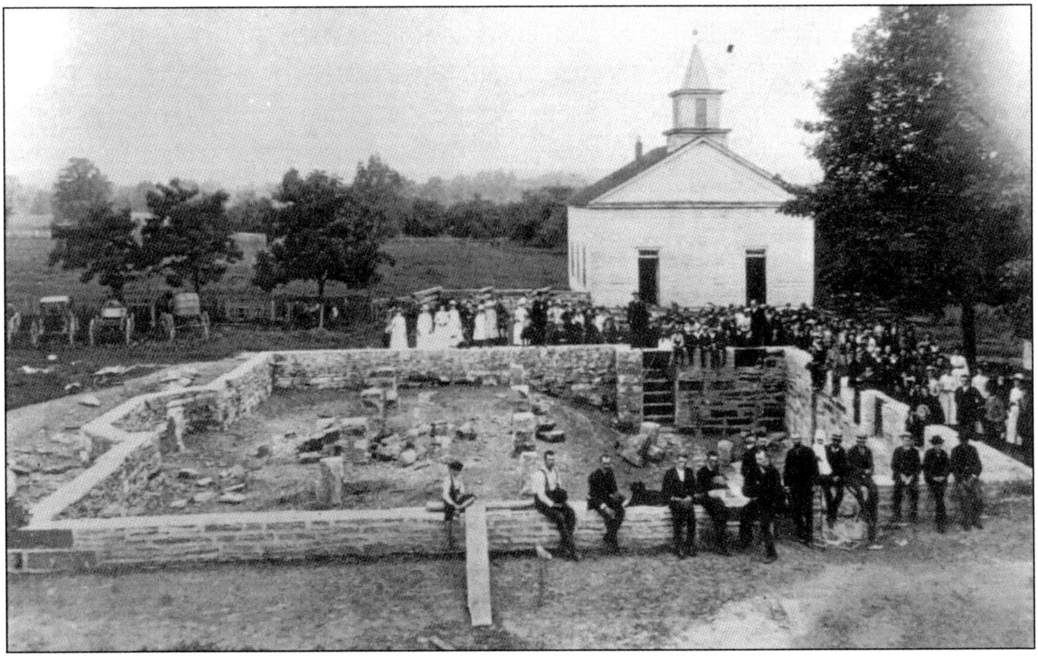

Building the New Presbyterian Church, Pulaski, 1912. The Presbyterian congregation turned out in its best finery for this occasion, which might have been the placing of the cornerstone of the new church. Two infants and a fine dog can be seen in the front row of the gathering. (Courtesy of Pulaski Historical Society.)

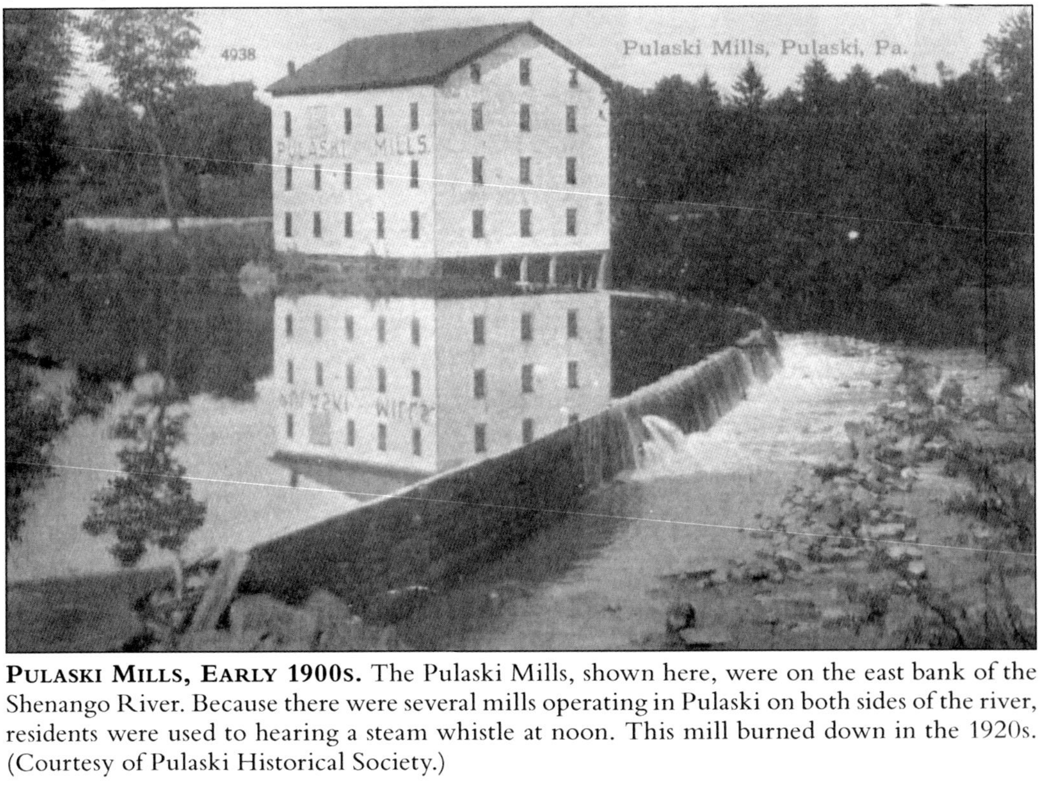

Pulaski Mills, Early 1900s. The Pulaski Mills, shown here, were on the east bank of the Shenango River. Because there were several mills operating in Pulaski on both sides of the river, residents were used to hearing a steam whistle at noon. This mill burned down in the 1920s. (Courtesy of Pulaski Historical Society.)

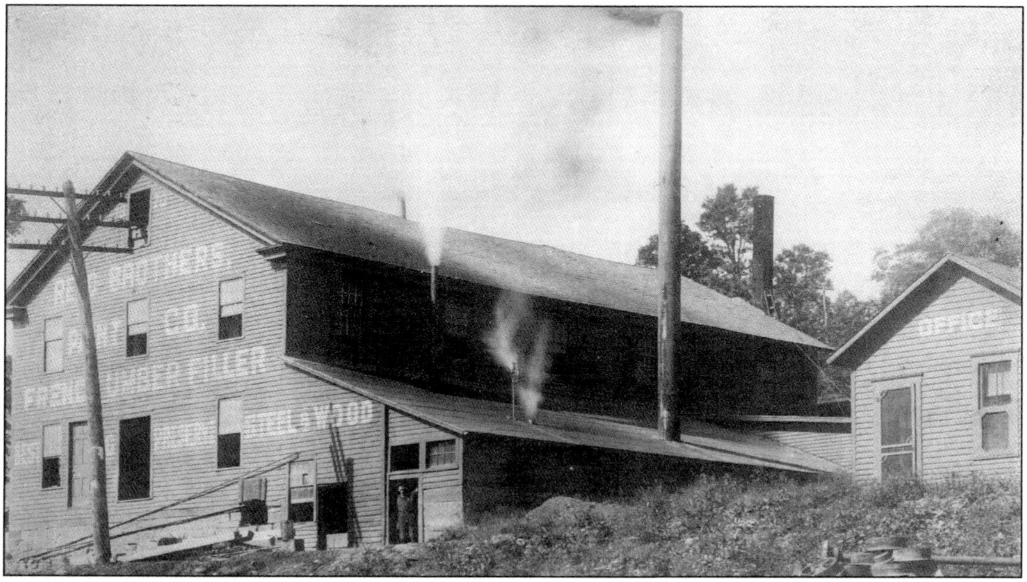

RENO BROTHERS PAINT COMPANY, PULASKI, EARLY 1900S. This factory near the Pennsylvania station produced french umber filler, a paint used by tinners and other metal workers. Umber, pigmented earth deposited by glaciers, was a mineral peculiar to Pulaski. A mine and this factory, built in the 1870s, were on the west bank of the Shenango, the mine about one and a half miles north of the bridge and the factory one and a half miles south. (Courtesy of Pulaski Historical Society.)

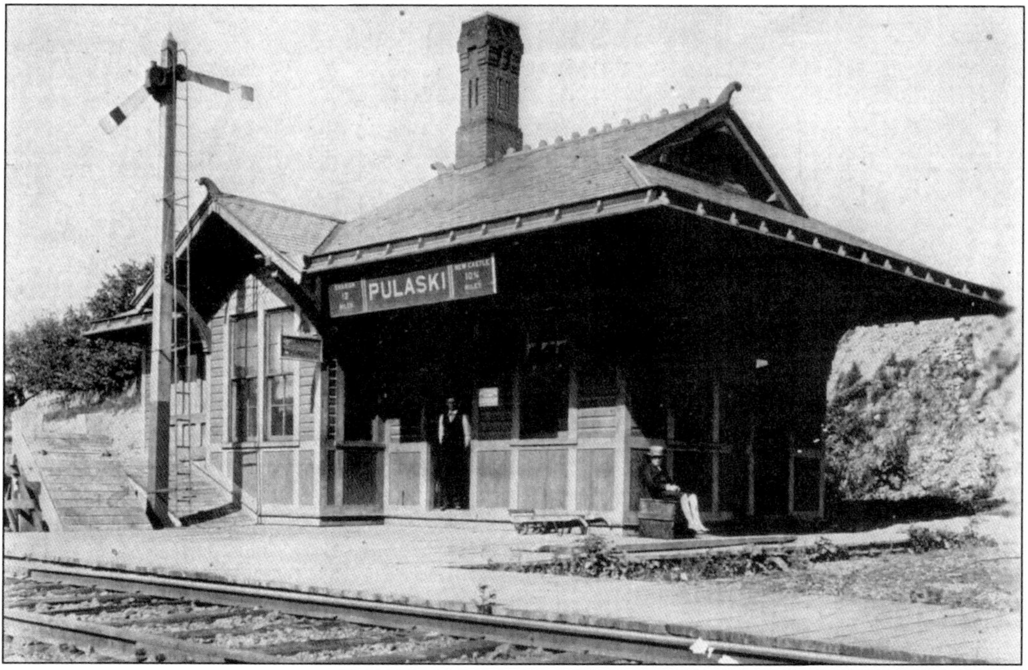

PULASKI STATION, 1920S. The Pennsylvania Railroad station was on the west side of the Shenango, 12 miles from Sharon and 10.5 miles from New Castle. Pulaski was thriving in the early 1900s with railroads, hotels, livery stables, and shops. Businessmen came to buy umber, the clay used to color paints. People seeking cures or recreation visited Nancy's Island, the "pleasure resort" with picnic grounds, mineral springs, and amusements. (Courtesy of Pulaski Historical Society.)

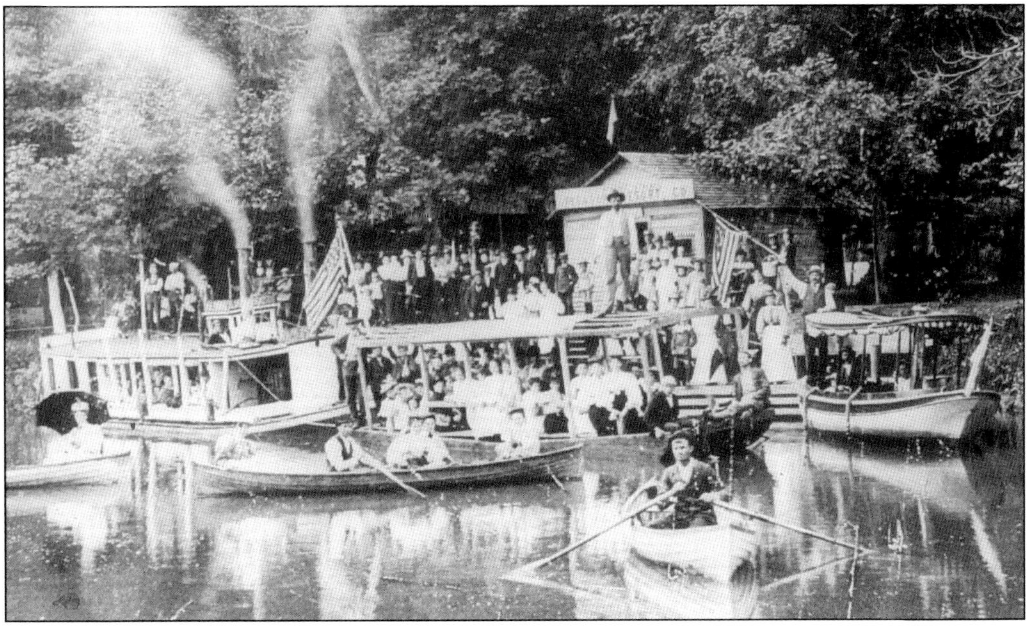

NANCY'S ISLAND, PULASKI, *C.* 1900. From 1896 to 1904, a 14-acre island known as the "pleasure resort" offered amusements, dancing, picnic tables, a bicycle track, and natural beauty. About a mile north of Pulaski, the island is named for Nancy Arnott, who was once trapped on the island when she made one of her regular trips to tap the sugar maple trees. (Courtesy of Pulaski Historical Society.)

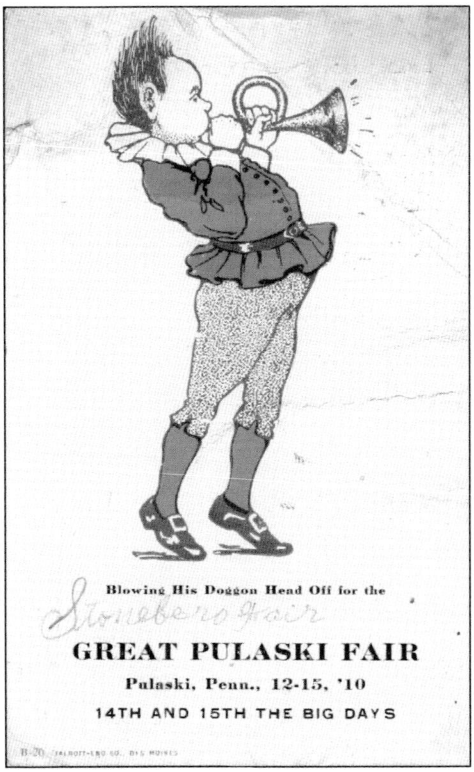

ADVERTISING CARD OF THE GREAT PULASKI FAIR, 1910. The railroads in Pulaski ran special trains to the Great Pulaski Fair, ensuring good attendance. This postcard was probably a souvenir of the fair because it is postmarked after the fair days. In addition to all the amusements, concessions, races, and exhibits, the Pulaski Cornet Band played at the annual fairs.

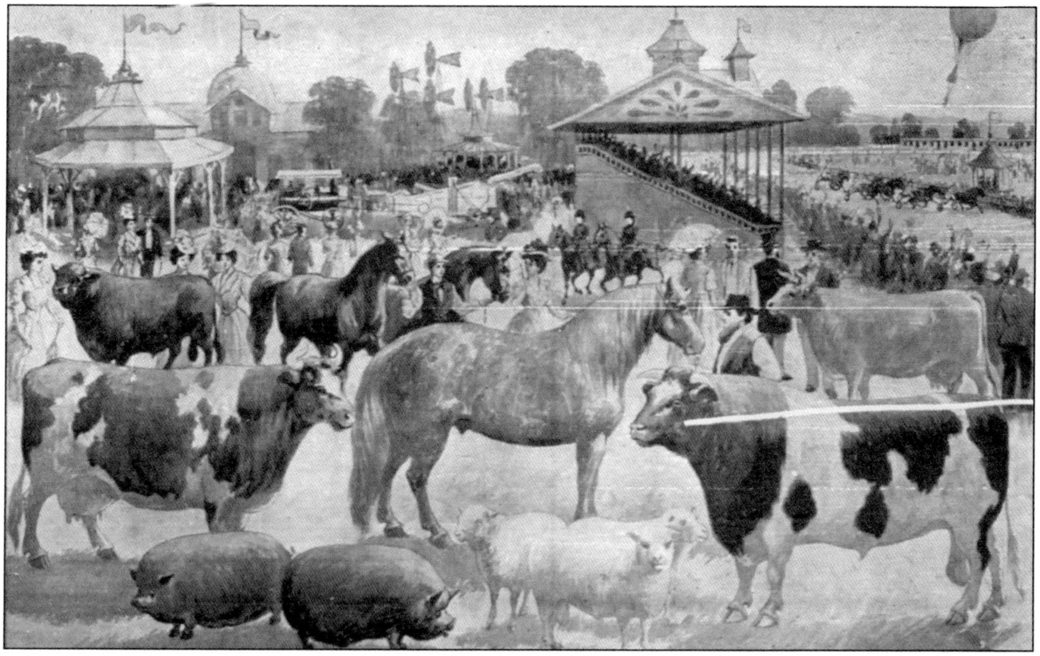

ADVERTISING CARD FOR PULASKI FAIR EXHIBITS, 1908. Animal exhibits and running races were the features advertised on this postcard. A quarter-mile bicycle track was there, as well as music and good food. The stylized animals on this card are whimsical; the pennants, gazebos, hot-air balloons, and windmills declare that the Great Pulaski Fair was indeed a festive one.

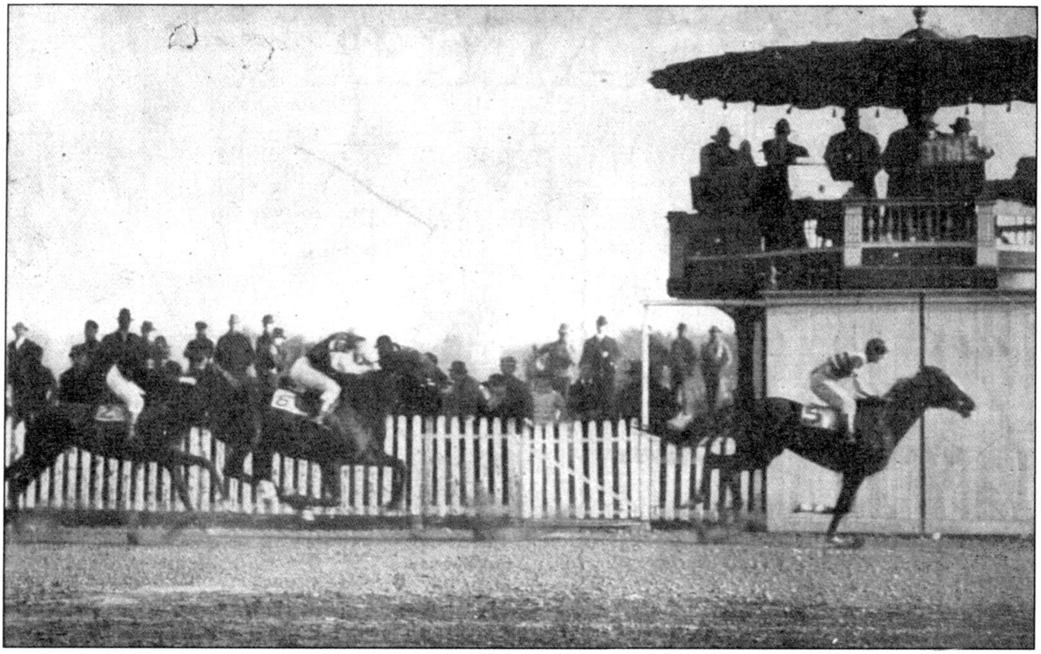

ADVERTISING CARD FOR RACING AT THE GREAT PULASKI FAIR, 1908. Pulaski Station was a busy place in September 1908. Hundreds of people arrived during the four days of the Great Pulaski Fair, and racing was one of the varieties of amusements awaiting them. The fair was held in September and was an event all ages could look forward to.

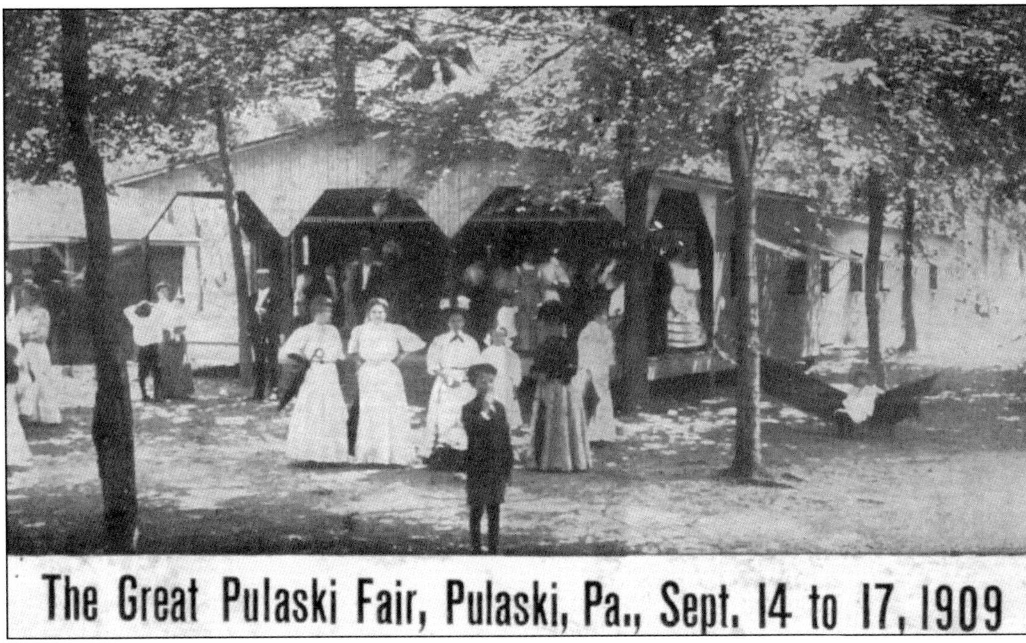

THE GREAT PULASKI FAIR, 1909. This photograph of fairgoers shows the elegant hats and dresses women wore to the fair in spite of the lingering summer heat of September. This advertisement from 1909 shows the wooded grounds and open-air pavilions at the fair. (Courtesy of the Pulaski Historical Society.)

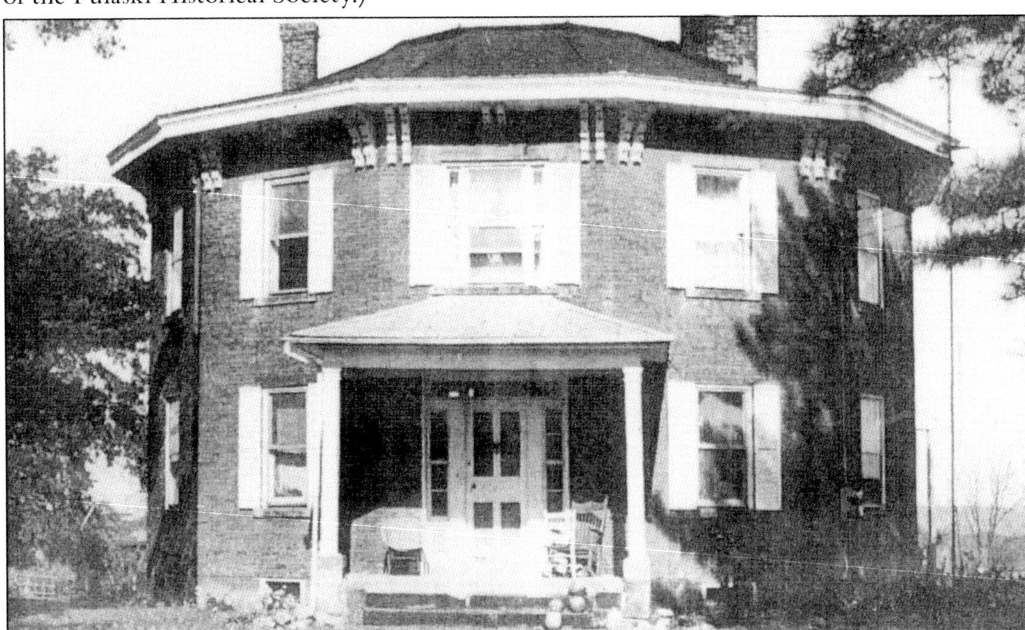

THE 10-SIDED HOUSE, NEW BEDFORD. This house between Pulaski and New Bedford was built around the 1850s with five equal sides in front and four narrow sides and one wide side in back. Some claim the 10 sides offer less resistance to wind. Others claim that whoever lived there "could not be cornered by the devil." It was well known to fugitive slaves traveling north on the Underground Railroad.

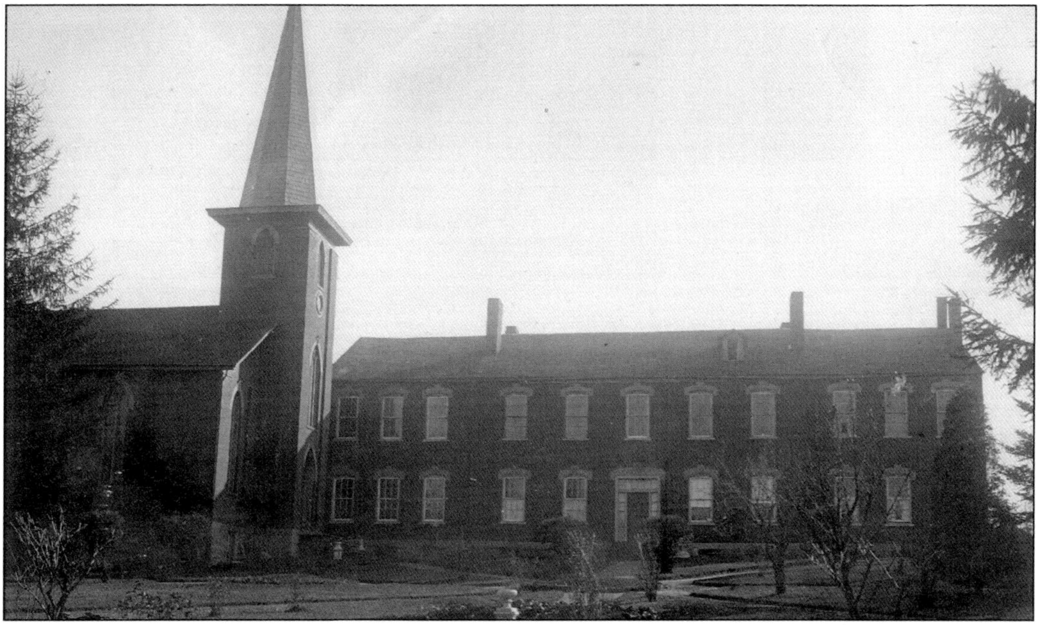

ENTRANCE TO VILLA MARIA CHAPEL, NEW BEDFORD, 1895. Mother Madelaine, the founder of the Sisters of the Humility of Mary in France, believed that "to educate a woman is to educate a family." Accordingly, their ministry has always included education for girls. Its high school ran from 1921 to 1989, with about 250 students enrolled in the peak years. Most graduates went on to higher education. (Courtesy of Villa Maria Archives.)

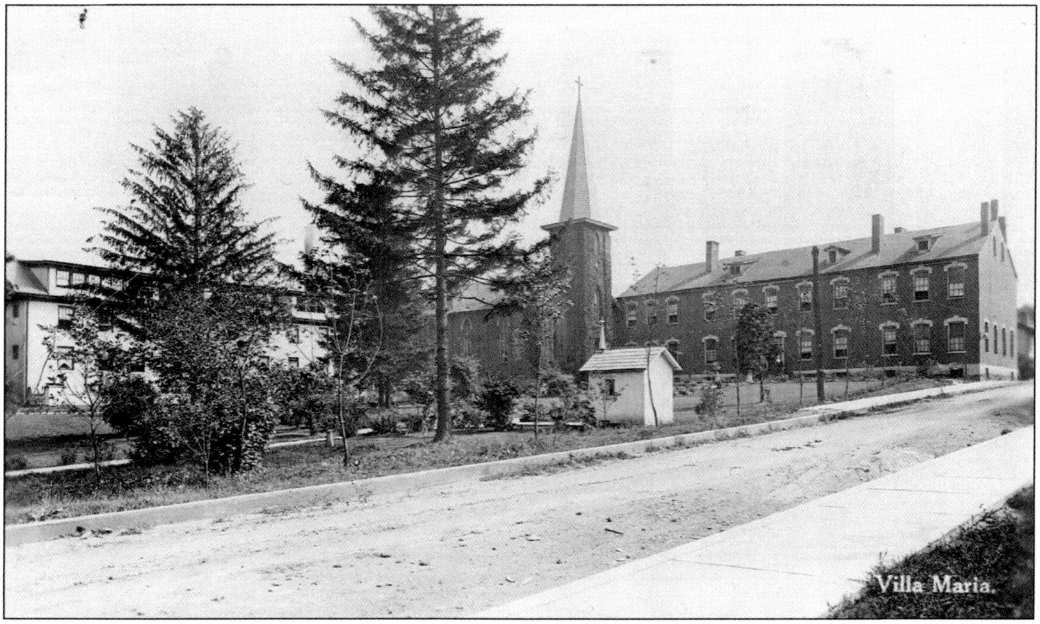

VILLA MARIA CHAPEL AND CONVENT, NEW BEDFORD, 1919. The Villa Maria chapel is adjacent to the convent of the Sisters of the Humility of Mary. The convent, originally built as a seminary, dates back to the 1850s. The small white structure in the foreground is the Wish House, where a French statue of the Virgin and Child used to be kept for visitors seeking the prayerful intercession of the Virgin Mary. (Courtesy of Villa Maria Archives.)

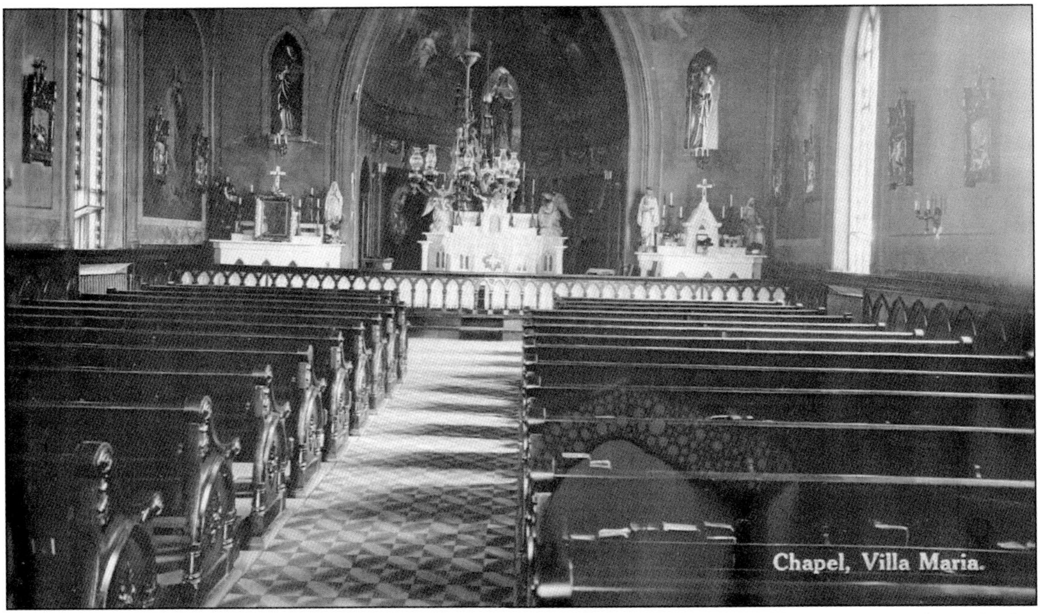

INTERIOR OF VILLA MARIA CHAPEL, NEW BEDFORD, 1899. Villa Maria Chapel, with the characteristic use of marble and wood, serves the spiritual needs of the Sisters of the Humility of Mary and Roman Catholic parishioners. The congregation of religious sisters arrived at New Bedford from France in 1864. The motherhouse property was named Villa Maria in 1889, when a U.S. post office opened there. (Courtesy of Villa Maria Archives.)

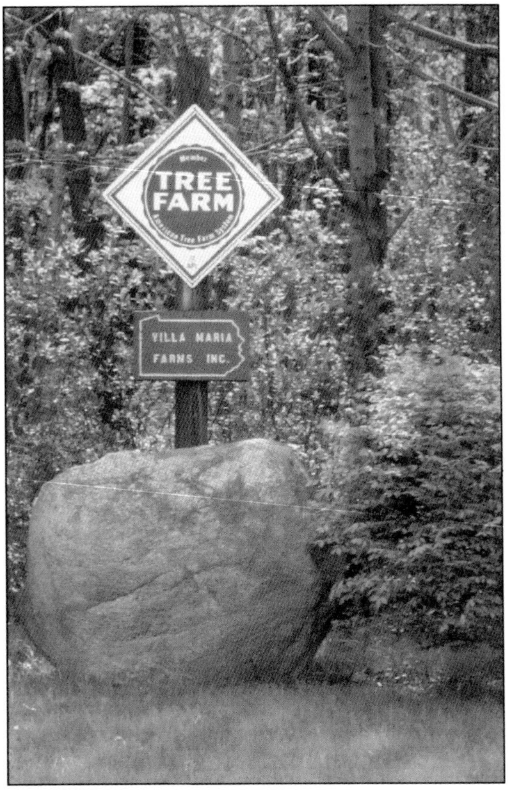

VILLA MARIA TREE FARM, NEW BEDFORD. Villa Maria's 728 acres include farmlands, an organic garden, wetlands, a bird sanctuary, and nature trails. The Evergreen staff regularly conducts workshops and programs on ecology and environmental awareness. The education center, community center, and retreat center address the needs of local children and senior citizens as well as visitors from other areas.

Six

Bessemer and Mount Jackson Area

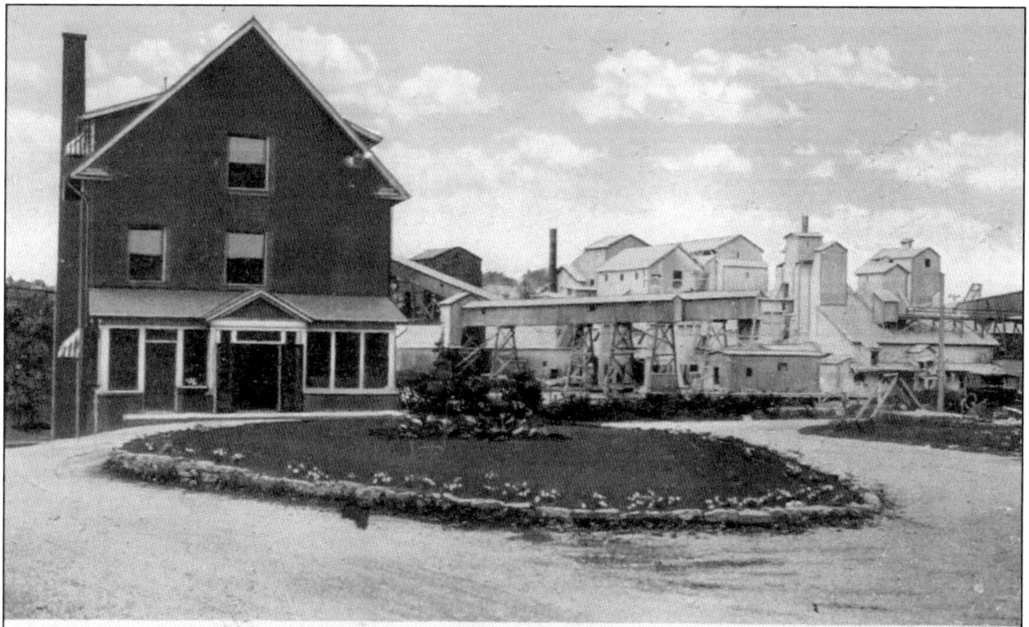

Bessemer Limestone and Cement Company, c. 1920. These offices and stone crushers are still in use in Bessemer, although the name of the company has changed. Since 1990 it has been Italcementi, a subsidiary of Essroc. Limestone has been a mainstay of Bessemer's economy since 1887, when a group of furnace men from Ohio and West Virginia chartered the Bessemer Limestone Company. The first cement plant went up in 1907.

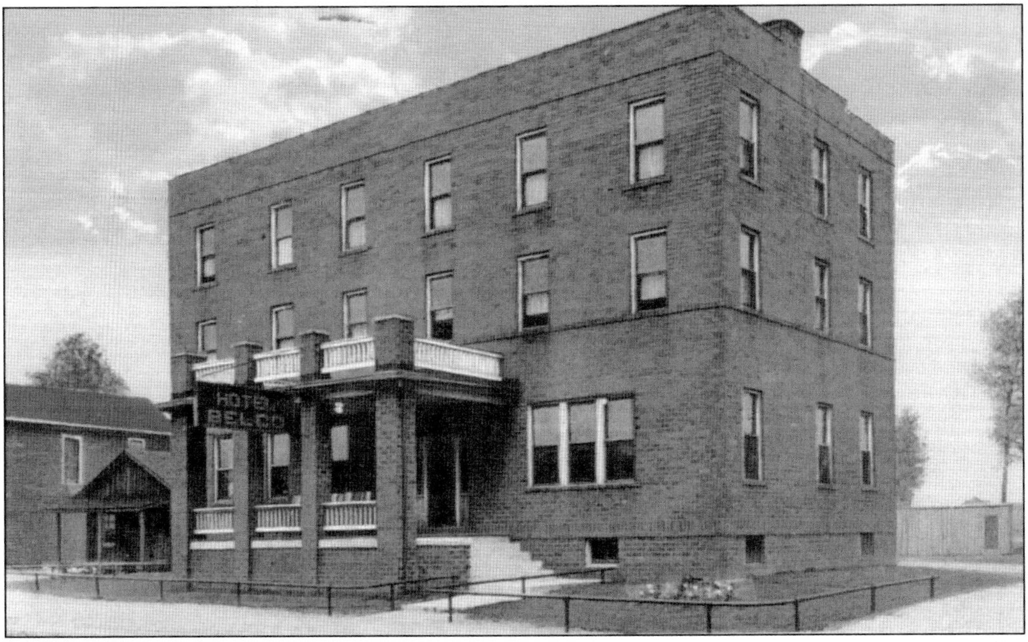

HOTEL BELCO, BESSEMER, *c.* 1921. Belco stands for Bessemer Limestone Company. The hotel operated from about 1910 to the early 1930s. The second and third floors were removed in the 1950s, and by the 1960s the building was being used for offices of the Bessemer Cement Company. In 1983, it became the F. D. Campbell Memorial Library. The hotel's former dining room is now the main room of the library.

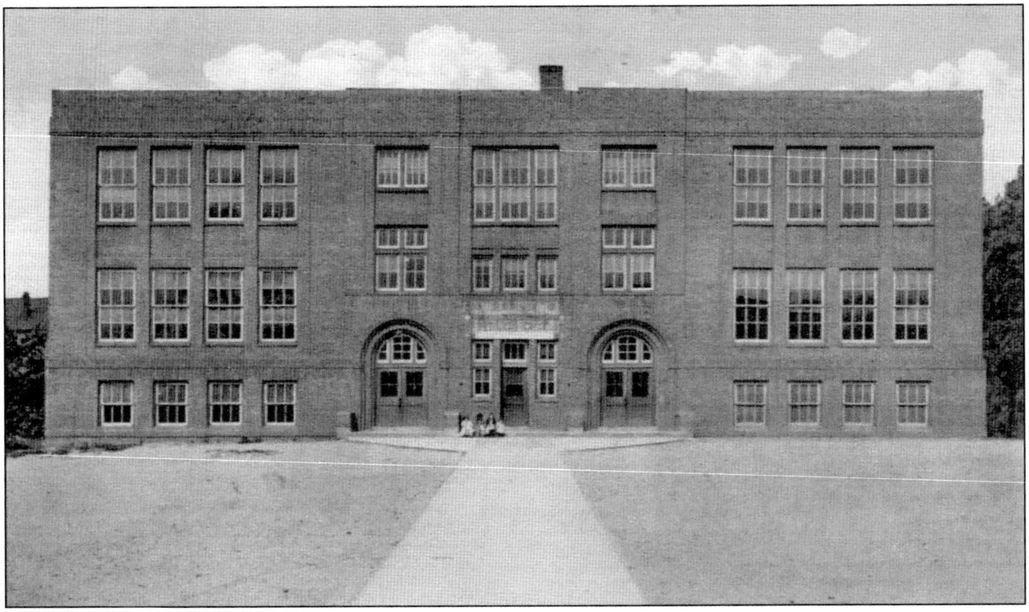

PUBLIC SCHOOL, BESSEMER, *c.* 1937. In the 1930s, this school served all grades. Bessemer had grown rapidly with the establishment of the Bessemer Limestone Company in 1887. The opening of quarries attracted workers from Sweden, Finland, and Austria, and Italian immigrants from Hillsville began to move in. Within six years after its founding, Bessemer became a borough of Lawrence County.

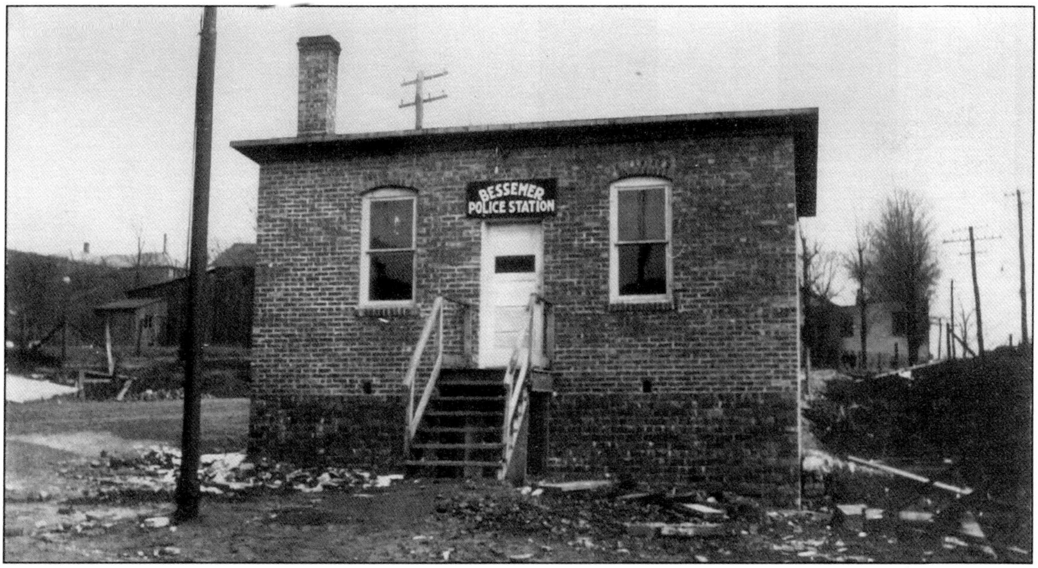

BESSEMER POLICE STATION, 1931. This brick building served the Bessemer police officers until they moved into the new borough building in 1963. U.S. representative Frank Clark was Bessemer's police chief for many years before he was elected to Congress in 1954.

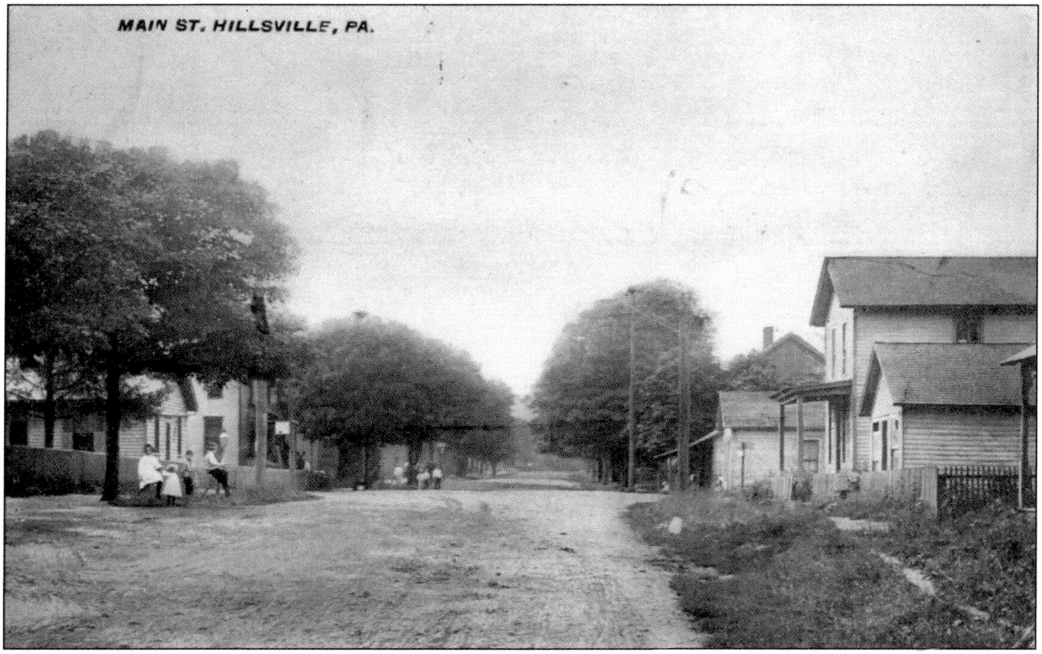

MAIN STREET, HILLSVILLE, *c.* 1913. John Hill laid out the town that he called Hillsburg in 1824. Some years after that, the name of the town became Hill Town, and eventually it was called Hillsville. In the early 1900s and thereafter, quarries and the production of limestone drove the economy of the town.

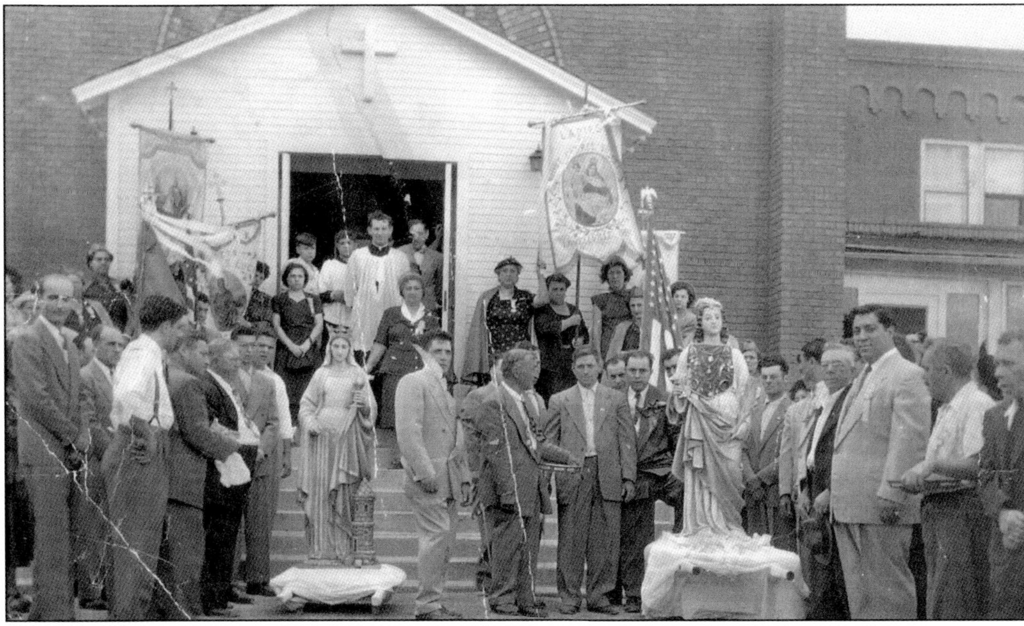

Labor Day Celebration, Hillsville, 1940s. Since 1905, many Hillsville residents have been celebrating Labor Day with a mass at St. Lawrence Church and festivities in honor of St. Lucy and St. Barbara. In this photograph, Fr. Joseph Mastrangelo, a few years after his ordination, greets the members of the congregation. A procession of the saints is being organized for the walk to St. Lucy's Club. (Courtesy of Mike Sackin.)

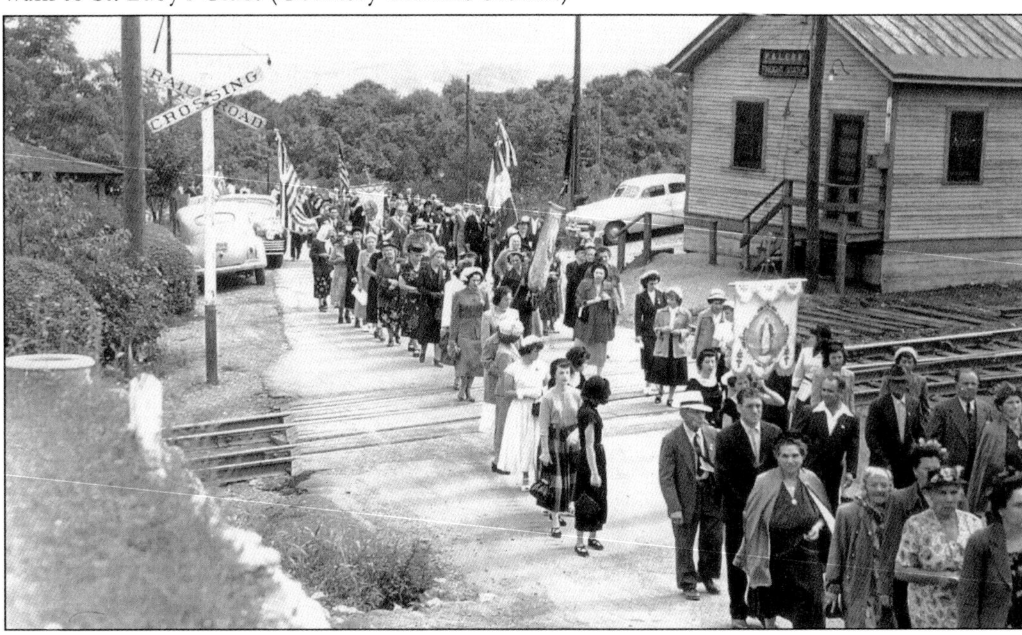

St. Lucy Society Procession, Hillsville, 1950s. The St. Lucy Society of Hillsville has been honoring St. Barbara and St. Lucy for more than 100 years. In this photograph, members of the society walk from St. Lawrence Church past the P&LE freight station to the society hall. They will continue the celebration with food, speeches, band music, a baby doll dance, and fireworks. (Courtesy of Mike Sackin.)

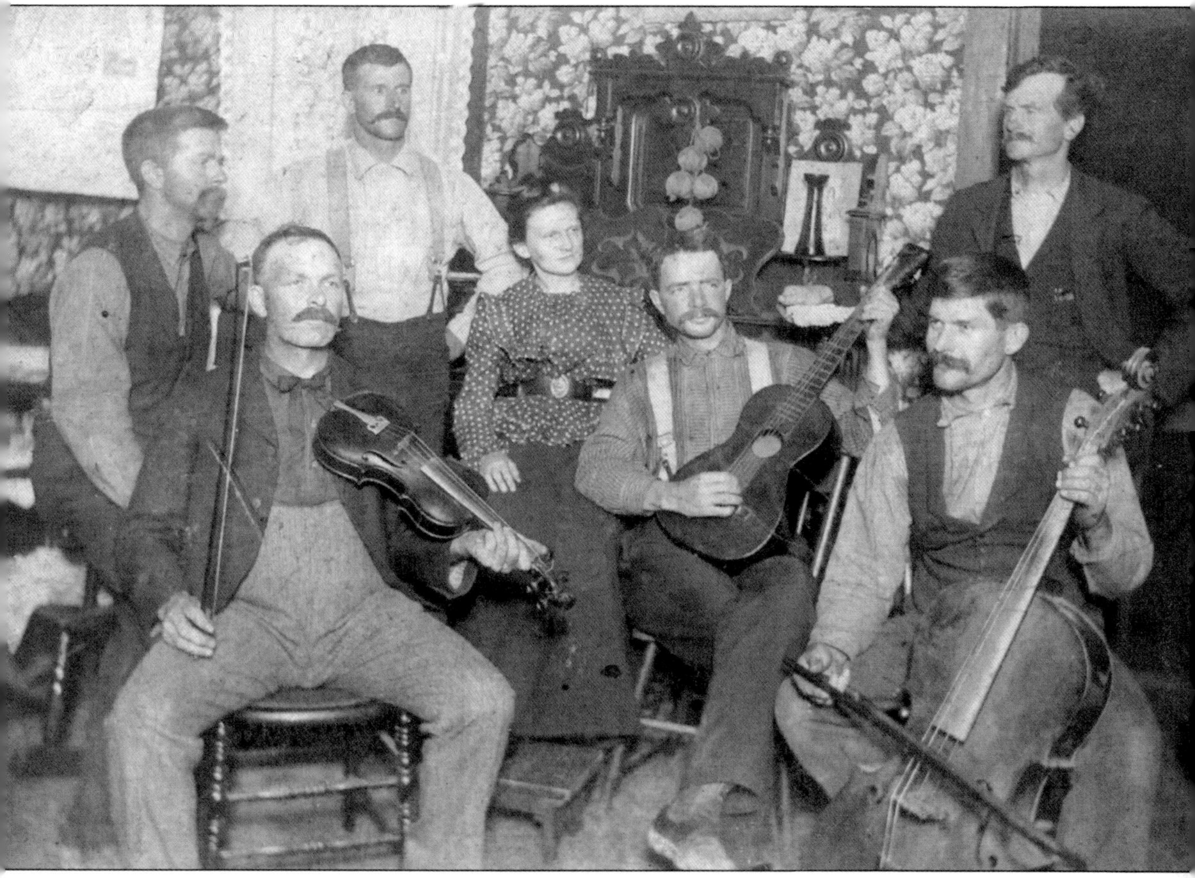

Mount Jackson Fiddle Band, Late 1800s. The town of Mount Jackson was laid out in 1815 by John Nesbit on his farmland. The War of 1812 was being waged at that time, so the new town was named for Gen. Andrew Jackson ("Old Hickory"), who led the U.S. Army to victory against the British in the 1815 Battle of New Orleans. Mount Jackson was largely a rural community with merchants and tradesmen offering necessary services. The village photographer was Harry L. (Bird) Camblin, son of village undertaker James Camblin. Harry recorded scenes like this one for the families of the town. The musicians in this group were evidently affluent enough to afford a cello, a guitar, and a violin. In the background is a parlor organ, also called a pump organ, often identified with family sing-alongs. The back of this old photograph carries the names Camblin, McKim, McMurray.

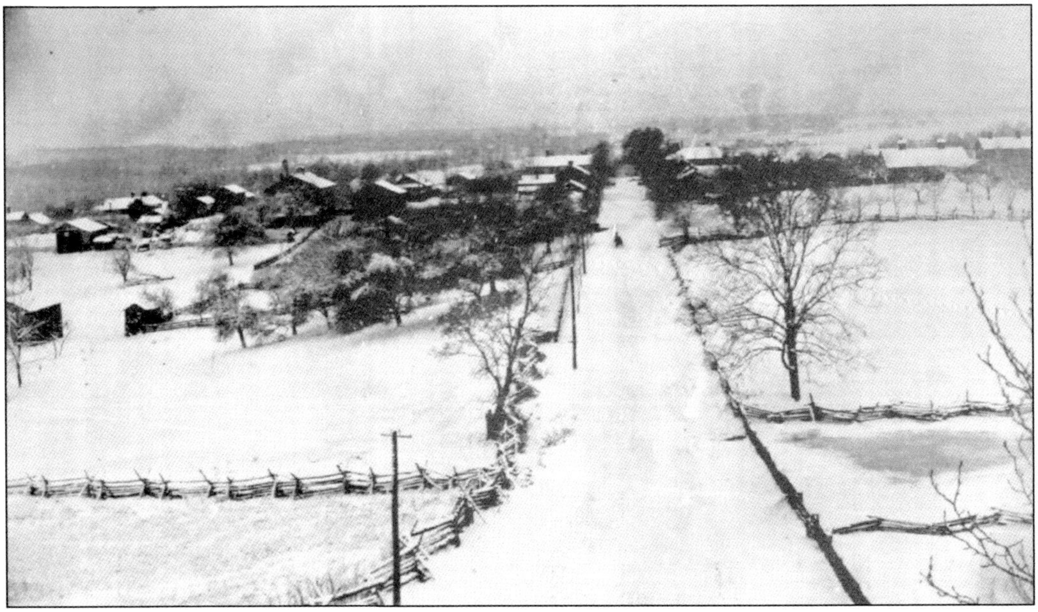

MOUNT JACKSON, LOOKING SOUTHWEST, 1870S. This postcard is another Harry L. Camblin photograph. It was taken from the belfry of the Methodist church looking southwest into Mount Jackson. An unsigned handwritten note on the back of the card, dated 1965, reads "Taken by moonlight almost 100 years ago."

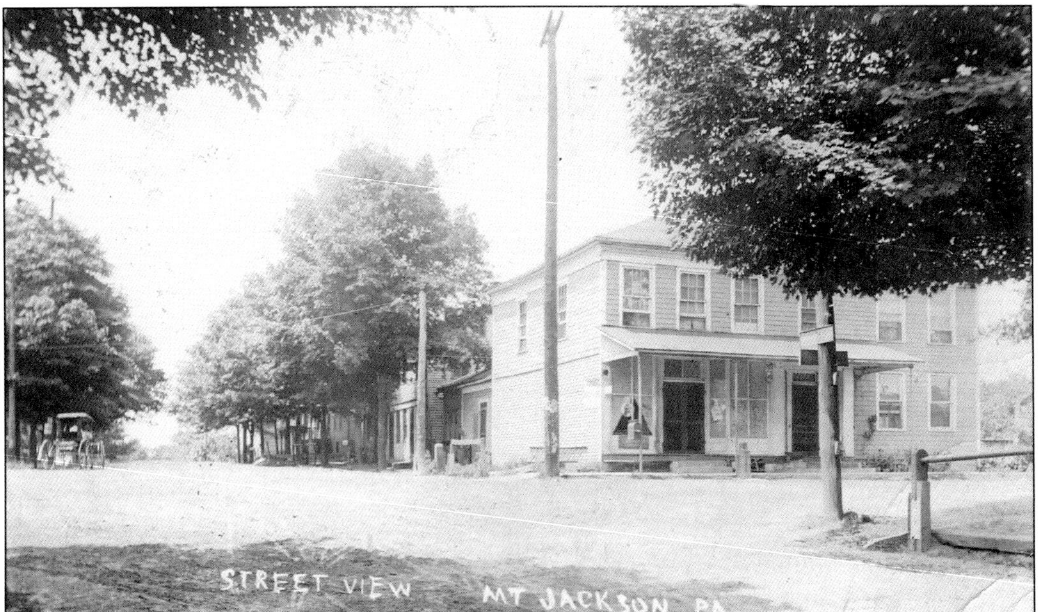

MOUNT JACKSON STREET VIEW, EARLY 1900S. Most of the businesses in Mount Jackson were close to the intersection of Mill Street and Market Street. In this scene is a storefront on Mill Street. Market Street heads west. A mailbox is in front of the store, and a sign on the storefront advertises the Lawrence Laundry Company.

BATTERY B MONUMENT, MOUNT JACKSON, C. 1912. In April 1862, 14 days after the Confederate states fired on Fort Sumter, the Mount Jackson Guards were organized as Battery B, 1st Regiment Light Artillery. The 78 men who volunteered marched to Enon Valley to take a train to Pittsburgh, where they were formally mustered into the Army of the Potomac. The battery fought 27 battles, including Antietam, Fredricksburg, Gettysburg, and Petersburg.

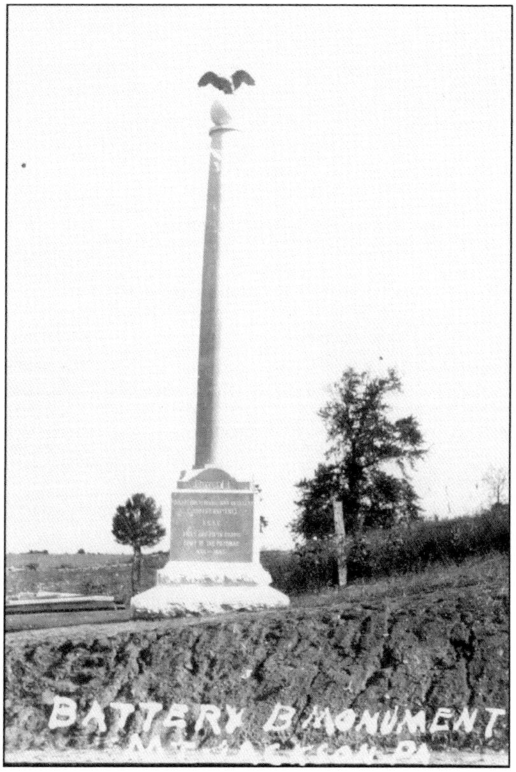

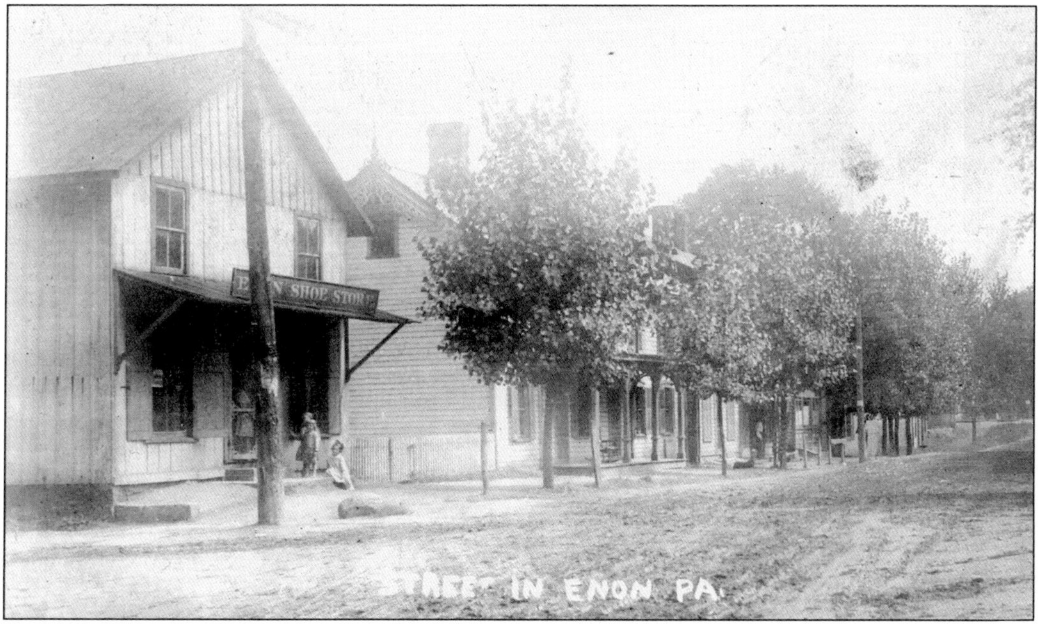

STREET IN ENON, EARLY 1900S. Called Enon, Enon Station, or Enon Valley, the town was the location of New Castle's closest railroad station from 1851 until 1864. The Pittsburgh, Fort Wayne, and Chicago Railroad attracted residents of Old Enon several miles away. The railroad created jobs and opportunities for businesses like the shoe store shown here. *Enon* translates to "Valley of Many Waters," which refers to the two Little Beaver Creek tributaries nearby.

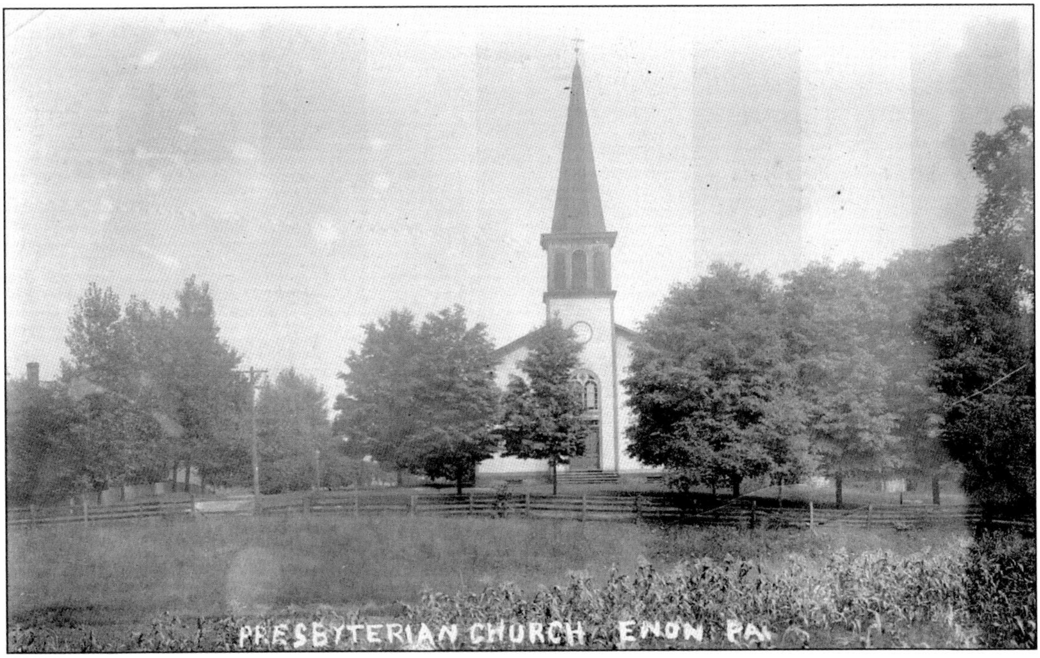

PRESBYTERIAN CHURCH, ENON, *C.* 1912. This steeple with its graceful spire accentuates the simple beauty of this church built in 1873. Some years after the date of this view, a thunderstorm damaged the steeple, and it was replaced with one of another design. The original church had no basement, but in the late 1940s, the men of the congregation carefully dug one by hand.

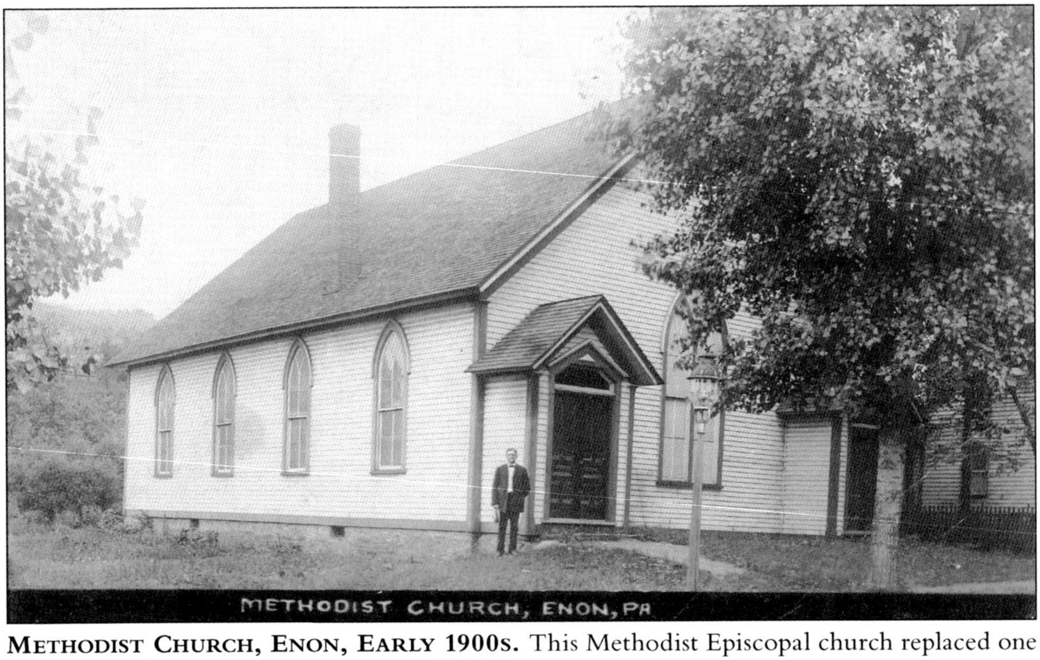

METHODIST CHURCH, ENON, EARLY 1900S. This Methodist Episcopal church replaced one that had been torn down in 1886. Located on the corner of Main and Kossuth Streets, this church served its congregation until about 1916. It fell into disrepair after years of being used for basketball games, meetings, and storage and was torn down in the 1970s.

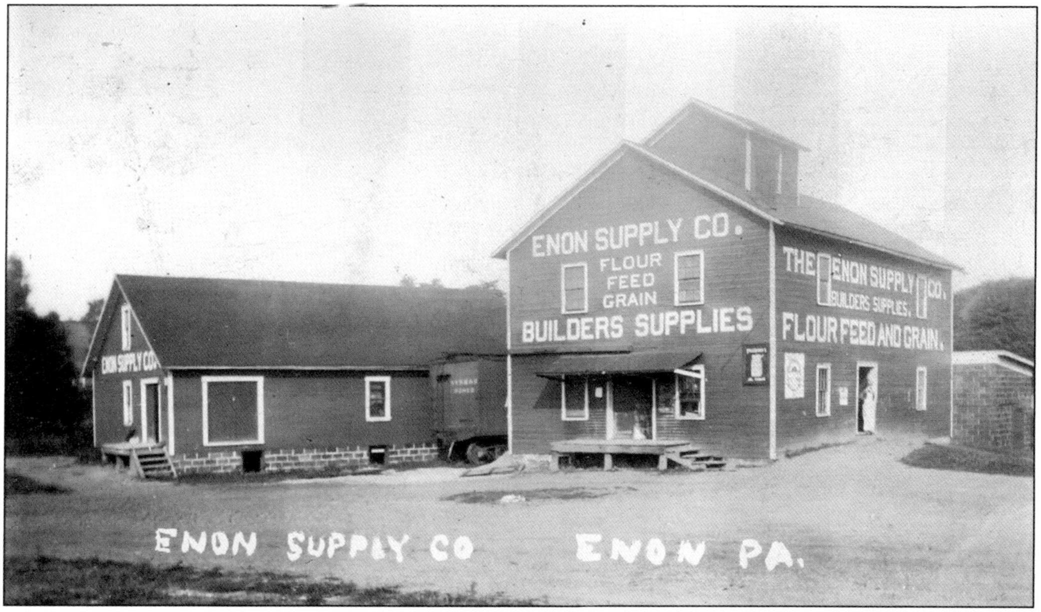

ENON SUPPLY COMPANY, *C.* 1912. This building started as a sawmill in 1892. It became Enon's first feed mill in 1899 and added the supply store in 1911. Over the years a number of owners operated the business, and in 1973, the Musguire Milling and Feed Company acquired the building. That company is still in operation.

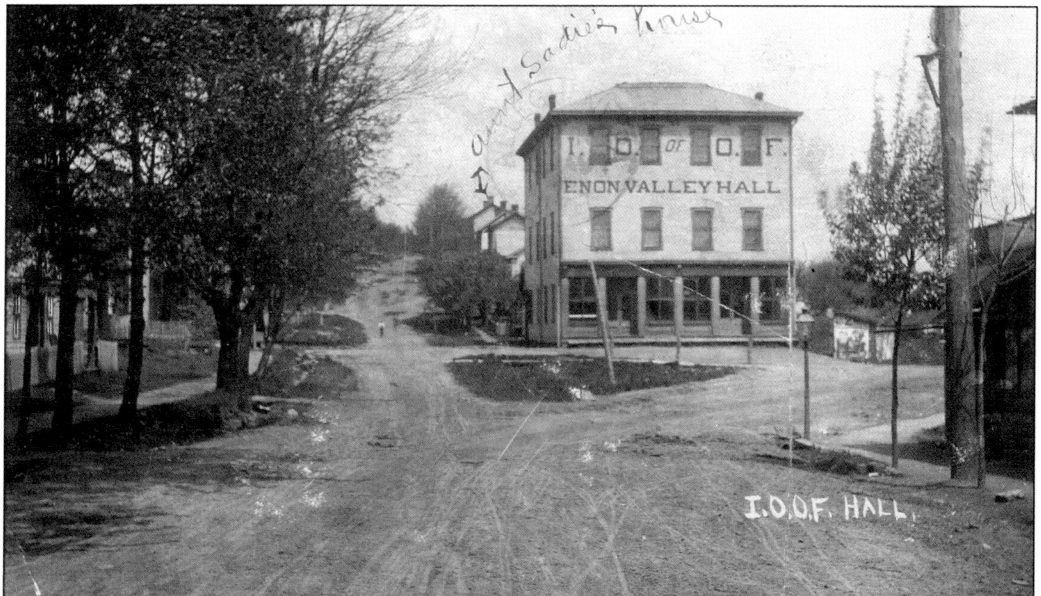

IOOF HALL, ENON VALLEY, *C.* 1907. The IOOF had several lodges in Lawrence County. In Enon Valley, their building, dating back to the 1870s, was in the center of town. Its first floor housed businesses, its second floor was used for community events and served as the town hall for a period, and its third floor was for the lodge. The building was demolished in 1965.

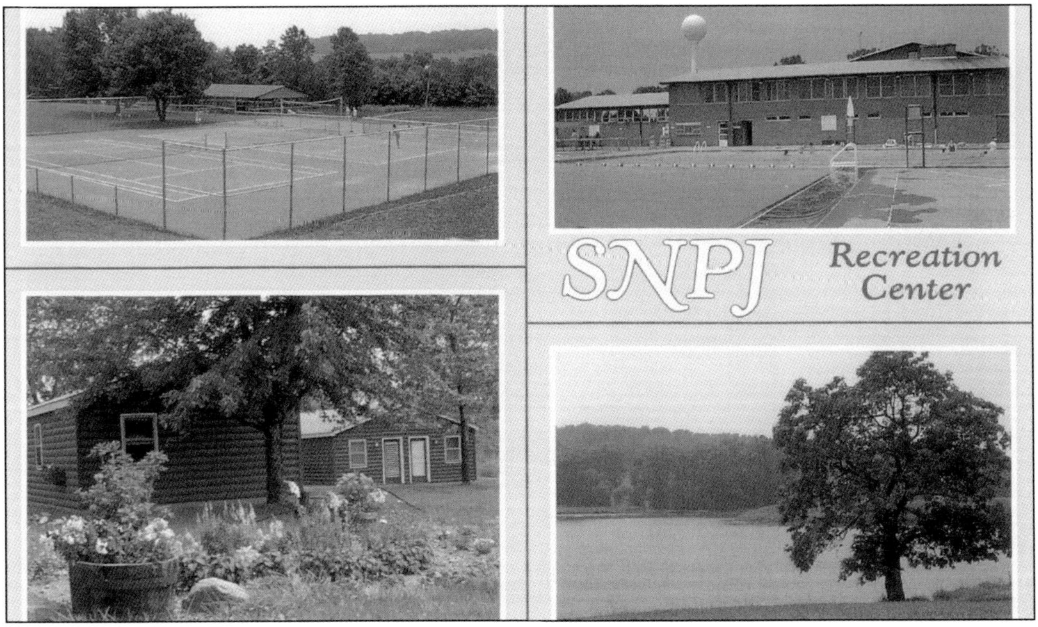

SNPJ Recreation Center, SNPJ Borough. In 1964, SNPJ, a national fraternal insurance organization, bought several hundred acres of land near Enon Valley. It was meant to serve as a campsite for young people of Slovenian descent, but it became a recreation center for Slovenians of all ages. The initials stand for *Slovenska Norodna Podporna Jednota.* (Courtesy of Slovene National Benefit Society [SNPJ], Imperial, Pennsylvania.)

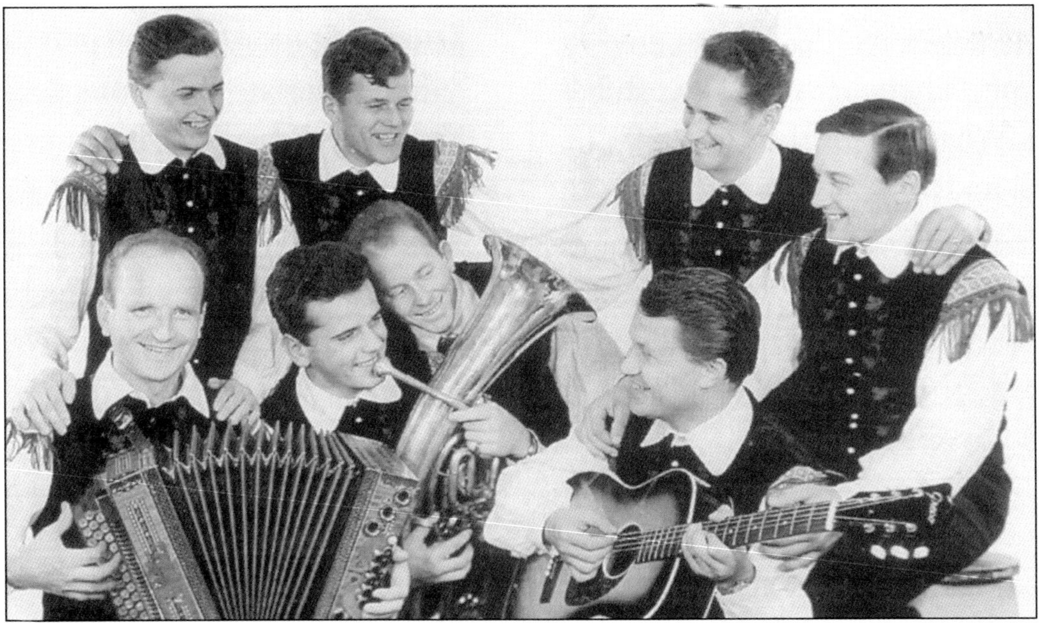

Slak Ensemble. In 1970, the performance of this famous musical group from Slovenia was the highlight of the SNPJ national convention, which met at the recreation center that year. The group's special appearance was in appreciation and recognition of SNPJ's contribution to the interests of Slovenia and Yugoslavia over several decades. (Courtesy of Slovene National Benefit Society [SNPJ], Imperial, Pennsylvania.)

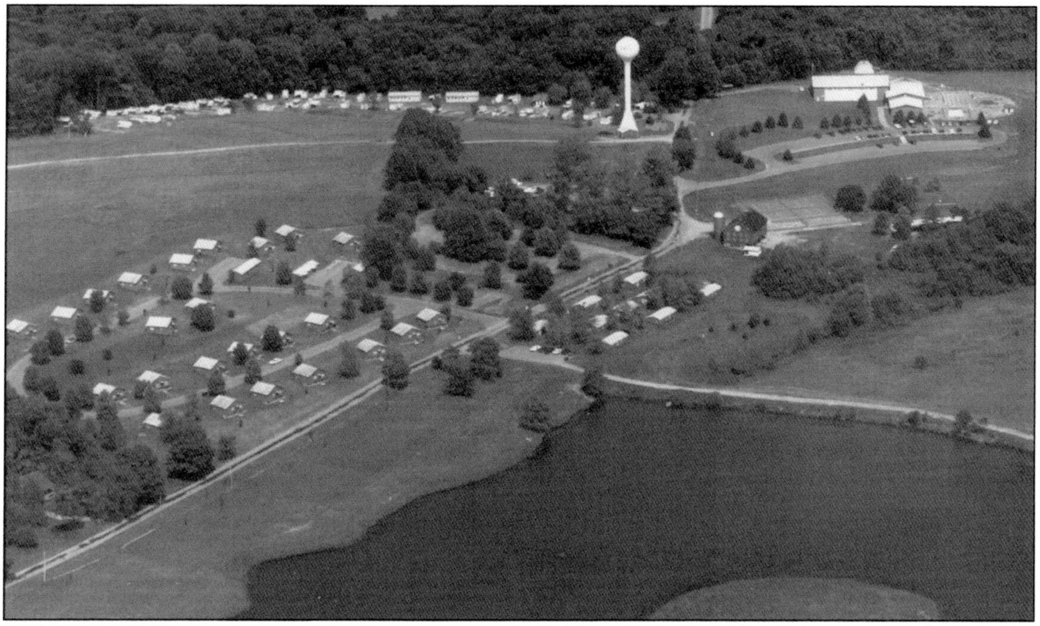

BIRD'S-EYE VIEW OF SNPJ. This rolling farmland is a state-of-the-art recreation center and campground. The extensive layout includes a 25-acre lake, an Olympic-sized swimming pool, vacation cottages, a trailer court, dining facilities, meeting rooms, a ballroom, and tennis, bocce, and volleyball courts. A museum-like Heritage Room exhibits historic photographs, crafts, and artifacts related to Slovenian origins and traditions, as well as SNPJ's history.

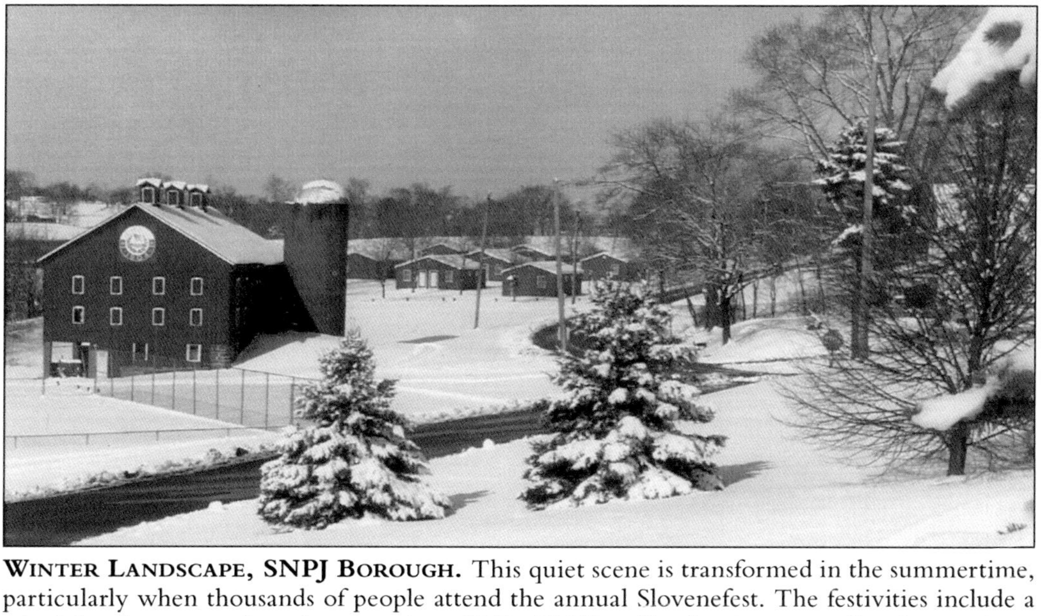

WINTER LANDSCAPE, SNPJ BOROUGH. This quiet scene is transformed in the summertime, particularly when thousands of people attend the annual Slovenefest. The festivities include a schedule of events such as the crowning of Miss SNPJ, polka dancing, accordion jam sessions, traditional food, and fireworks. It is hard to believe that, according to the 2000 census, the population of the borough of SNPJ is only 14 residents.

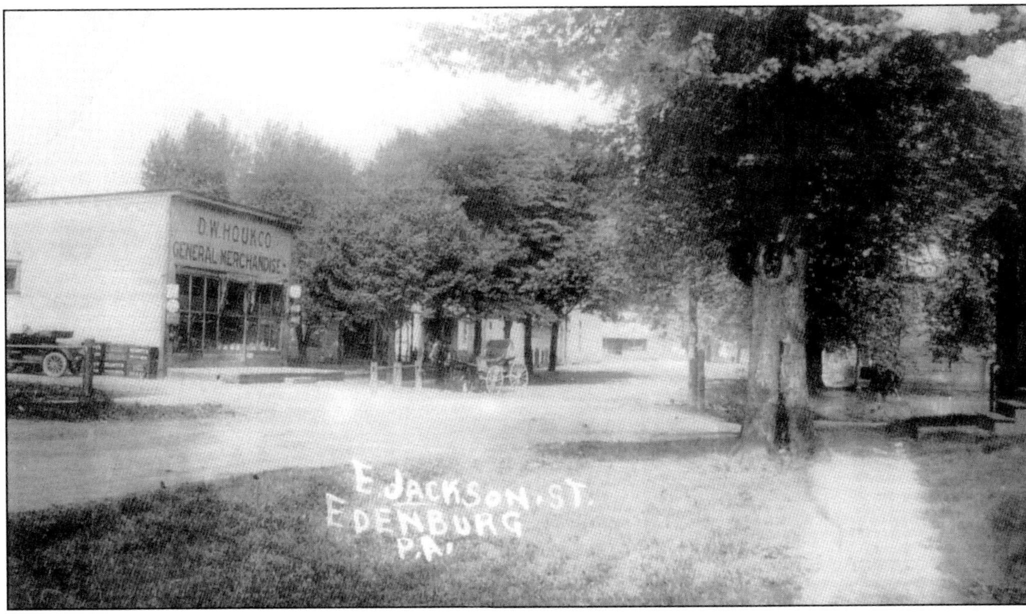

EAST JACKSON STREET, EDINBURG, EARLY 1900S. Whether it is spelled Edenburg or Edinburg has been a question since Crawford White laid out the town in 1824. William McFate bought the first lot and the privilege of naming the town. McFate was a native of Edinburgh, Scotland, and preferred "Edinburg." White thought the site resembled the Garden of Eden and preferred Edenburg. Today the U.S. Postal Service spells it "Edinburg." (Courtesy of LCHS, Hitch Collection.)

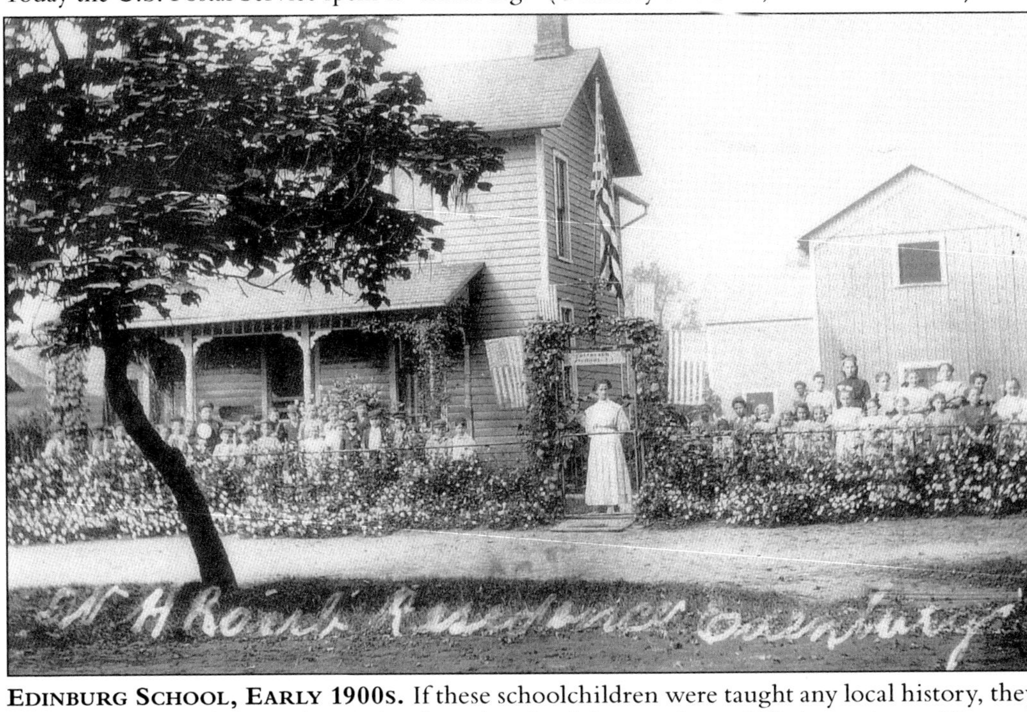

EDINBURG SCHOOL, EARLY 1900S. If these schoolchildren were taught any local history, they would have learned about the Native American burial ground near Edinburg. Aaron Hazen, a historian writing in their time, reported a burial mound 50 feet in circumference and six feet high. In 1960, a team excavated one such burial mound with prehistoric artifacts.

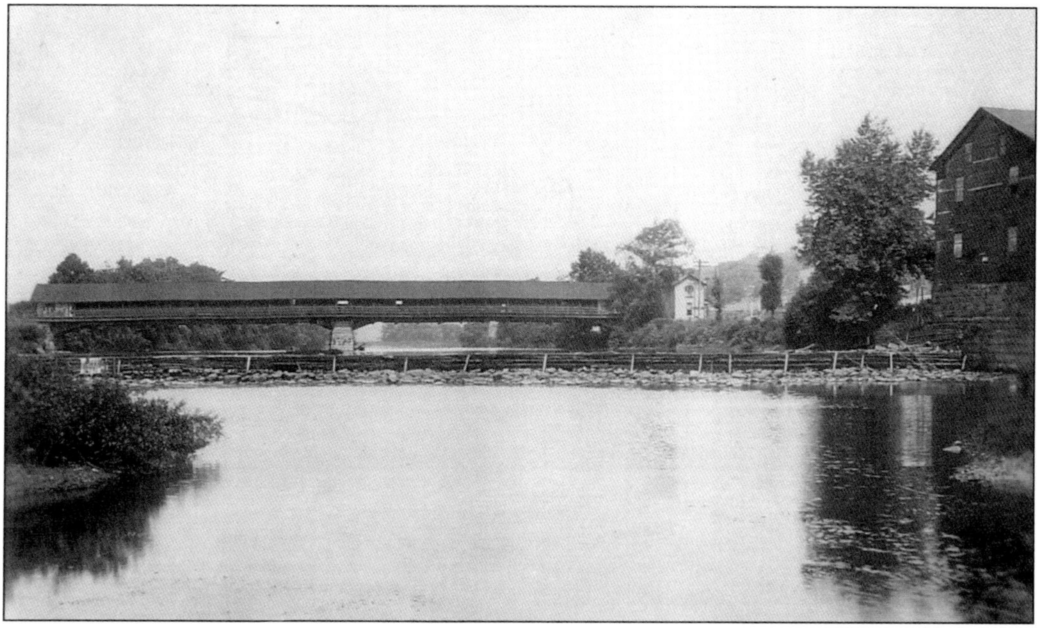

Edinburg Covered Bridge, c. 1910. This long covered bridge crossed the Mahoning River a little south of the present bridge on Route 224. A dam ran parallel to the bridge, with a sawmill operating on one side of the river and a gristmill on the other. In the 1800s, Edinburg had a broom factory, a foundry, an oil well, and even a boatbuilding enterprise. (Courtesy of Tom Walczak.)

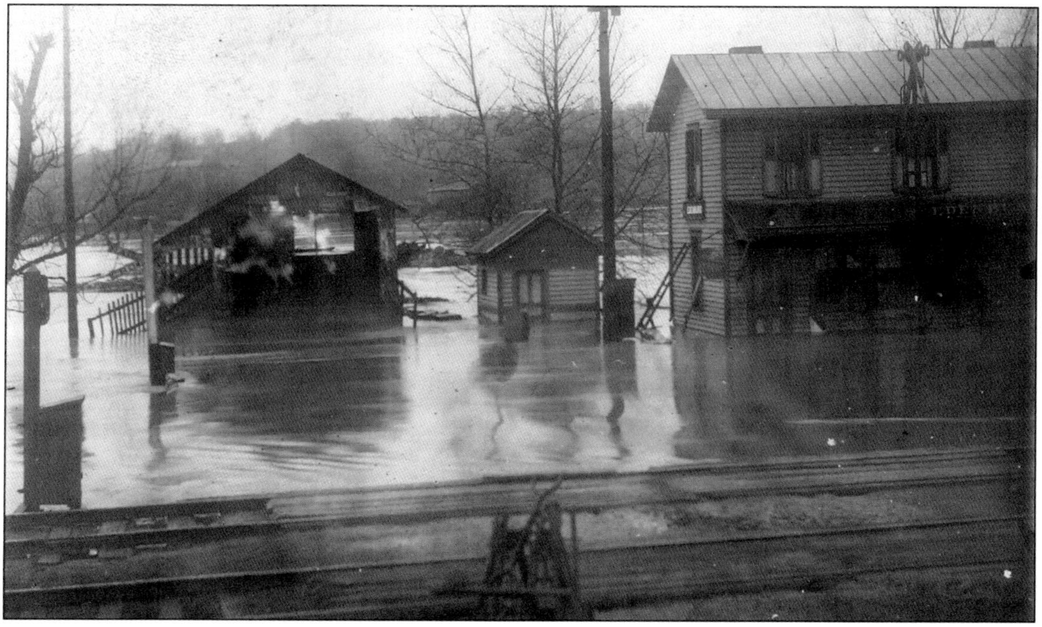

Edinburg Flood, Early 1900s. This postcard shows the B&O railroad station inundated by the Mahoning River. Transportation in Edinburg, mostly on the north side of the river, included the Cross-Cut Canal built in 1838, the B&O in the 1870s, and the Penn-Ohio trolley line between New Castle and Struthers, Ohio. By 1906, the B&O was running where the canal had been.

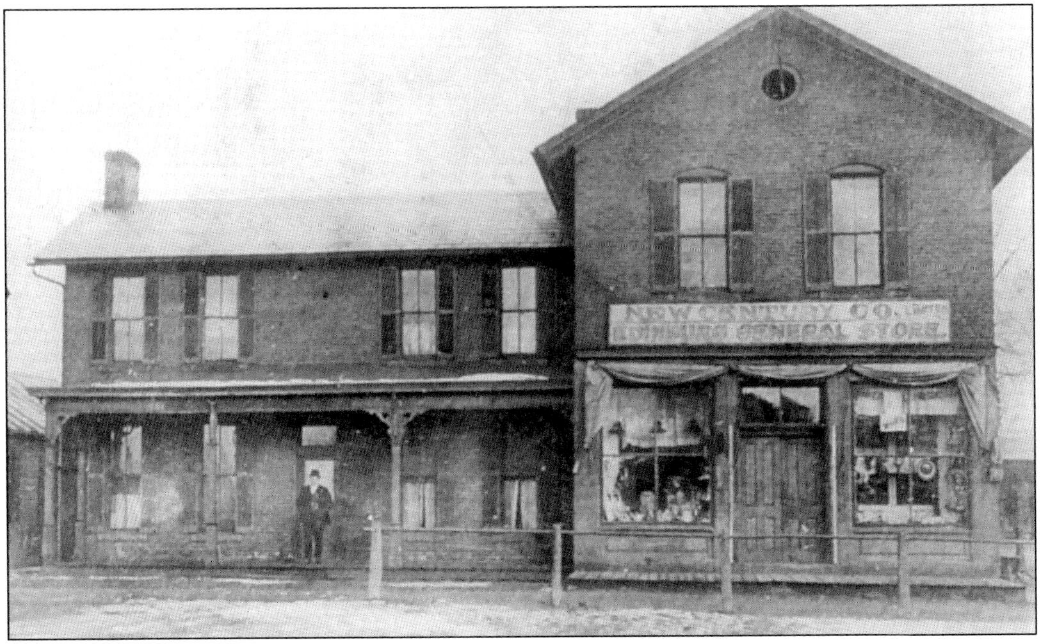

EDINBURG GENERAL STORE, EARLY 1900S. This is the New Century Company Limited, Edinburg's general store. Next to it is the residence of F. S. Webb. The building is located on the southeast corner of "the diamond" where Jackson Street and Erie Street intersect. It is still standing, housing an archery business.

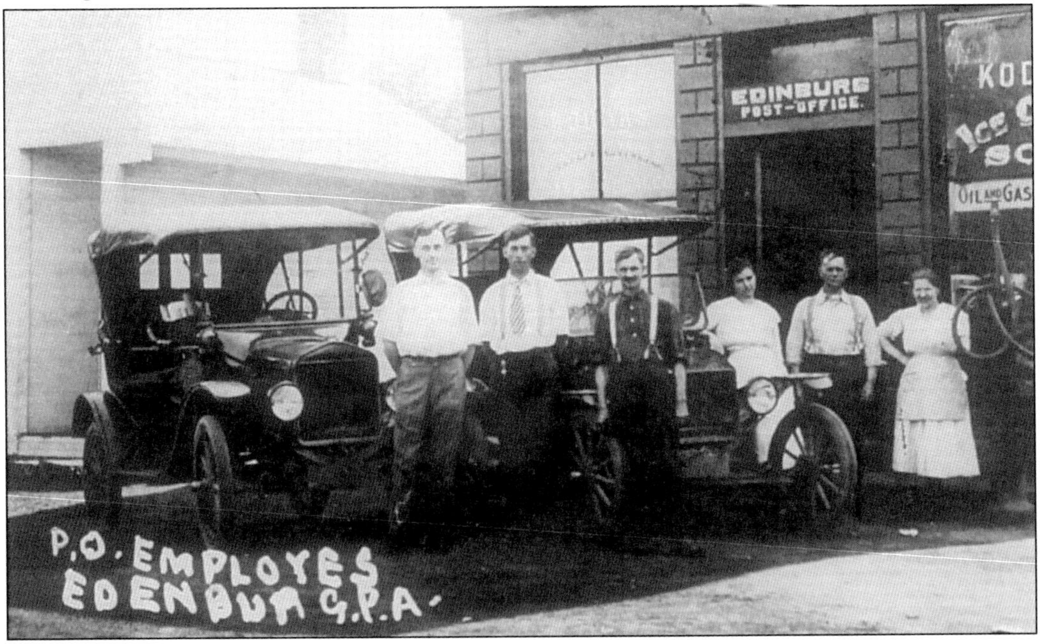

EDINBURG POST OFFICE, 1920S. Erie Street's post office was also a general store, drugstore, and gas station. In 1960, the present post office was built at Erie and Jackson Streets, the site where, in 1840, Ira Sankey was born. He was the world-famous evangelist, hymn writer, and gospel singer who gave New Castle a YMCA building in 1885. Sankey's father was Edinburg's first postmaster and an important figure in the founding of Lawrence County.

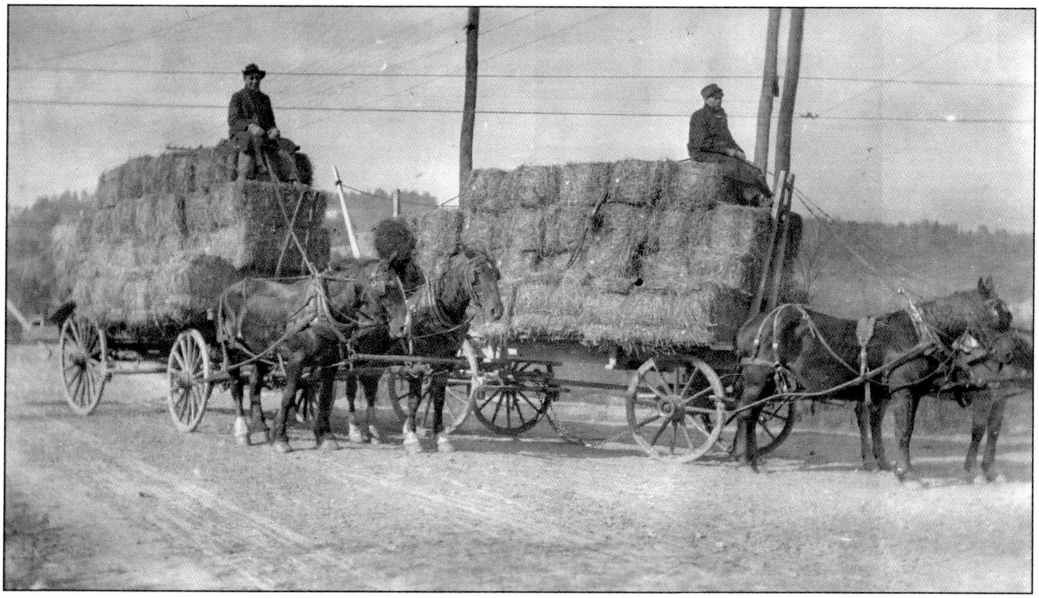

HAY WAGONS, STOP 88 AT THE HARBOR, 1910. Farmers sold hay at Stop 88 on the Harbor interurban trolley line. Largely a rural community, the town of Western Reserve Harbor was laid out in 1835, about the time the Beaver Division of the Erie Canal reached New Castle. The Harbor, called Western Reserve Harbor then, became a center for great business activity. (Courtesy of LCHS, Hitch Collection.)

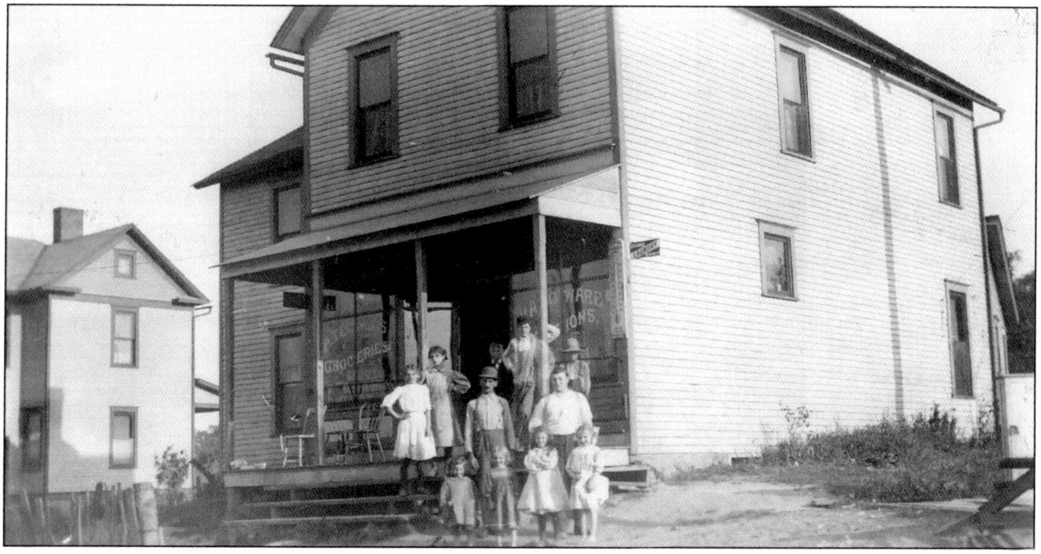

ECKLES FAMILY, STOP 88 AT THE HARBOR, 1920S. The A. T. Eckles General Store was important to the community that developed around Stop 88. The interurban trolley line at Stop 88, established in the early 1900s, carried Harbor residents to Ohio from this convenient stop on the line. (Courtesy of LCHS, Hitch Collection.)

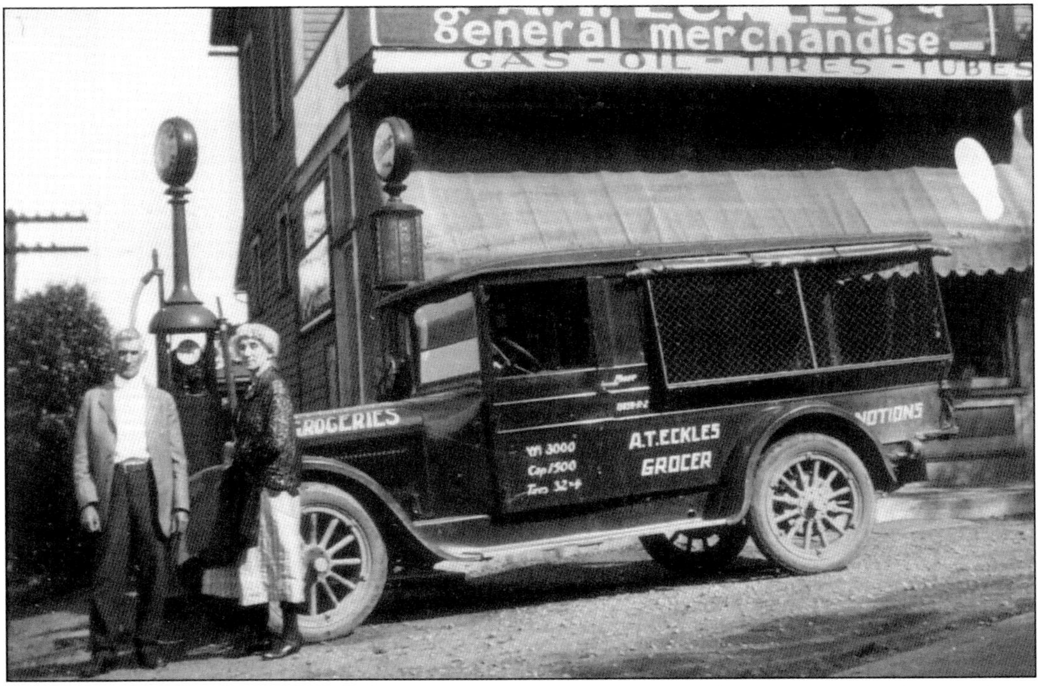

Eckles General Store, Stop 88 at the Harbor, 1920s. The A. T. Eckles General Store expanded its services. Besides groceries and notions, the store also offered gas, oil, and other automobile necessities. Note the vintage gas pump in the background. Eckles and his sister pose in front of the delivery truck. (Courtesy of LCHS, Hitch Collection.)

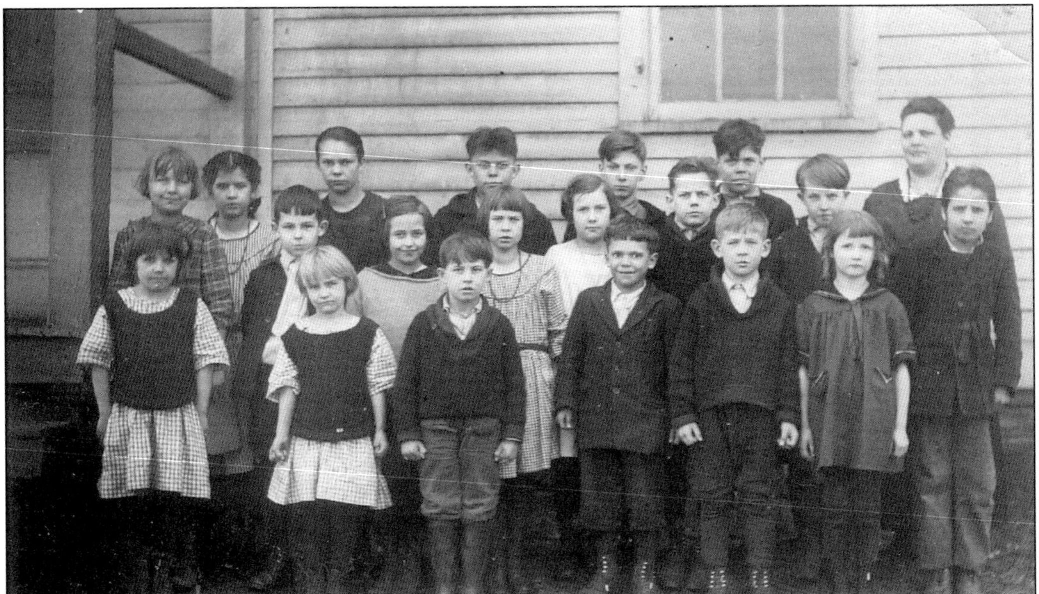

Old Harbor Elementary School, Early 1930s. Although the Harbor lost its importance as the canal and trolley lines disappeared, there were enough families in the area to support a school. These pupils attended the Old Harbor School. Like other county schools, it was a typical frame building.

Seven

Volant and Harlansburg Area

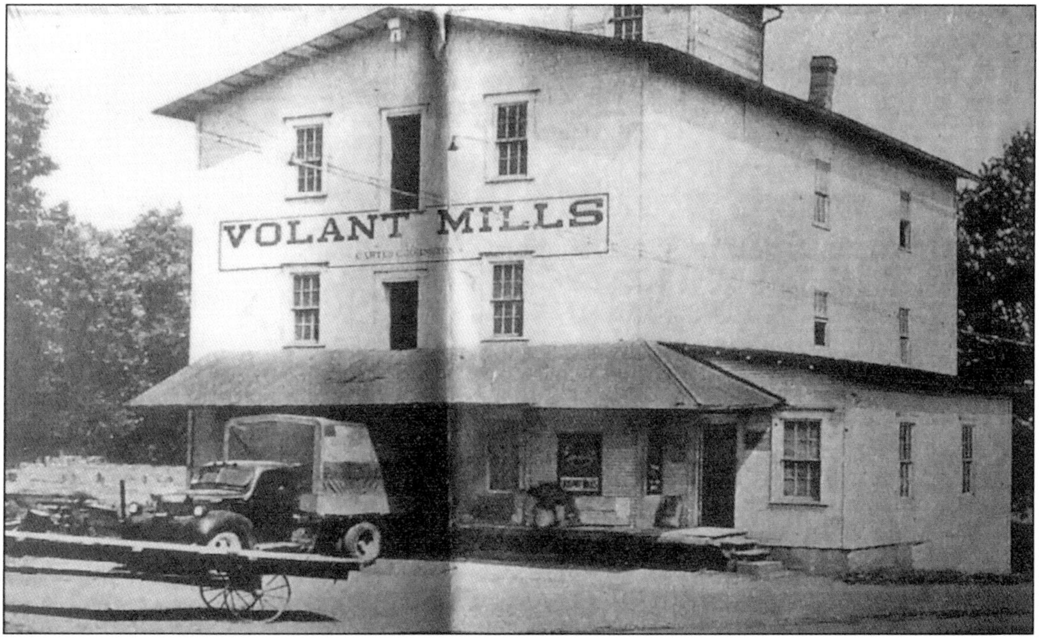

Volant Mills, 1930s. This building dates back to the early 1800s. In 1868, J. P. Locke bought the mills and 100 acres of land and called it Lockeville. When the New Castle and Franklin Railroad was completed in 1873 and an existing post office was moved to Lockeville, the town became Volant, the Latin word for "they fly." The borough was incorporated in 1893. (Courtesy of Betty Steve.)

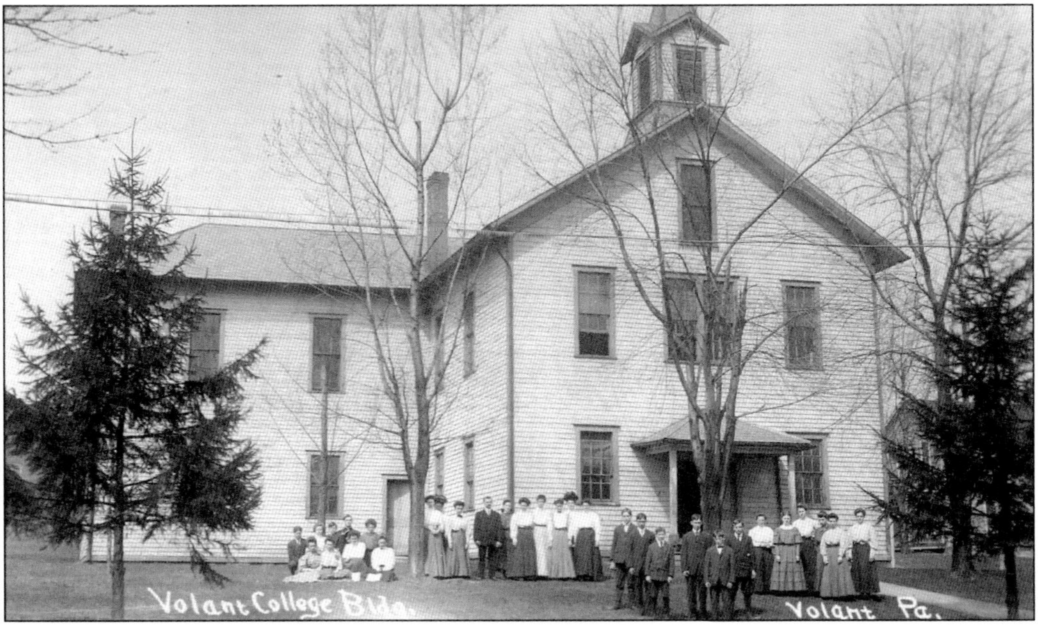

VOLANT COLLEGE, C. 1908. Volant Normal Academy was founded in 1889 with 37 students in its first term. It functioned as a high school when high schools were few. In 1890, it became Volant College. Many students went on to prominence, among them two Lawrence County judges, three county superintendents of education, and one hall of fame baseball pitcher, Rube Waddell. The college was destroyed by fire in 1911.

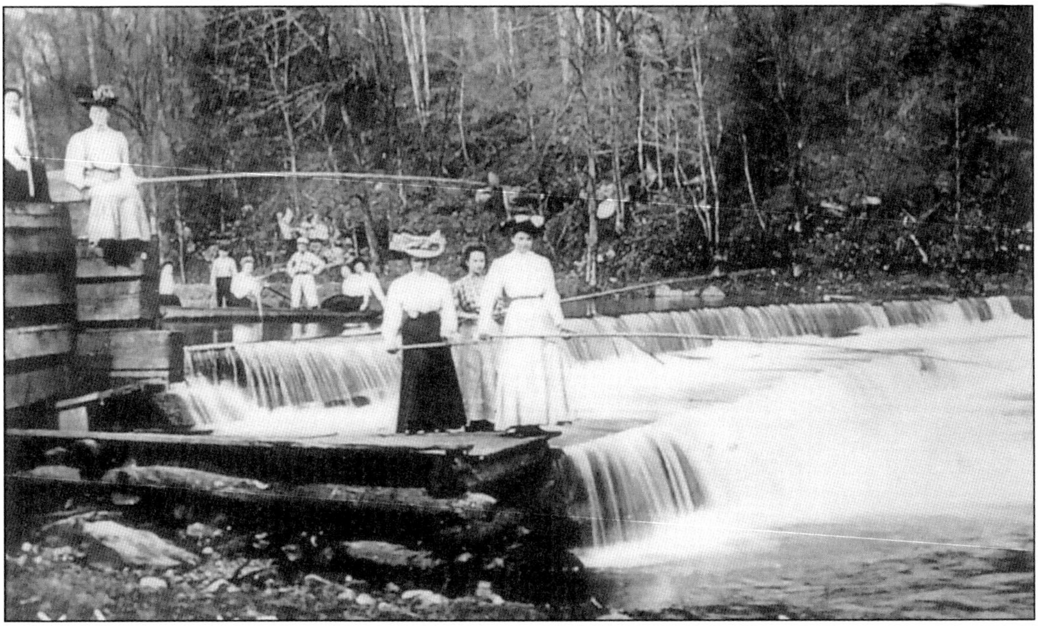

NESHANNOCK DAM, VOLANT MILLS, EARLY 1900S. These beautiful ladies wear hats and carry bamboo poles as they fish near the mills. Over time, the building has served as a flour mill, feed store, general store, furniture shop, antique store, and gift shop. Presently oak pins and beams, and the works of the mills itself, are being restored as part of the borough's development plan. (Courtesy of Betty Steve.)

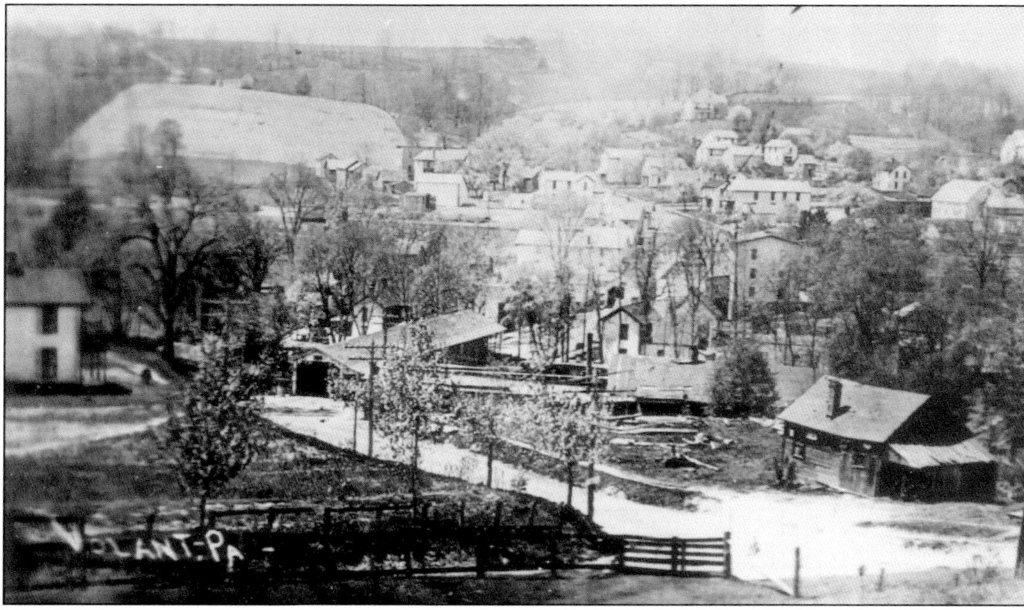

Bird's-Eye View, Main Street, Volant, Early 1900s. Volant once had two covered bridges. The first one, in the foreground, had a covered walkway across the Neshannock Creek. It was reportedly built in 1890 and was removed in 1931. A second smaller covered bridge was several hundred yards beyond and crossed the millrace. (Courtesy of Tom Walczak.)

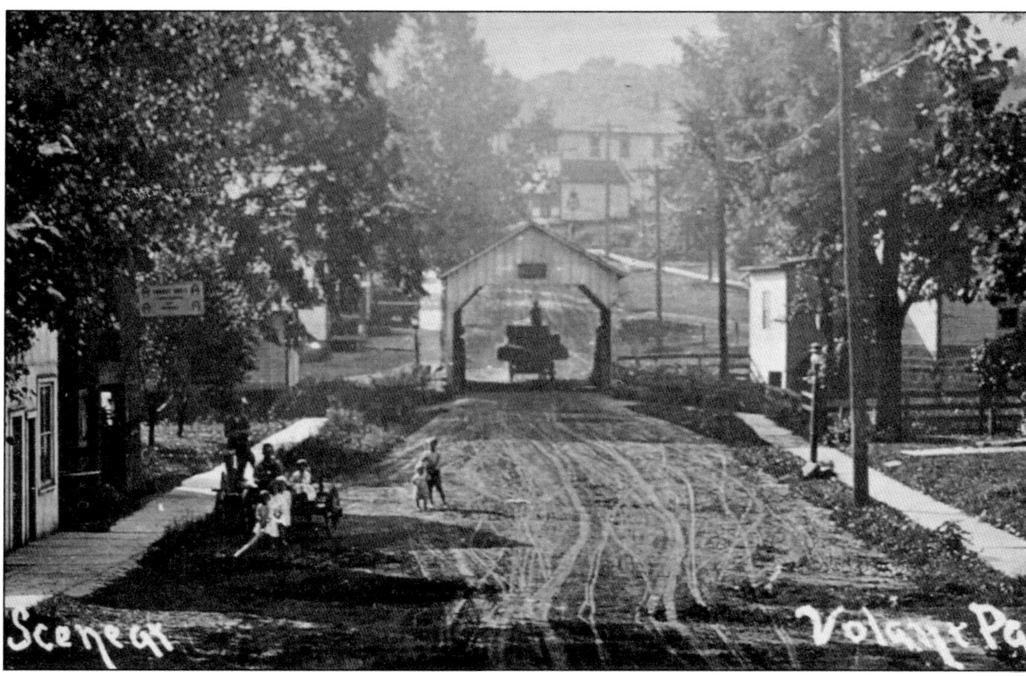

Millrace Bridge, Volant, Early 1900s. This is a close-up view of the covered bridge across the millrace. Volant Mills is partially obscured to the right of the bridge. The loaded wagon is probably taking grain to the mills for processing. The bridge was built around 1891 or 1892 and was removed in 1931. (Courtesy of Tom Walczak.)

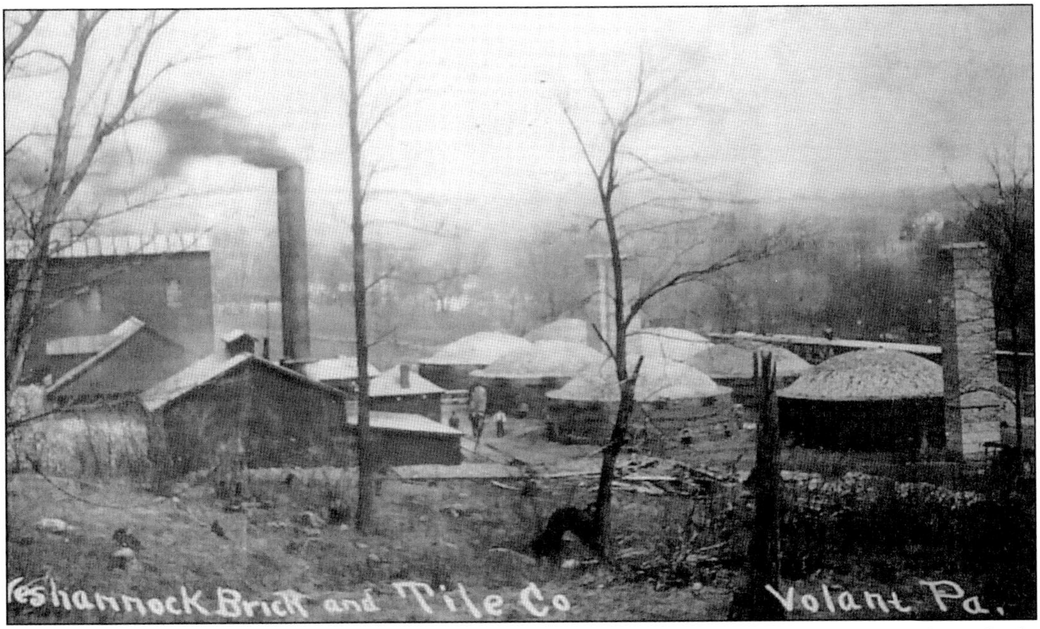

NESHANNOCK BRICK AND TILE COMPANY, VOLANT, EARLY 1900S. This brick and tile company operated in the early 1900s with the beehive kilns seen here. Early brick making used clay or shale in a long operation, crushing, grinding, forming, and baking at extremely high temperatures. It could take days to load the kilns, more days to fire them, and even more to cool down the bricks. (Courtesy of Betty Steve.)

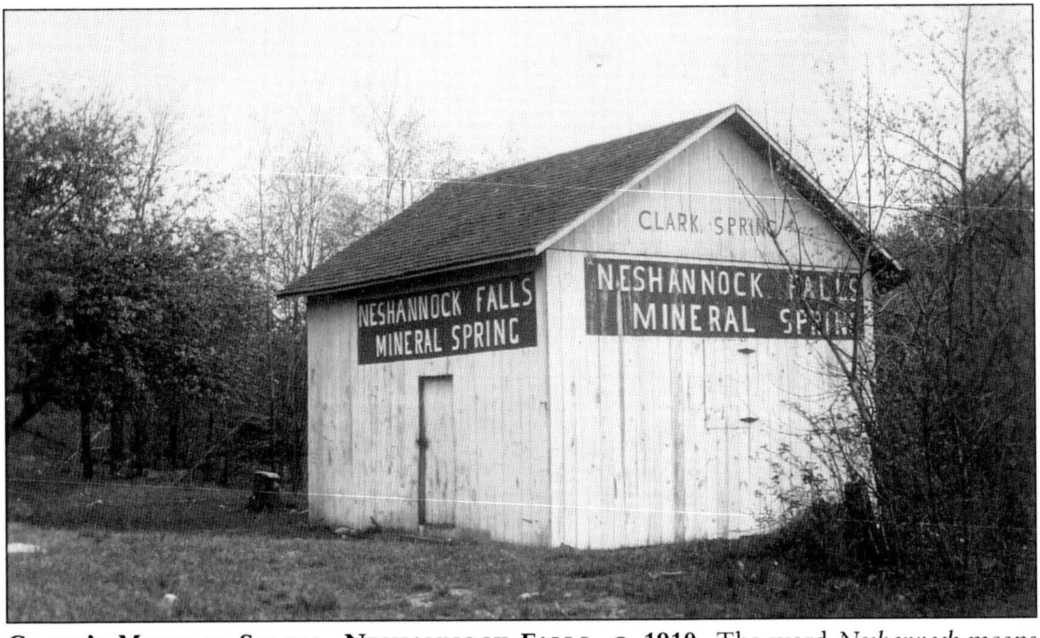

CLARK'S MINERAL SPRING, NESHANNOCK FALLS, *C.* 1910. The word *Neshannock* means "place between the waters." This mineral spring operating in Neshannock Falls was said to have curative powers. The mineral water was bottled and sold. The artesian well is still flowing in a little building outside Daley's Country Pantry. It is said to have the highest rate of flow of the wells in Lawrence County.

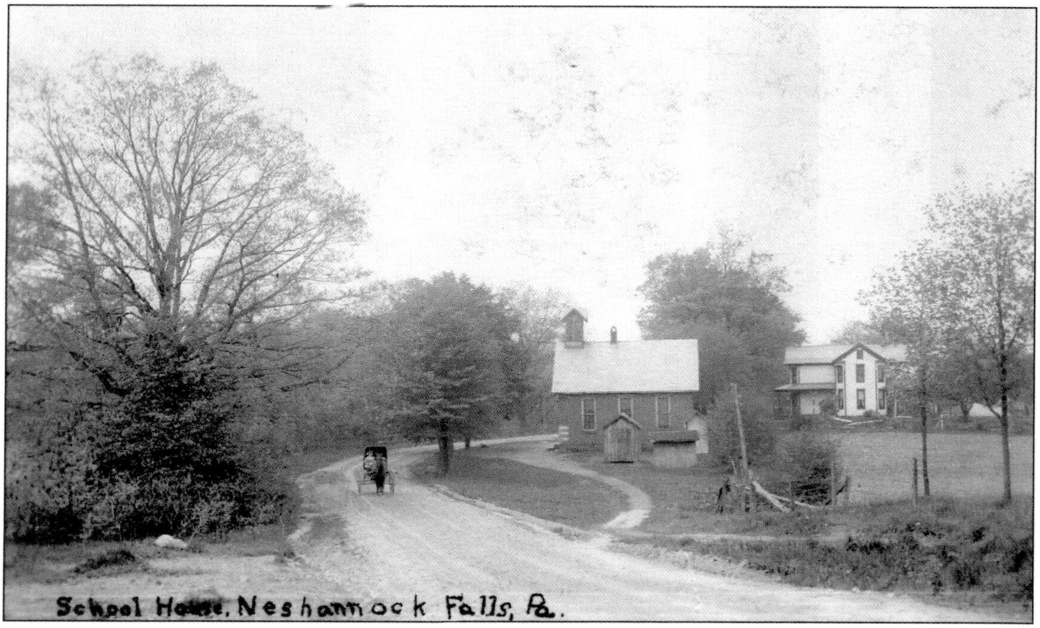

SCHOOLHOUSE, NESHANNOCK FALLS, *c.* 1910. The first schoolhouse in Neshannock Falls was built in 1872 on what was to become Route 956. The New Castle and Franklin Railway ran behind the school, a convenience for one of the schoolteachers who boarded a train in West Pittsburg and rode to the school. The schoolhouse, still standing, is now owned privately. The belfry is gone. The house in the background is still a residence.

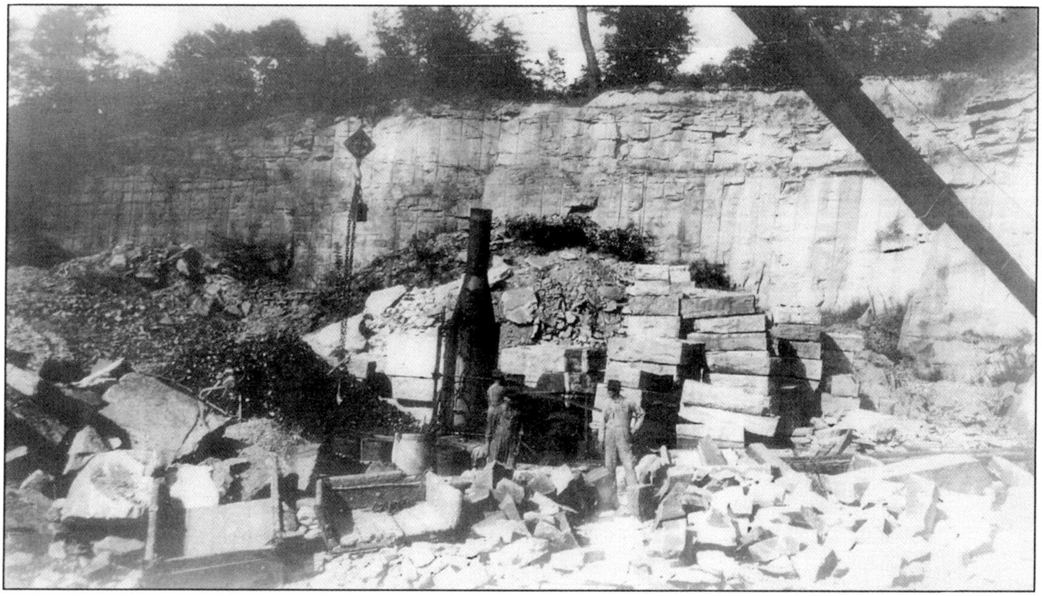

LIMESTONE QUARRY, NESHANNOCK FALLS. This limestone quarry in Neshannock Falls probably could not compete with the numerous quarries near Bessemer and Hillsville, but the limestone was quarried, nevertheless. In addition to limestone, iron ore and coal deposits were in the area. Those products were of good quality, but they were too near the surface to mine successfully. (Courtesy of LCHS, Hitch Collection.)

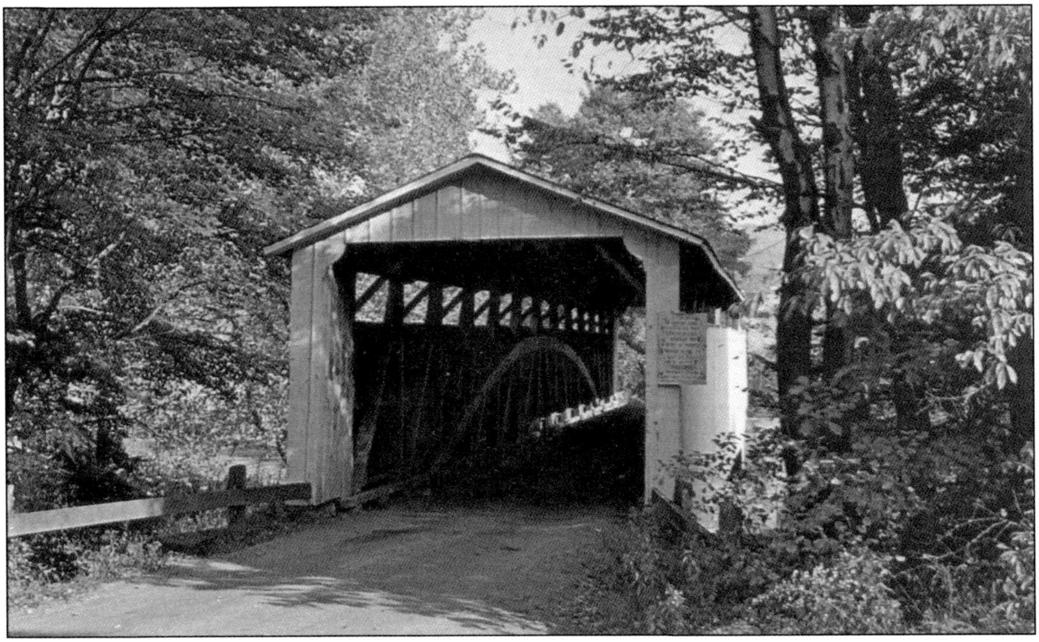

BANKS BRIDGE, NESHANNOCK FALLS. The Banks Bridge on Covered Bridge Road is one of two covered bridges still standing in Lawrence County (the other is at McConnell's Mill.) Built in 1889 in Burr arch truss style, it is 121 feet long. Today it is reinforced with steel beams and supported by a steel pier understructure. It is on the National Register of Historic Places.

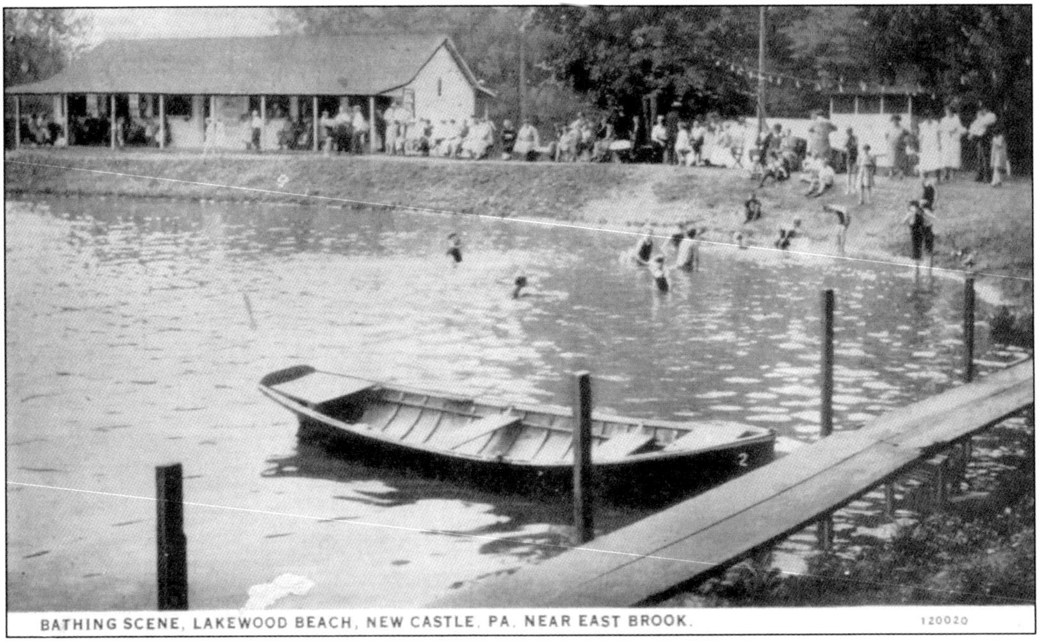

LAKEWOOD BEACH, *c.* 1934. In 1917, five doctors built a dam with a spillway to form a lake from Hettenbaugh Run. They hauled in sand for a beach and built a lifeguard stand and dance hall. The dance hall burned down in 1939. A second dance hall had the same fate in the late 1990s. The lake was eventually declared polluted by the Environmental Protection Agency and is now dry as a result of a break in the dam.

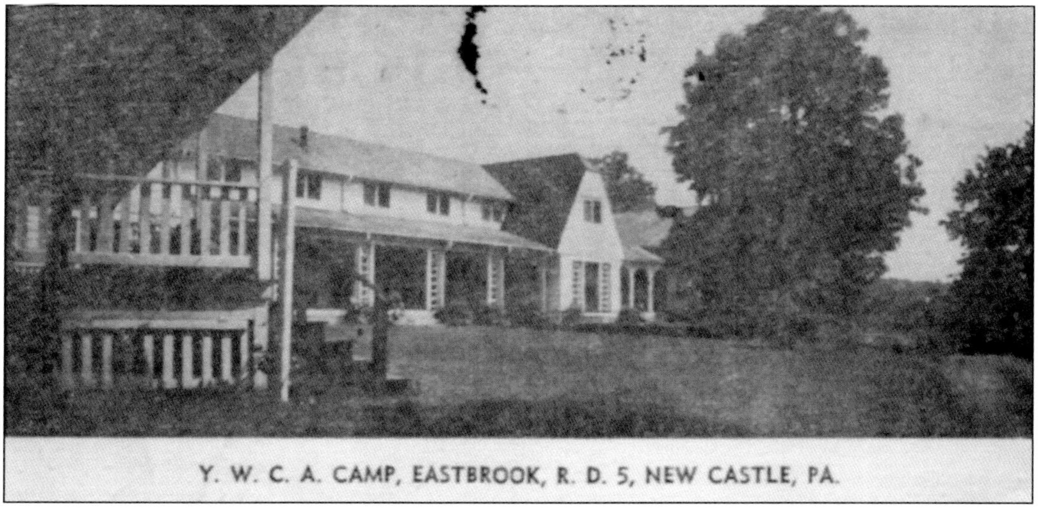

YWCA CAMP, EASTBROOK, *c.* 1956. This private residence in Eastbrook became a YWCA camp. The message on the other side of the card was written in the summer of 1956 by a minister's young daughter. She reported to her family that she was having a nice time swimming three times a day and that she had learned the side stroke and breast stroke.

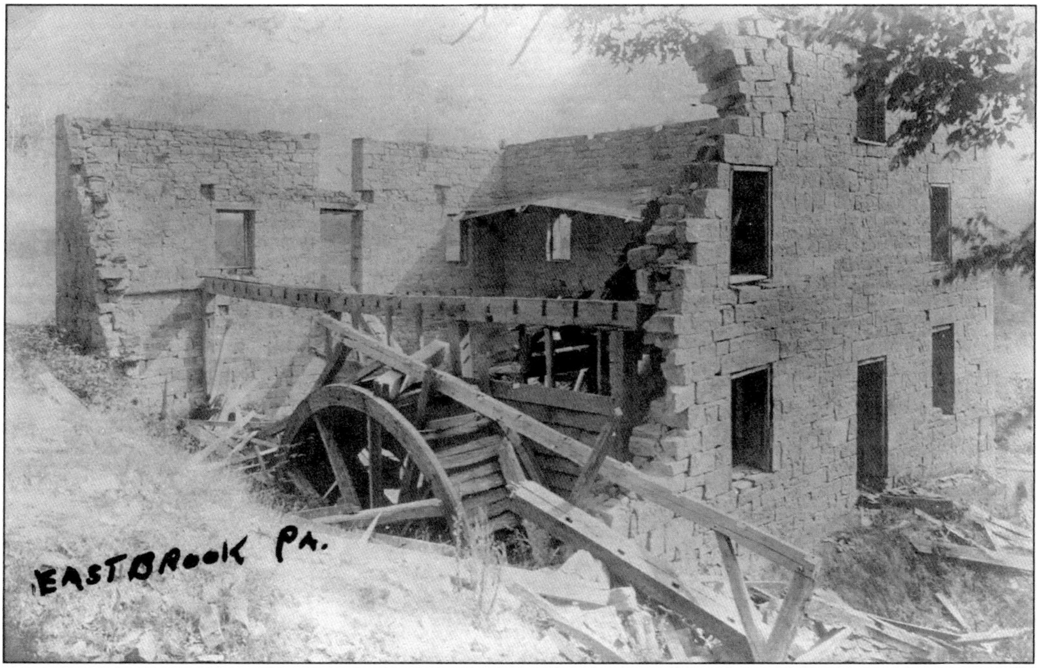

EASTBROOK MILL, 1907. This gristmill was about a mile west of Eastbrook near Eastbrook Station, which served the New Castle and Franklin Railroad. The village of Eastbrook was named for the stream passing through town, Hettenbaugh Run (also called Hottenbaugh and Huttenbaugh). The run attracted early gristmills, sawmills, and woolen factories. The Eastbrook Post Office was established in 1837, before Hickory Township was formed.

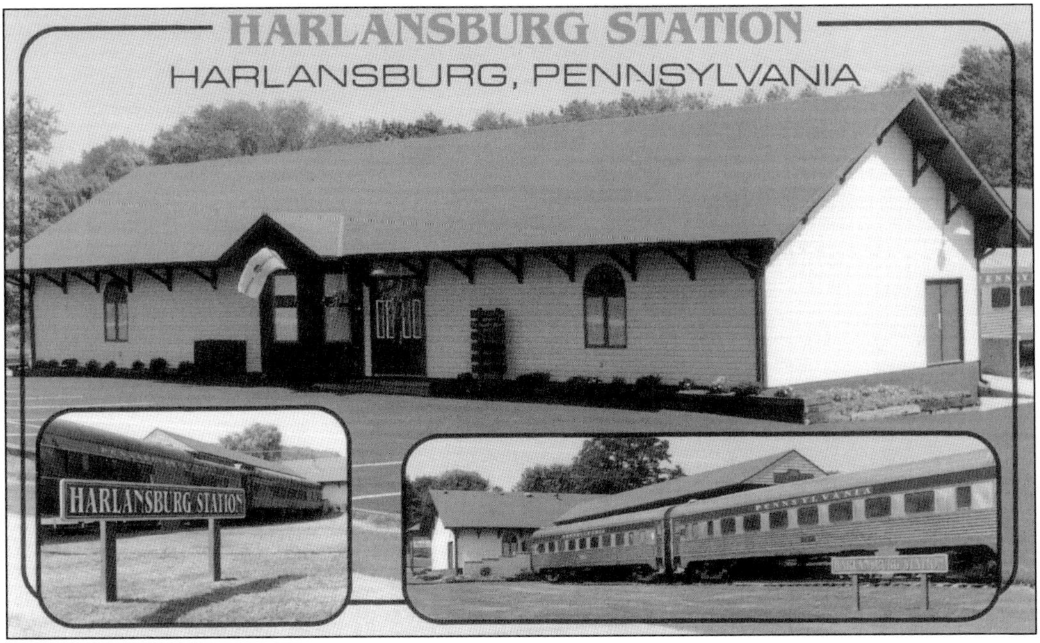

HARLANSBURG STATION AND MUSEUM OF TRANSPORTATION. Harlansburg Station is one of three historic buildings at the intersection of Routes 19 and 108. Route 19, Perry Highway, was originally the Pittsburgh-to-Erie stage road. It is named for Adm. Oliver Hazard Perry, who in the War of 1812 marched troops from Pittsburgh to Erie. It was Perry who, at the Battle of Lake Erie, said "We have met the enemy and they are ours."

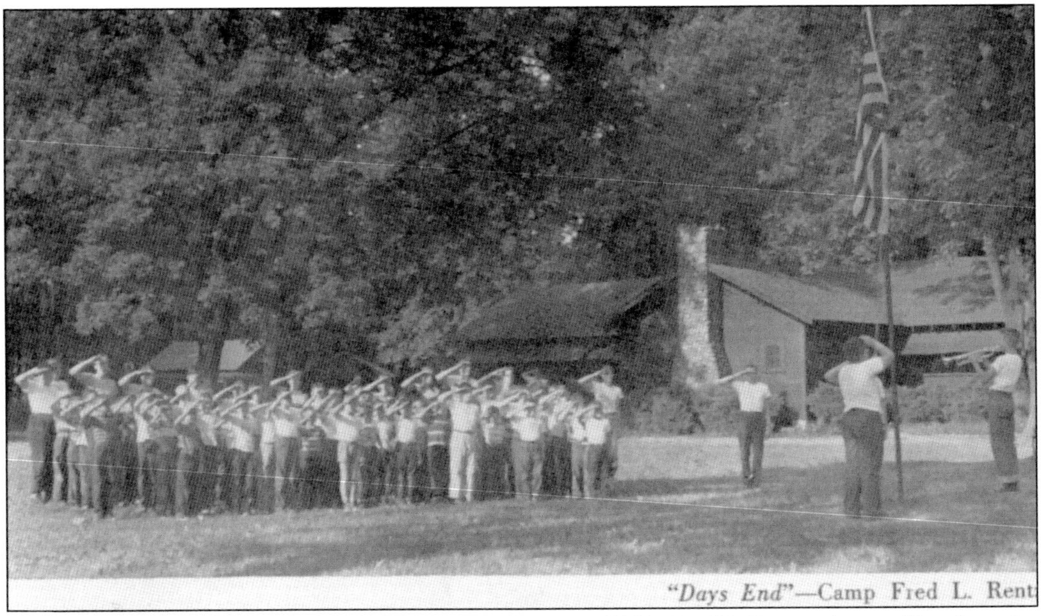

CAMP FRED L. RENTZ, HARLANSBURG, *C.* 1955. In 1931, Fred L. Rentz donated land on the Slippery Rock Creek to the YMCA. Rentz started at the *New Castle News* as a printer's devil, then became part owner and publisher. Noted for civic service and generosity, he was briefly mayor of New Castle in the 1920s. For many years, Rentz presented a $5 bill to county babies born on March 12, his birthday.

PITTSBURGHER INN, HARLANSBURG, 1930S. The Pittsburgher Inn was on the southeast corner of the intersection of Routes 19 and 108. Its heated cabins, lunchroom, and service station made it a popular stopping place for tourists. It attracted local people because of the bears, monkeys, and other animals in cages. The inn burned down in the late 1950s, and an A-frame building is on the site.

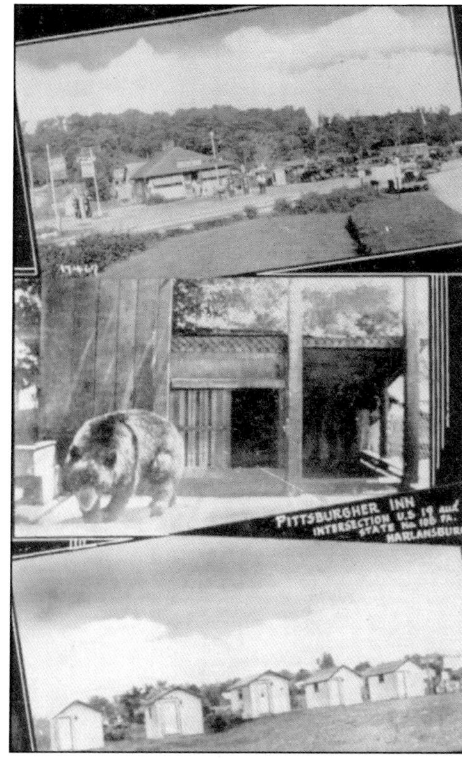

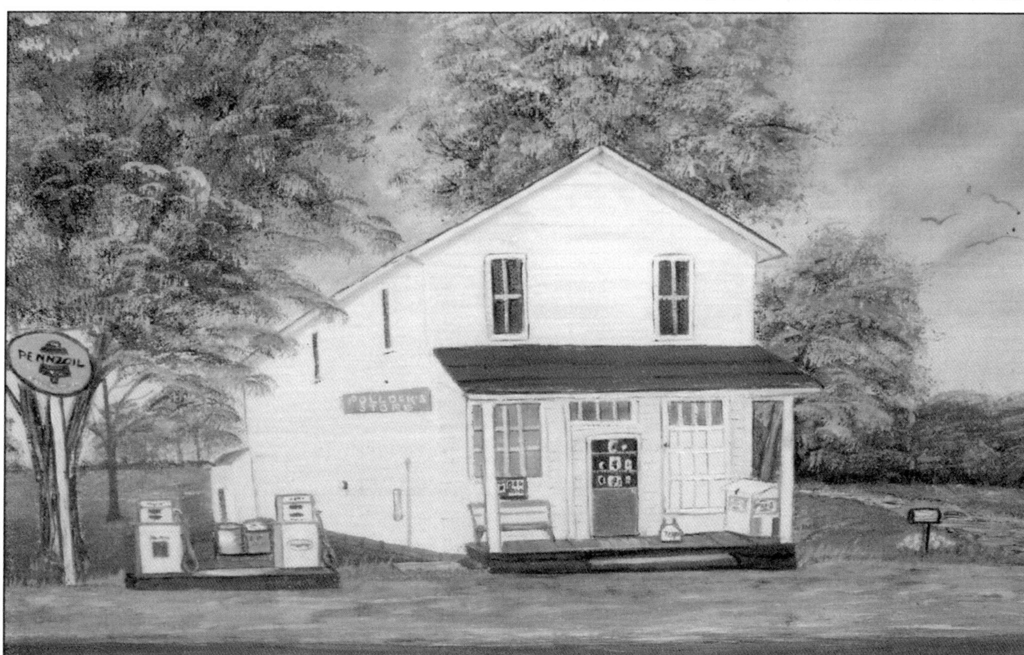

COUNTRY STORE, PLAIN GROVE, 1990. Built in the early 1800s, this building was moved to its present location in the early 1870s. For many years it was Cliff Pollock's General Store, the only store in the township. It is now Maria's Country Store and is still the only store in Plain Grove. (Courtesy of Maria Getz and Adam Pivovar.)

BIBLIOGRAPHY

Art Work, Beaver and Lawrence Counties, Pennsylvania. Chicago: W. H. Parish and Company, 1894.

Atlas of the County of Lawrence and the State of Pennsylvania. Philadelphia: G. M. Hopkins and Company, 1872.

Burmester, Bill. *Legends of Lawrence County.* New Castle, PA: New Castle News Company, 1992.

Currie, Dale. *McConnell's Mill: Yesteryear and Other Stories.* New Wilmington, PA: Globe Printing Company, 1990.

Currie, Dale. *McConnell's Mill: Echoes of the Past.* New Wilmington, PA: Globe Graphics, 1992.

DeWitt, H. Dewey, Paul Gamble, Delber L. McKee, Eugene G. Sharkey, and G. Alan Sternbergh, eds. *The History of New Wilmington, Pennsylvania 1797–2003.* New Wilmington, PA: New Horizons Publishing Company, 2004.

Diamond Jubilee Committee. *Bessemer Diamond Jubilee, 1913–1988.* Bessemer, PA.

Durant, S. W., and P. A. Durant. *History of Lawrence County, Pennsylvania.* Philadelphia: L. H. Everts and Company, 1877.

Ellwood City Historical Association, ed. *History of Ellwood City, 1892–1942.* Ellwood City, PA: Lion's Club.

Fox, Donald W., ed. *Bridges to the Past: A Pictorial History of Lawrence County.* New Castle, PA: Lawrence County Historical Society, 1994.

Hazen, Aaron. *20th Century History of New Castle and Lawrence County, Pennsylvania.* Chicago: Richmond-Arnold Publishing Company, 1908.

Petrich, Sheri L. *Enon Valley: A Community of Friends and Neighbors.* Philadelphia: Starry Night Publishing, 2005.

Richards, Bart. *Lawrence County.* New Castle, PA: New Castle Area School District, 1968.

Sesquicentennial Committee. *Mount Jackson Sesquicentennial, 1815–1965.* Mount Jackson, PA: 1965.

Wood, Wick W., compiler. *History of Lawrence County.* New Castle, PA: News Company, 1887. Reprint, New Castle, PA: J. V. Lamb, 1987.

Index